WOMEN AND PEACE:
THEORETICAL, HISTORICAL AND
PRACTICAL PERSPECTIVES

WOMEN
AND PEACE

THEORETICAL, HISTORICAL AND
PRACTICAL PERSPECTIVES

Edited by RUTH ROACH PIERSON

with the assistance of Joanne Thompson,
Somer Brodribb, Paula Bourne

CROOM HELM
London • New York • Sydney

© 1987 Ruth Roach Pierson
Croom Helm Ltd, Provident House, Burrell Row,
Beckenham, Kent, BR3 1AT
Croom Helm Australia, 44-50 Waterloo Road,
North Ryde, 2113, New South Wales

Published in the USA by
Croom Helm
in association with Methuen, Inc.
29 West 35th Street
New York, NY 10001

British Library Cataloguing in Publication Data
Women and peace: theoretical, historical
    and practical perspectives
    1. Women and peace
    2. Pierson, Ruth Roach
    327.1'72 JX1965
    ISBN 0-7099-4068-8

Library of Congress Cataloging-in-Publication Data

Women and peace.

    Bibliography: p.
    Includes index.
    1. Women and peace — History. I. Pierson, Ruth
Roach, 1938-
JX1965.W44   1987   327.1'72'088042   87-6778
ISBN 0-7099-4068-8

Printed and bound in Great Britain
by Billings & Sons Limited, Worcester.

CONTENTS

PART III CONTEMPORARY PRACTICES

ACKNOWLEDGEMENTS

All published works are collaborative efforts and none more so than a publication of conference proceedings, as is the case here. Of the many deserving thanks, I should like to single out: Kathy Arnup for helping with the initial Conference on "Women and Education for Peace and Non-Violence"; Susan Hall, secretary of the OISE Centre for Women's Studies in Education, for transcribing the Conference tapes; Somer Brodribb for her faith in the project of publication when all doors to its realization were slamming shut in our faces; Deborah Gorham for approaching Croom Helm on our behalf; Naomi Roth, editor at Croom Helm, for her enthusiastic interest in and support of the book; the Ontario Institute for Studies in Education for small-scale grants to hire typing, editorial and indexing assistance; Paula Bourne for her skillful editing of the contributions translated from French; Michèle Fillion and Joanne Thompson for working so assiduously on the compilation of the Index; and Joanne Thompson for her meticulous attention to detail during the many rounds of editing and proofreading in the "endless" final stages of manuscript preparation.

Margaret Brennan, secretary in the Department of History and Philosophy of Education at the Ontario Institute for Studies in Education, is in a category all her own. The cliche "without whose help this book could not have been completed" is, in this instance, absolutely true. As the one who entered the entire manuscript into the computer and worked countless hours to achieve the proper formatting for a camera-ready copy, she served as the typesetter of this book. That she, throughout this ordeal, not only preserved her good humour and sharp wit but also cheered up the rest of us when our spirits flagged, is nothing short of remarkable. My gratitude to her is immense.

Any royalties generated by the
sale of this book will be contributed
to the Voice of Women of Canada

LIST OF CONTRIBUTORS

Yvonne Aleksandra Bennett received her Ph.D. from McMaster University, Hamilton, Ontario, in 1984. She is currently teaching in the History Department of Carleton University in Ottawa, Ontario, and continuing work on the Peace Pledge Union, and on wartime issues from a pacifist perspective, 1939-1945.

Berenice A. Carroll is Director of Women's Studies and member of the faculty of Political Science at the University of Illinois at Urbana-Champaign. Her research, teaching and publication are in the fields of women's history, peace studies, and feminist theory.

Sandi E. Cooper, Professor of History at the College of Staten Island, City University of New York, has written many essays on the history of peace movements for Peace and Change and many introductions to books published in the Garland Library of War and Peace reprint series. She has served as president of the Berkshire Conference of Women Historians and is vice-president of the Conference on Peace Research in History.

Micheline de Sève teaches in the Department of Political Science at the Université du Québec à Montréal and is the author of Pour un féminisme libertaire (Montréal: Boreal Express, 1985).

Deborah Gorham, Associate Professor of History at Carleton University, Ottawa, Ontario, is the author of The Victorian Girl and the Feminine Ideal (Croom Helm, 1982) and is currently at work on a book about Vera Brittain to be published by Basil Blackwell.

Ursula Herrmann, Professor and Doctor of Science at the Institut fuer Marxismus-Leninismus, Berlin, has published a number of books about the German labour movement before 1914 and the struggle of the working class for peace. She is an active member of the socialist women's movement of the German Democratic Republic.

Margaret Hobbs is a doctoral candidate in the Department of History and Philosophy of Education at the Ontario Institute for Studies in Education, Toronto, Ontario. She is currently researching her dissertation on the experience of Canadian women during the Great Depression.

Nadine Lubelski-Bernard is chief research assistant at the Université Libre de Bruxelles where she earned a Ph.D. in Political Science. Her dissertation focused on the Belgian peace movement before the First World War and was entitled: "Les mouvements et les idéologies pacifistes en Belgique (1830-1914)."

Ruth Roach Pierson teaches women's history and history of feminism at the Ontario Institute for Studies in Education, Toronto, Ontario, and is the author of "They're Still Women After All": The Second World War and Canadian Womanhood (Toronto: McClelland and Stewart, 1986).

Veronica Strong-Boag is an Associate Professor in History and Women's Studies at Simon Fraser University, Burnaby, British Columbia, and publishes regularly in the field of Canadian women's history.

Dorothy Thompson teaches Modern British Social History at the University of Birmingham, England. She has published a number of works on the history of working men and women in nineteenth century Britain, the latest of which is The Chartists: Popular Politics in the Industrial Revolution (London: Pantheon, 1984). She is married to the historian E. P. Thompson and they have three children and five grandchildren.

Setsuko Thurlow grew up in Hiroshima and survived the atomic bombing. She received a B.A. in English Literature and Education from Hiroshima Jogakuin College, a B.A. in Sociology from Lynchburg, Virginia, and a bachelor's and master's degree in social work from the University of Toronto. She is presently employed as a school social worker by the Toronto Board of Education and has worked for almost three decades with women's and peace groups in Japan and Canada.

Jo Vellacott, born and educated in England, now teaches Women's Studies at the Simone de Beauvoir Institute of Concordia University in Montreal. As a Quaker, she is an active member of the Canadian Friends Service Committee and also participates in the activities of the Voice of Women and other peace organizations. She is the author of Bertrand Russell and the Pacifists in the First World War (Harvester, 1980; St. Martin's Press, 1981).

Margaret Wells has worked as a teacher for sixteen years and contributed to the formation of two alternative school programmes with the Toronto Board of Education. She is a founding member of Educators for Social Responsibility (originally named Education for Nuclear Disarmament) and co-chairperson for 1986.

Judith Wishnia teaches women's history and Women's Studies at the State University of New York at Stony Brook, Long Island, New York. She has recently completed a manuscript on the unionization of civil service workers in France and is currently preparing a monograph on women feminists-unionists-pacifists in France. She herself is a long-time political activist in the peace movement, the feminist movement, and the union movement.

INTRODUCTION

Ruth Roach Pierson

As Blanche Wiesen Cook has pointed out, "the most vigorous aspects of the peace movement today are organized and staffed by women."[*] On those grounds alone, we have a right and a need to learn more about women's relation to peace, both in theory and in historical and contemporary practice. The study of women and peace, however, goes against the grain of societies which remain male-dominated and committed to the use of organized violence to contain and resolve conflict. Women's ideas and activities are considered to be of secondary or marginal interest, and war and the preparation for war are regarded as intrinsically more important and interesting than peace and the preparation for peace.

The papers collected here stem from two academic gatherings organized to counteract that orientation: the September 1984 conference at the Ontario Institute for Studies in Education (OISE), in Toronto, on "Women and Education for Peace and Non-Violence" and the August 1985 round table at the Sixteenth International Congress of the Historical Sciences, in Stuttgart, on "The History of Women and Peace Movements." The contributors are all women educators, scholars, and peace activists whose research and writing reflect only one side of their commitment to the contemporary peace movement. For this volume, the papers have been grouped into three sections: one of theoretical reflections, one of historical case studies, and one of statements arising from contemporary practice. Where we had transcriptions of comments and questions from the audience of the OISE Conference, we have appended them to the individual paper which they addressed.

Leading off the theoretical section, indeed the entire volume, Berenice A. Carroll examines the "Historical and Theoretical Connections" between "Feminism and Pacifism." She attempts to disentangle the concept of "women and peace" from that of "feminism and pacifism" by distinguishing between "feminism" and "the women's movement," "peace movements" and "pacifism," and "pacifism" and "pacific behaviour." It is powerlessness which, according to Carroll, has linked women historically to peace. Nonetheless, she seeks a logic linking feminism to pacifism and finds it above all in the liberal principle of the inalienable right to life and liberty underlying both ideologies.

---

[*] Blanche Wiesen Cook, "Feminism and Peace Research: Thoughts on Alternative Strategy," Women's Studies Quarterly XII, 2 (Summer 1984): 18.

While Carroll concentrates on the contemporary situation and the recent past, Dorothy Thompson surveys the whole of western recorded history in her interrogation of the relationship between gender and war. By means of historical "example and counter-example," Thompson advances an argument against a mono-causal explanation for war, particularly the tracing of all evil to the male half of the human species. In contrast to the complexities and ambiguities shading Carroll's and Thompson's conceptions of human society, Micheline de Sève claims that establishing "the relationship between women and peace is relatively simple." With a selection of images, she conjures up a nightmare world dichotomized between militarist men and innocent, pacifist women. Her poetic, apocalyptic vision is designed to impart a sense of urgency and galvanize us into action.

European and North American women have been actively organizing for peace for the past hundred years or so, as the nine papers contained in Part II document. That the period covered extends no further into the past than the nineteenth century can be explained in terms of another angle to the tripartite women/peace/power relationship. The majority of women may well have been opposed to war for centuries; they certainly have had their share of suffering from armed conflicts. As Ursula Herrmann suggests, however, it was only with the emergence of the women's movement in the last century, and of the movement of women out of the home into the public sphere on a large scale, that the politicization of women became possible and, with it, women's involvement in peace movements.

By examining bourgeois women's participation in European peace movements prior to World War I, Sandi E. Cooper puts the famous 1915 International Women's Peace Congress at the Hague into historical perspective. She demonstrates that the meeting was not unique for the resolutions it passed on strategies for peace--women and men in European peace societies had been recommending these for decades. Rather, its uniqueness lay in the women's determination to come together in the name of peace despite the dangers posed by traveling through a world at war and the fierce opposition they faced from their nationalistic compatriots. Nadine Lubelski-Bernard outlines the particular social and political conditions impeding Belgian women's anti-war activities in the late 19th and early 20th centuries as well as the general international developments so inimical to European peace in this period.

The subject of Ursula Herrmann's paper is the role of German Social Democratic women in the struggle for peace before and during the First World War. She stresses the degree to which their opposition to war was related, on the part of leaders like Rosa Luxemburg, to the purity of their commitment to revolutionary Marxism and to the international community of workers and, on the part of ordinary women, to their experience of overwork, deprivation and death in wartime Germany.

In her study of pacifism and feminism in France in the years before and during the First World War, Judith Wishnia has unearthed a remarkable group of women teachers whose opposition to war was joined not only to the campaign for women's rights but also to the working-class struggle. For these teachers the causes of peace and social justice for women and for workers were inseparable. Educational practices, from curriculum reform to pamphlet distribution, were at the centre of their efforts as teachers to transform society.

Jo Vellacott performs a similar service of historical recovery in her paper on "Feminist Consciousness and the First World War," this time for a group of British non-militant suffragists. Until recently either the militant suffragette leaders Emmeline and Christabel Pankhurst or the mainstream non-militants aligned with Millicent Fawcett have occupied centre stage in the literature on the suffrage movement in Great Britain. In contrast to the former's as well as the latter's subordination of women's rights to the war effort, Vellacott's "renegade members" of the National Union of Women's Suffrage Societies did not abandon the conviction that "there was an intimate connection between the women's suffrage issue and opposition to militarism." Indeed, under the impact of the First World War, these radicals not only preserved the feminist-pacifist connection, they also broadened their feminist theory to embrace a socialism of non-violence.

The English writer and feminist Vera Brittain and the Canadian writer and suffragist Flora MacDonald Denison, the subjects of Deborah Gorham's study of the impact of the First World War on women's consciousness, tell a different story or, rather, two different stories. Denison's pre-war pacifism survived the outbreak of war in 1914 but not her son's departure in October 1916 for France and combat service on the western front. Unlike the mature, maternal Denison, Brittain was but a young woman in 1914 and in the grip of an untested feminism. Her future pacifism, as Gorham mentions, dates from Brittain's experience as a VAD in France, nursing the mutilated casualties of both German and Allied fire power. Gorham turns her attention to what has been less well understood: the fatal attraction that war held for Brittain and other women of her class and generation. In the case of both Denison and Brittain, ties to men played a crucial part in shaping their responses to the Great War.

The later life of Vera Brittain is taken up by Yvonne Bennett in the last contribution to the section of historical case studies. Brittain did not, according to Bennett, make the journey from romantic patriotism to principled pacifism in one leap. A growing disenchantment with the internationalism of the League of Nations

Union and an intensification of her Christian faith prepared the way for her eventual conversion in 1937 to total renunciation of war and membership in the Peace Pledge Union. Bennett's paper explores Brittain's ideas from the 1930s on women and peace, as well as her deliberate decision to absent herself from the Peace Pledge Union's Women's Peace Campaign of 1939-1940. As Bennett shows, it was on the basis of her humanity, rather than her feminine gender, that Brittain threw herself into an exhausting round of writing and speaking for peace during the Second World War.

Writing in the United States before and during the First World War, Charlotte Perkins Gilman was a feminist pacifist of an entirely different ilk. As Margaret Hobbs demonstrates in her examination of the "Pacifist Elements in the Feminist and Socialist Thought" of the American theorist, sex and gender were integral to the analysis of war and peace for Gilman. There was no doubt in her mind that the belligerent instincts, traceable to the male sperm cell, formed the essence of masculinity and "unbridled masculinity" meant war. According to Hobbs, however, even though the principle of social motherhood underpins the society of Herland, Gilman proves to be rather less than consistent in her association of the maternal traits of nurturance and caring, the essence of femininity, with either women or peace.

Despite the blow dealt it by the First World War, the equation of female nurturance with peaceful proclivities "died hard," as Veronica Strong-Boag observes in her review of "Peace-Making Women" in Canada between the wars. She has located women working for peace within the United Church of Canada, the League of Nations Society, the National Council of Women of Canada and its affiliated Local Councils, and in the Canadian branches of the Women's International League for Peace and Freedom (WILPF). Convinced as they may have been "of their sex's particular sensitivity to the costs of armed conflict," only a small minority, according to Strong-Boag, were absolute pacifists. She draws a necessary distinction between the internationalism which sought to induce world-mindedness in women and girls but put its faith in collective security backed by military sanctions, and a principled pacifism that renounced all recourse to violence. Openness to the latter perspective as well as left-wing leanings set WILPF apart from other groups advocating peace and international understanding; and these differences mounted as the international climate worsened preceding World War II. Nevertheless, Strong-Boag credits the peace-minded women of Canada, "for all their shortcomings," with keeping the "Canadian peace conscience" alive into the nuclear era.

The third and final section of the book contains examples of women taking up the anti-nuclear arms struggle of the post-Alamogordo world: only two examples, but impressive ones. Margaret

Wells, currently a teacher in an alternative high school in Toronto, is in the tradition of Judith Wishnia's women teachers in France before and during the First World War. Wells was a founding member of Educators for Social Responsibility (formerly Educators for Nuclear Disarmament) and has helped develop peace studies curricula for the Toronto Board of Education. Her paper is a lucid exposition of the principles that guide her practice in teaching about war and peace in the nuclear age.

Setsuko Thurlow, author of the concluding piece, is herself a survivor of the August 6, 1945, atomic bombing of Hiroshima. In her account of the role of Japanese women in Japan's post-war peace movement, Thurlow recalls the horror of living death suffered by survivors in the aftermath of the nuclear bombings, a horror unspeakably intensified by the U.S. Occupation policies of censorship and monopolization of information about the medical effects of radiation. Like the women in her moving account of recovery through resistance, Setsuko Thurlow derives from her experience of the apocalypse the will to transcend her own "personal trauma and tragedy" and take on "the prophetic mission of warning the world of the dangers of nuclearism." She pursues her anti-nuclear mission tirelessly. A long-time member of the Canadian women's peace organization, the Voice of Women, in 1974 she founded Hiroshima-Nagasaki Relived to house and distribute information on the known effects of nuclear weapons. Testifying as a defence witness in recent trials of peace activists, she has exposed herself and her painful memories of August 1945 to the prosecution's charge of irrelevance. Setsuko Thurlow's contribution to this volume is but one of her many acts of witnessing to the horrors of nuclear war.

Diverse as are the perspectives on women and peace represented in this volume, some thematic concerns recur. Many of the papers emphasize the importance that peace-minded women have assigned to education for peace, in the schools and in the popular media. Germane to this topic is Vera Brittain's lament that the study of war has traditionally had a greater capacity to excite the imagination, especially of the young, than has the study of peace, a problem that still plagues peace researchers and activists.

The historical case studies of Part II tend to confirm Berenice Carroll's contention that, as one cannot equate "pacifism" with "peace movement," neither can one make the concept of "feminism and pacifism" interchangeable with that of "women and peace." Indeed a number of authors treat as problematic the equation of women with moral superiority and an innate pacifism. The distinction which Gorham draws between "feminine pacifism" and "feminist pacifism" makes a valuable contribution to the analysis of this problem.

While contesting the automatic linkage of women with peace, most authors hold out hope for the potential linkage of feminism and pacifism. Feminist critiques of patriarchy as fostering militarism and war, albeit in need of further elaboration as Carroll suggests, provide an important ground for the joining of pacifism and feminism. That a connection exists between male dominance and war was a truism for many pre-World War I feminists, however rudimentary their analyses may have been. According to Gorham, the chief message of the Canadian suffragist Flora MacDonald Denison's pre-war pamphlet <u>War and Women</u> was that "militarism results from the dominance of men in public life." Charlotte Perkins Gilman, as already mentioned, also put war down to excessive masculinity. Ironically, once the First World War was underway, women in the Anglo-American world made frequent reference to the greater male dominance of German society in order to mobilize women's support for the anti-German war effort.

Another more fully developed argument advanced in these pages for the joining of feminism with pacifism derives from the opposition of both ideologies to the supremacy of force. Vera Brittain attributed the very emergence of the women's movement to the dawning perception that "the operation of reason was superior to force" in the ordering of human affairs. Jo Vellacott identifies rejection of the doctrine that "might is right" as a key element in the thought of her feminist pacifists of the First World War. Seventy years later Carroll forges the same link when she reasons that "feminists committed to securing the rights of women as human beings" to life and liberty, "must question any right claimed by governments or armies or parties or individuals to enforce their will on others by force of arms," loss of liberty, and threat of death.

This commitment to non-violence led many women to oppose any and all violently enforced oppression. Cooper tells us that, to the radical French feminist Eugénie Potonié-Pierre, "both women's and working people's rights were inseparable from peace." And Vera Brittain argued, we read in Bennett's paper, that "the struggle against war, which is the final and most vicious expression of force, is fundamentally inseparable from feminism, socialism, slave emancipation and the liberation of subject races." Thus feminism embraces pacifism and both in turn link arms in the struggle for universal social justice. While some may dismiss such a vision as utopian, others, as Micheline de Sève reminds us, regard it as our only bulwark against annihilation.

PART I

THEORETICAL PERSPECTIVES

Patriotic !—At the Sham Fight, Beacon Hill, May 24.

Papa's Boy—" Gee ! Don't I wish I was a cannon firing solger."
Mama's Boy—" I'd rather be a solger hidin' in the broom."
Sally—" And I'm glad I'm a wummon !"

Emily Carr
Source: credit #42673 Provincial Archives, Victoria, British Columbia

FEMINISM AND PACIFISM: HISTORICAL AND THEORETICAL CONNECTIONS

Berenice A. Carroll

In an essay entitled "Peace Studies and the Feminist Challenge," Beverly Woodward wrote:

> Peace studies is a discipline rooted in our passions--in fear, in revulsion, in love, in hope, in stubbornness: in the fear of what humankind may yet do to itself, in revulsion at the cruel destruction that has already been wrought, in the love of life and the potentialities it bears, in the hope that we may still affect our common human future, in the stubborn refusal to give up in the face of the seemingly insuperable obstacles to the creation of a peaceful and just world order.[1]

As I read this it struck me that Woodward could as readily have begun with the words "feminist studies" instead of "peace studies." The statement then takes on some subtle changes of meaning, but still rings true.

This strikingly easy translation from "peace studies" to "feminist studies" (or vice-versa) in such a passage corresponds to an intuitive feeling--a "gut feeling" of mine, which I know at least some others share--that there is some fundamental bond between feminism and pacifism, some inherent and inevitable logic that binds them ultimately together.

Yet there are many facts and arguments that dispute this intuition. Despite the frequent stereotypical association of women with pacifism, women do not find it easy to work for peace. In the peace movement, we often find ourselves outsiders: if not excluded, then accepted mainly as exception or as servant. In the world of national and international "politics," we find doors closed in our faces, deaf ears turned to our pleas and demands alike. And if we turn to the history of feminist politics, we find sister pitted against sister, suffragette against pacifist, moderate against militant, conservative against radical. The goals of feminism and pacifism may appear to some of us to be in excellent harmony, yet the women struggling for these goals find themselves continually in conflict, not only with the declared enemies of both feminism and pacifism, but with our supposed friends and even with each other.[2]

Efforts to integrate feminism with pacifism have come mainly from the pacifist side, or rather, from the side of pacifist women. Women in the peace movement have sought to combine their own concerns, to respond to male dominance in the peace movement, and at the same time to promote peace as a feminist issue. Feminists, though widely supportive of peace and internationalism, have been more reluctant to identify themselves with pacifism.

I

One line of argument against linking feminism with pacifism comes from those who see feminism as primarily concerned with opening opportunities for women on an equal basis with men in all aspects of our present-day society, including those relating to war.[3] This position is allied with another which holds that women's subordination and dependency are perpetuated by stereotyped associations between women and pacifism.

This is the view represented, for example, by Emily Stoper and Roberta Ann Johnson in their paper, "The Weaker Sex and the Better Half: The Idea of Women's Moral Superiority in the American Feminist Movement."[4] Stoper and Johnson argue that feminists have often asserted women's moral superiority over men, and in particular have claimed a special role for women as peacemakers. Unfortunately this may be turned against us:

> Once women admitted that there was a significant difference between the sexes, the argument could be reversed once more and used against them again. Women's uncorrupted nature, it could be argued, might make her too soft in hard negotiations and too naive in policy-making. . . .[The claim of moral superiority] has made [women] vulnerable to the charge that being different makes them inferior; has reinforced their traditional roles; and has saddled them with a self-defeating approach to politics. In these ways, it has severely limited women's access to and effectiveness in the political arena.

Others have argued that for women to refuse participation in military policy and armed forces of nation-states leaves these key arenas of power and control in exclusively male hands and constitutes a failure of responsibility. "By accepting a categorical prohibition against women's exercise of society's force, all women become protectees and all men potential protectors," writes Judith Stiehm. But the "protection" is of a very dubious character. "Not having direct access to force makes women appear as potential victims, while men who are accustomed to acting with force become potential attackers. . . ." We must then wonder "when protection becomes a racket--when 'protectors' align themselves to their mutual advantage while offering false protection to persons forbidden to participate in their own defence." And Stiehm suggests: "While one does not want to fall into the trap of demanding something simply because it is denied, shared risk and responsibility would seem to be the *sine qua non* of citizenship."[5]

Elizabeth Janeway, in *The Powers of the Weak*, while not rejecting nonviolence, also cautions that it "may suit women too well."[6] Avoidance of the use of force is so "typically feminine," she suggests, that it may fail to have the impact of nonviolent tactics carried out by men. Even radical feminists committed to nonviolence may be uneasy on this point. The Feminism and Nonviolence Study Group, concerned that "traditional nonviolence" has been male-led and male-defined, acknowledge too that "certain women's actions for peace can tend to perpetuate our subordination by portraying women as natural peacemakers and not as powerful activists for change."[7]

Source: *Breaching the peace* (London: Onlywomen Press, 1983)

The Onlywomen Collective, in *Breaching the Peace*, have argued strongly against the women's peace movement on the grounds that it is an arena of cooptation and diversion of energies from feminism, that it rests on dangerous "biological" assumptions, that it presents a "reactionary reinforcement of the stereotyping of women," obstructs us in "taking our own oppression seriously" (by emphasizing the goal of "saving the children" and working for a "greater cause"), and uses arguments very similar to those of "Women for Defence" (protecting the children, keeping the peace, etc.). "We see the women's peace movement as a symptom of the loss of feminist principles and processes--radical analysis, __Acriticism and consciousness raising."[8]

The charge that the women's peace movement has been sexist may seem strange, but the evidence of it surrounds us still today in many quarters. An example is the striking advertisement circulated by Women Strike for Peace and published in the *New York Times* on June 1, 1980, declaring "We Are Angry Women."

WE ARE ANGRY WOMEN

**A Message to the Leaders
of Nuclear Nations**

WE DO NOT WANT OUR CHILDREN
TO BE THE LAST GENERATION

WE ARE ANGERED by the continuing build-up of **arsenals which** threaten the world with nuclear extinction by **plan or accident.**

WE ARE ANGERED at the spectacle of men who claim they are for peace while they build for war — who confuse their own political fortunes with the fortunes of humanity.

WE ARE OUTRAGED that nations spend hundreds of billions of dollars for weapons while children starve by the millions.

WE CONDEMN the use of military force by one government against another for such acts can ignite into nuclear war.

WE SPEAK AS AMERICAN WOMEN who believe that no government should hold the power to condemn all humanity to death.

Source: *The New York Times*, Sunday, June 1, 1980

The textual reference to "angry women" calls to mind images of feminism, but what is the picture actually used in the ad? Not women in a protest march or some other militant collective action, but a single, stern-looking woman, attractive and fairly young, with a baby held over one breast and another child leaning against the other, under her protective arm, her hand spread tensely over the child's shoulder. The subliminal images silently projected are: woman as mother, woman as an isolated being, surrounded only by children, woman as stern moralist, woman as sex object (pencilled eyebrows, emphasis on breasts), woman as anxious and fearful, woman as nurturant and protective.

One of the most recently established organizations in the women's peace movement, Peace Links, founded by Betty Bumpers, also emphasizes women's mothering role. The *New York Times* wrote on May 26, 1982: "'The disarmament campaign is directed toward women,' Mrs. Bumpers said, 'because it is the ultimate parenting issue.'" And the Peace Links brochure says: "We hope that the women of the Soviet Union, just as all women of the world, share our concern for the future of our children."[9] Peace Links and Women Strike for Peace might argue that they are seeking to appeal to a mass audience, and must use images acceptable to that audience. Whether this is a valid position is debatable, but for our purposes the point is that the priority is clear: one wants to get across a message concerning the danger of the nuclear arms race (the "greater cause"); if one can do this by projecting a stereotyped image of woman, one does it, regardless of the possible effects of perpetuating the stereotype.

II

The tension between the women's peace movement and the organized feminist movement is not new. Historically, relations between the two have been complex and ambivalent.

To begin with, it is necessary to distinguish between women's organizations and feminist organizations, and even between "the women's movement" and "feminism"; and likewise to distinguish between "peace movements" and "pacifism." There are today and have been historically many women's movements and many peace movements, in different times, places, cultures, and classes. These movements have been highly diverse and internally complex and among them there have been profound disagreements on many issues. Among the women's movements have been many that decline to identify themselves as "feminist"; among the peace movements there are many that decline to identify themselves as "pacifist." It is therefore not obvious that peace movement women were or are "feminist pacifists."

Indeed there has been much debate as to whether women's reform groups and peace organizations in the late nineteenth and early twentieth century can be characterized as strongly feminist. For many decades, for example, the Women's International League for Peace and Freedom refused to support the Equal Rights Amendment. It is true that Dorothy Detzer and WILPF worked hard (though with very little success) to secure representation of women in disarmament negotiations and international organizations in the 1920s and 1930s, but in general the women's peace organizations and women active in mixed groups in the peace movement for many decades gave little priority either to feminist concerns or to women's representation in the top echelons of the peace movement as a whole, preferring to concentrate attention on what is often called "the issues," meaning, issues of war, peace and disarmament as they have traditionally been defined by the male-dominated leadership.[10]

Similarly, some leading pacifist women of the nineteenth century, such as Bertha von Suttner, gave little attention to the status of women. As Sandi E. Cooper points out, "Feminist questions were not central to her; she was a successful, independent woman who lived by her pen. The civil disabilities that constrained other women were not her main interest; peace was." Moreover: "For von Suttner, it was crucial to keep the peace movement separate from movements of social reform and revolution."[11] Though von Suttner did argue in 1910 at the Stockholm Universal Peace Congress that "women's and peace movements were two sides of the same cloth," her priority was unquestionably the peace movement.[12]

It is true that there were some close personal links among the leaders of the women's peace movement and the organized feminist movement in the late nineteenth and early twentieth centuries. In a recent paper on "Pacifism and the Roots of Feminism," Carolyn Stephenson argues on this basis that early feminists saw "a logical linkage between feminism, socialism or social reform, and pacifism," and that this linkage "formed the basis of feminism's roots."[13] Stephenson presents evidence to show that in three major periods of modern feminism (1830-1870, 1910-1925, and 1970-present), "substantial parts of the women's movement have been involved in peace and radical social change movements." This is certainly undeniable, but that it proves an essential historical and logical linkage between pacifism and the origins of feminism is doubtful.

To begin with, the historical linkage revolved strongly around the traditional stereotypic images of women as nurturers, mothers, and natural peacemakers. Many feminists of this early period linked their demands for women's rights and political and legal equality with the view that women would raise the moral tone of political life. As Angelina Grimké wrote in 1836, in her "Appeal to the Christian Women of the South," women would raise the issue of slavery "in the best possible manner, as a matter of *morals* and *religion*, not of expediency or politics."[14] This linkage was made repeatedly during and after World War I. As Ellen Key put it in *War, Peace, and the Future* in 1916: "To everybody with any depth of insight the warring woman must seem a painful contradiction in terms. To be a woman implies the giving and protecting of life, and the whole future significance of women's increased rights is dependent on her reverence for this mission and her abhorrence of all destruction of life, especially of the mass destruction of war."[15]

The same theme was sounded repeatedly by many others. In 1915, the Woman's Peace Party declared: "As women, we are especially the custodian of the life of the ages. We will not longer consent to its reckless destruction."[16] Jane Addams argued in similar terms in *Peace and Bread in Time of War*: ". . . so it seemed to me the millions of American women might be caught up into a great world purpose, that of conservation of life; there might be found an antidote to war in woman's affection and all-embracing pity for helpless children."[17]

Moreover, while the linkage between feminism and pacifism in the past often has been based on stereotypes that contemporary feminism questions, it has also been a linkage all too readily breached when put to the test of war, when the majority of women's organizations, including those we may call feminist and those we might call pacifist alike, abandoned their alleged pacifism to support their governments in prosecuting the war at hand. One may argue that this means only that both betrayed the logic of their cause, but evidently that logic was not so compelling in feminism's early roots as to persuade most of the women's organizations of that period that pacifism was absolutely essential to feminism.

Thus Matilda Joslyn Gage, in the *History of Woman Suffrage*, looked back with pride on women's contributions to the war effort in the Civil War:

> At this eventful hour the patriotism of woman shone forth as fervently and spontaneously as did that of man; and her self-sacrifice and devotion were displayed in as many varied fields of action. While he buckled on his knapsack and marched forth to conquer the enemy, she planned the campaigns which brought the nation victory; fought in the ranks when she could do so without detection; inspired the sanitary commission; gathered needed supplies for the grand army; provided nurses for the hospitals; comforted the sick; smoothed the pillows of the dying; inscribed the last messages of love to those far away; and marked the resting-places where the brave men fell.[18]

In World War I most of the main women's suffrage or women's rights organizations rallied to their national war efforts, though this war split the feminists not only across the warring lines but also internally. The National American Woman Suffrage Association (NAWSA), the largest women's suffrage organization in the United States, gave active support to the war after US entry, and all but the most radical branches even of the Woman's Peace Party gave some degree of support.[19] In England both the moderate and the militant branches of the suffrage movement split, with the established leadership preferring support for the war.

Millicent Fawcett, president of the British National Union of Women's Suffrage Societies, declared on the day after the outbreak of war in 1914 that members of the National Union would "bind ourselves together for the purpose of rendering the greatest possible aid to our country at this momentous epoch."[20] Her counterpart in Germany, Gertrud Baumer, president of the Federation of German Women's Associations, made the same commitment, with somewhat greater nationalist fervour: "We are swept up in this great, serious unification of all national endeavor into a great consensus: that is, to defend the power and greatness of our nation in this war that has been forced upon us."[21] Even the most uncompromising English suffragists, Emmeline and Christabel Pankhurst and the Women's Social and Political Union (WSPU), rallied to the war effort, urging men to enlist in the armed forces and women to join the National Service. "Directly the threat of foreign war descended on our nation," wrote Emmeline Pankhurst, "we declared a complete truce from militancy." Christabel, returned from her exile in Paris, declared: "Everything that we women have been fighting for and treasure would disappear in the event of a German victory. The Germans are playing the part of savages, overriding every principle of humanity and morality." On July 17, 1915, Emmeline Pankhurst, who had for years waged an implacable struggle against the British government and stood close to death before the outbreak of the war from ten hunger strikes in the previous eighteen months, conducted a government-financed "Right to Serve" demonstration of 30,000 women.[22] At the same time the leaders of the mainstream French feminist movement were also urging their members to support the war, and, after the war, to "give to the nation the children who would replace those who died."[23]

Some feminists, certainly, opposed World War I and adopted a strongly pacifist stance. Alice Paul, Crystal Eastman, and the Congressional Union in the United States, Catherine Marshall, Sylvia Pankhurst and the East London Federation of Suffragettes in England, and Hélène Brion and the syndicalist teachers' union in France, all resisted the war and saw their feminism and pacifism as closely interrelated, even inseparable.[24] But the vast majority of those who had struggled for women's rights both long and ardently for decades past saw no contradiction, when the war came, between feminism and support for their warring national governments. On the contrary, most were convinced that support for the war was in the interest of the cause of women's rights: that it would gain women opportunities, respect, and a claim to equal citizenship too strong for men to deny after the war. Whether they were right in this remains in debate among historians of the suffrage movement; some argue that the war only delayed the achievement of woman suffrage. But it is clear that the compelling logic linking feminism and pacifism escaped them at the time.

III

The problem is complicated by the fact that women face the issues of support or resistance to war, and the puzzles of achieving peace, in a context very different from that of men. One of the key differences in the social and political context is the fact that women have been overwhelmingly *disarmed* through most of the history of "civilization." I don't say "through most of *human* history," because both men and women appear to have been *un*armed through most of the very long period of human evolution prior to the establishment of what we call "civilization" (which essentially corresponds to the appearance of patriarchy, warfare, and class society).[25] Nor do I say "*un*armed" of the condition of most women since the appearance of patriarchy, because it is not clear to what extent women have had the *choice* whether to be armed or not, and it is clear that at least in modern civilization women have been for the most part explicitly excluded from bearing arms in military and police forces. Moreover, there is considerable evidence that many women (not necessarily "most," but clearly at least thousands or tens of thousands of women) when given the choice do take up arms and enter combat and sometimes kill, either for personal reasons or for patriotic or revolutionary goals. Hence, I think it is probably more correct to say that women as a group have been *dis*armed, kept from bearing arms by others, more particularly, by armed men.

Now for women to live *dis*armed in a world dominated by men most monstrously armed has very peculiar, perhaps contradictory, consequences.

On the one hand, as some pacifist women have argued, it gives women a special vantage point and special skills with which to assess the role of weapons and war in human affairs and to offer alternative models of behaviour in dealing with conflict and social change.

This view has been suggested most strongly, for example, by Elise Boulding (a past president of the Women's International League for Peace and Freedom), in her book, *Women in the Twentieth Century World*, where she argues that women provide the central hope for world social transformation. "Who will create the images needed for such a transformation?" asks Boulding, and replies:

It will be those who are marginal to the present society, who are excluded from the centers of power, who stand at the world's peripheries and see society with different eyes. . . .It happens that the category of human beings I have been writing about in this book fulfills the requirements of marginality, of exclusion from the centers of power, and of possession of practical everyday skills at the micro and

intermediate levels of human activity--the family, the
neighborhood, the town . . . I am referring, of course, to
women.[26]

On the other hand, since women have not consciously *chosen* their
*dis*armed and marginal status, and since the armed might of male
dominance is often turned against us in many hideous forms of physical
and mental violence to which we are subjected daily at least as threat if
not as actual experience, it is not surprising that many feminists today
question the male *monopoly* of violence more than they question the use
of violence itself.

This questioning of the male monopoly of violence has taken four
main forms: (1) the demand for entry for women on the same basis as
men into military and police forces, including combat duty; (2) the
spread of physical self-defence training for women, including or
excluding the use of firearms, and advocacy of physical retaliation by
women on identified rapists and batterers; (3) Amazonian art and
literature projecting images of societies in which armed women defend
their territories, fight wars of extermination against men, or build a
new social order from which men have been eliminated; and (4)
encouragement of women's participation in revolutionary or
liberationist armed struggles.

I find myself strangely in sympathy with all of these challenges to
male violence, even though I would not choose them myself or urge
them as preferred political choices. And I know I am not alone in such
feelings, among pacifist feminists. For example, Pam McAllister, in her
introduction to *Reweaving the Web of Life*, describes her visit to a
women's collective in Florida that "armed themselves, slept with pistols
beneath their pillows and talked freely about the significance of women
becoming willing, able, and prepared to use guns for self-defence":

> They took me to the police range where they practiced and
> gave me one lesson in how to shoot. I remember that
> afternoon as one of the most satisfying I'd spent in months--
> standing beneath a sunny, vividly blue sky with six women
> absolutely committed to the "I'm-not-a-victim-anymore" spirit
> . . . . I ringed the bull's eye with all but two of the bullets! . . .
> "McAllister, you're a natural killer!" shouted Maryanne,
> congratulating me with her version of a compliment. And I
> loved these women with all my heart. I felt one in spirit with
> these fine sisters--in their rage and their solid commitment to
> resistance and in their boisterous laughter--even though I
> couldn't affirm their adopting the patriarchy's answer-to-
> everything (threat of death).[27]

I feel less sympathy with Sally Gearhart's proposal for returning
"species responsibility" to women by reducing the male population
through a conscious and extensive policy of genetic engineering and

11

control of reproductive technology. Through ovular merging and other techniques, she proposes, "the proportion of men must be reduced and maintained at approximately 10% of the human race."[28] Despite Gearhart's rejection of violent means to achieve this end, I find both the objective itself and the logic of the argument chillingly reminiscent of genocidal policies, not only of Nazis against Jews and Slavs but of white imperialists and settlers against conquered peoples around the globe. Though Gearhart differentiates her proposal from such policies by arguing that it would "have to be done within cultures themselves, without outside intervention," one wonders whether men would agree that a deliberate and drastic reduction in their numbers through genetic engineering controlled by women was "without outside intervention."

Gearhart's proposal, relying on a "masculine" style of logic distancing the speaker and reader from objects (Jews, blacks, Indians, etc.; in this case, men) who are thus dehumanized, is unusual even among those apocalyptic writings of women portraying a future society entirely devoid of men. These excursions into a future freed from the manifold violence purveyed so widely by men in contemporary society offer opportunities for that process of imaging future alternatives suggested by Boulding as one of women's potentially unique contributions. But these visions seldom envisage a systematic policy of male depopulation by technological means. In general they either assume some *deus ex machina*, such as a male-chromosome-linked disease, or they involve women breaking the male monopoly of violence by resorting to it themselves in extremity. Charlotte Perkins Gilman, in *Herland*, combines these approaches: she disposes of most of the men through their own wars and a natural disaster, but finally has women turn on the remaining male oppressors and kill them in desperation.[29]

Gilman passes over these events quite hurriedly, as do a number of other writers of women's utopian fiction, but at least one contemporary writer dwells on the apocalyptic visions with poetic ecstasy. Monique Wittig, in *Les Guérillères*, celebrates the revolt and victory of women in an epic war for freedom from male domination and for the reconstruction of a female society. It may be worth pausing to consider an example of the tone and flavour of this vision. Wittig describes dark images of the war itself:

> They say, hell, let the earth become a vast hell. So they speak crying and shouting. They say, let my words be like the tempest the thunder and lightning that the mighty release from their height. They say, let me be seen everywhere arms in hand. They say anger hate revolt. They say, hell, let the earth become a vast hell destroying killing and setting fire to the buildings of men, to theatres national assemblies to museums libraries prisons psychiatric hospitals factories old and new from which they free the slaves. They say, let the memory of Attila and his warrior hordes perish from history

because of his meekness. They say that they are more
barbarous than the most barbarous. Their armies grow
hourly. Delegations go before them when they approach the
towns. Together they sow disorder in the great cities, taking
prisoners, putting to the sword all those who do not
acknowledge their might.[30]

But interspersed with these are other images of freedom and joy in
women's victory over oppression:

> CONSPIRACIES REVOLUTIONS/FERVOUR FOR THE
> STRUGGLE/INTENSE HEAT DEATH AND
> HAPPINESS/IN THE BREASTED TORSOS/THE
> PHOENIXES THE PHOENIXES/FREE CELIBATE
> GOLDEN/THEIR OUTSPREAD WINGS ARE HEARD . . .
> THE CRIES THE LAUGHS THE MOVEMENTS/THE
> WOMEN AFFIRM IN TRIUMPH THAT/ALL ACTION IS
> OVERTHROW.[31]

Such writings are more the exception than the rule among
feminist writers and activists. Much more widespread and broadly
accepted among many feminists are the demand for equal access to arms
in military and police forces, and encouragement for women to
participate in revolutionary or liberationist armed struggles. The
former, for example, is currently being pursued in the United States by
WEAL (Women's Equity Action League) through their "Women and the
Military Project," which serves an advocacy role for military women in
all matters of benefits and opportunities. WEAL specifically supports
"including women in defence policy-making roles" (i.e., all top military
and combat policy roles) and urges "repeal of all sections of the US code
and alteration of regulations and policies that restrict the assignment
and promotion of military women" (i.e., restrictions on combat and
"combat-related" assignments).[32]

The issue of the draft has drawn lines very sharply between many
feminist and pacifist women. Major feminist organizations, like the
National Organization for Women (NOW) in the US, have adopted the
position that, while they oppose conscription in general, women and
men should be subject to draft registration and conscription on the same
basis, without regard to sex. To many pacifist women, the spectacle of
women in effect demanding to be conscripted (even with the caveat "if
men are") has seemed ludicrous and shocking. But to many feminist
women, it has seemed equally ludicrous and shocking for women
demanding equality to claim the weakness and special status of their
sex against the obligation to military service. The pacifist women have
been further embarrassed by the fact that the most vociferous and
influential opponents of conscription and military service for women,
such as Phyllis Shlafly, have been on the anti-feminist right, closely
allied with the war hawks.

Pacifist women have also been embarrassed, confused, and sometimes silenced by the issue of women's participation in armed liberation struggles. The women's peace movement has tended to give strong support to liberation struggles around the world, from South Africa to Central America. But as the African National Congress has moved in recent years from its former commitment to nonviolent resistance towards growing pursuit of armed guerrilla action; and as the threat of U.S. intervention in Central America escalates, women are more and more directly involved in military units and combat operations. The anthology *Third World--Second Sex*, edited by Miranda Davies, carries interviews and reports of women in armed struggles in Namibia, Zimbabwe, Eritrea, and other countries. *Women: A Journal of Liberation*, in a special issue on women in peace and war, carried an article entitled "Up in Arms: Women in the Nicaraguan Revolution," noting that: "The Nicaraguan revolution has been acclaimed for the high level of participation by women. Hundreds of women joined the militia units."[33] Pacifist women have been rightly reluctant to repudiate the decision of Third World women to join the liberation struggles with arms, or to set themselves in opposition to the viewpoint expressed, for example, by a spokeswoman for the SWAPO (South West Africa People's Organization) Women's Council: "We have to make our women understand the need to participate fully in the armed struggle--not by saying that we should go to work in the kitchen, or carrying guns for our men, but participating to such a degree that today there are Namibian women commanders."[34]

IV

Thus feminist pacifists and pacifist feminists find themselves in a maze of conflicting and sometimes seemingly contradictory commitments and reasonings from which it is not obvious how to extricate ourselves, and in which it may seem increasingly doubtful that any inherent logic binds the two positions together. If pacifist women fall silent before the voice of the SWAPO Women's Council and the Nicaraguan AMNLAE (Asociación de Mujeres Nicaraguenses Luisa Amanda Espinosa/Nicaraguan Women's Association Luisa Amanda Espinosa) urging their women to take up arms; if feminist women find themselves demanding entry into armed forces on the same basis as men; if pacifist women feel love, solidarity, and exhilaration on the shooting range with a women's armed self-defence collective; if feminist women pursue visions of societies from which men have been banished by women's armed revolution--where is the unity and compelling logic joining feminism and pacifism?

I will argue in reply to this question that there is such a compelling logic, and that it has a specific location that is discernible if we proceed by a careful process of disentangling concepts that are deeply enmeshed in confusion.

14

The first step in this process is to disentangle the concepts of "women and peace" from the concepts of "feminism and pacifism." The linkage of feminism and pacifism must be placed squarely in the realm of political and ideological commitment and choice: it is not to be resolved by either biology or history. If there is any necessary connection between women and peace it is certainly not immutable, since women can and do fight, take up arms, kill, torture, brutalize and subjugate other human beings, including children. If we argue that it is only a small minority of women who do such things, we are bound to acknowledge that it is actually only a relatively small minority of men who do such things. In all societies men must be coerced by social pressure or conscripted to go to battle in large numbers; among volunteers for our armed forces, only about 4% volunteer for combat duty. Personal and domestic violence are more prevalent, and media violence is pervasive in our society, but even in these arenas women are perpetrators as well as victims, and we are still dealing with minorities rather than majorities of men as well as women.[35] Physical coercion of children is so widespread that we hardly notice it unless it is severe; the severity of the coercion and punishment of children may more often be greater when exercised by men, but slapping, pushing, pulling, and other forms of mild physical punishment and coercion are so commonly exercised by mothers against their own children that here we are probably in the realm of majorities.

That there is an historical connection between women and peace is undoubtedly true. But it is a connection imposed upon women along with their subordination, their disarmed condition, and their stereotyped roles. Out of this imposed connection arises also a widespread stereotypic association between *femininity* and *passivity*. But these must be clearly distinguished as concepts from "*feminism*" and "*pacifism*." Indeed, "femininity" is strongly rejected by "feminists," and "passivity" as such is equally rejected by both "feminists" and "pacifists," though some may use "passive resistance" as a form of direct action.

Similarly, we must disentangle ourselves from the stereotypic association between *pacifism*, or even *peace* itself, and "*effeminacy*." This is an old and widespread notion, expressed for example by Machiavelli in the early sixteenth century when he wrote that the Persians under Cyrus the Great had found their predecessors, the Medes, "weak and effeminate through long peace."[36] The concept of "effeminacy" is in itself an admission of misogyny and a weapon in the arsenal of propaganda used by patriarchal militarism to coerce men into accepting or adopting systems of violence. But beyond this, the fact is that *pacifism* has *not* been a prevalent part of women's traditional roles and "feminine" behavior.

One might argue that "pacific behavior" has been a part of women's traditional roles. Indeed, that is the basis of the argument by Elise Boulding and others that women have a special contribution to make to peacemaking. But "*pacifism*" is not equivalent to "*pacific behavior.*"

Pacific behavior is actually the human norm, for both men and women, which is why, for example, methods of physical intimidation are effective in securing power and privileges for governments and gangsters. If it were not, the minorities that rule would always be readily overcome by the vastly greater numbers of their victims responding in kind. But, in fact, it takes extreme duress and a variety of special circumstances to mobilize populations to overthrow by force of arms an oppressive regime or invading army. And even when the majority of the population is mobilized for support, it is always a minority that actually engages in combat operations. Indeed, the very notions of "courage" and "heroism" in battle imply that these are characteristics out-of-the-ordinary for men as well as women.

On the other hand, if "pacific behavior," the norm of human conduct, were equivalent to "pacifism," war would have been eliminated long ago, since the majority of the human population would have consciously chosen to eliminate it and taken concerted action to do so. Pacifism--like feminism--is a deliberate, conscious choice of principles and policies (the more necessarily conscious in that these principles and policies are often at odds with the predominant views of society). As we know, however, those who have consciously chosen *pacifism* as a political ideology and a basis for political action are a minority, indeed a very small minority, of the human population, both male and female.

That is indeed the central problem for pacifism, as Rosa Luxemburg recognized in her address to the judges who condemned her to prison for anti-militarist propaganda in 1914:

> We [Social Democrats] are of the opinion that the great mass of working people does and must decide about the question of war and peace--that this is not a matter of commands from above and blind obedience below. We think that wars can only come about so long as the working class either supports them enthusiastically because it considers them justified and necessary, or at least accepts them passively. But once the majority of working people come to the conclusion . . . that wars are nothing but a barbaric, unsocial, reactionary phenomenon, entirely against the interests of the people, then wars will have become impossible even if the soldiers obey their commanders. According to the concept of the prosecution it is the army who makes war; according to us it is the entire population. The latter have to decide whether wars happen or do not happen. The decision whether we shall or shall not have militarism rests with the working people, old and young, men and women . . .[37]

I am doubtful that Luxemburg was voicing here the position of the majority of the Social Democrats, who soon afterward voted to support the war and rally to the patriotic cause, just as Gertrud Baumer rallied the feminists to support the war. But I believe that Luxemburg's analysis was correct: the decision rests with the masses of the population. And despite their pacific behavior, they are not yet pacifists by conviction and they are not yet prepared to take action to create the conditions for peace or to dismantle the war system.

This is so for the majority of women as well as for the majority of men. It is true that there is evidence of a "gender gap" in opinion polls and voting behavior between men and women on issues of peace, war, defence spending, and welfare programmes.[38] This gender gap is significant statistically--it is not in the range of differences that could be attributed to accident. But neither is it in the range of majority vs. minority. A plurality or on some issues a majority of both men and women give general support to the war system, even where there may be a gap of as much as 20% between men and women on some questions.

It can be argued that women have a crucial role to play in altering the balance on such issues. One of the most powerful forms of influence exerted by women is in shaping the political socialization of the population, especially through establishing for children the legitimacy of authority exercised by government, church, and educational leaders. Should the "gender gap" reach a point at which the majority of women reject the authority of governments and other institutions to use armed force, we would certainly be at a point of enormous social transformation. To that extent, *women* may indeed have a special role to play in creating *peace*, not because of innate biological characteristics, but because of their traditional social and implicit political roles.

And to that extent, feminists may have a special obligation and a special role to play in creating peace, not because they speak *for* women, nor because they see any inherent or immutable connection between women and peace, but because they speak *to* women, and seek the development among women of a changed political consciousness. Thus the incorporation of a conscious policy of pacifist commitment into feminist programmes might ultimately have a powerful impact.

However, the question remains: is there any compelling reason, in the logic of feminist and pacifist ideologies, why feminists should accept this obligation and role? When Virginia Woolf urged, in *Three Guineas*, that feminists should *choose* to affirm and preserve, in reinterpreted form, those "four great teachers," poverty, chastity, derision, and freedom from unreal loyalties, she included among the latter those loyalties to "God and Empire," national pride, and other commitments leading men to pugnacity, greed and war. She urged women to draw on their own traditions to "make use of mind and will to abolish the inhumanity, the beastliness, the horror, the folly of war":

> And let the daughters of uneducated women dance round the new house, the poor house, the house that stands in a narrow street where omnibuses pass and the street hawkers cry their wares [in contrast with the wealthy and aloof universities of men], and let them sing, "We have done with war! We have done with tyranny!" And their mothers will

17

laugh from their graves, "It was for this that we suffered obloquy and contempt! Light up the windows of the new house, daughters! Let them blaze!"[39]

This is a powerful summons, and *Three Guineas* is an intricately argued and important theoretical contribution to feminist peace theory. Nevertheless, it does not clearly engage this central question: Is there something in the logic of feminism and pacifism that binds them inextricably together?

V

It must be stated at the outset that for those seeking to answer this question, to integrate feminism and pacifism on an intellectual level, there is almost no guidance in the theoretical literature. In the literature of the peace movement in general there is very little attention to feminism. In the literature of the women's peace movement, especially recent writings on feminism and nonviolence, the emphasis is on literary and "political" approaches, and the theoretical analysis is more implicit than explicit. In the literature of the feminist movement, there is considerable material on "women and peace," but very little on "feminism and pacifism." A number of feminist and pacifist women in recent years have been grappling with the practical, historical, social and intellectual problems of *combining* their feminist and pacifist commitments, but the logical grounds for this combination have not been much examined. And most of the literature of "feminist theory" as such is devoid of direct consideration of pacifism. At the conference on "The Second Sex: Thirty Years Later--A Commemorative Conference on Feminist Theory," held in New York in 1979, none of the conference papers dealt directly with pacifism or nonviolence. In several new collections of essays on feminist theory,[40] there are no essays on feminism and pacifism. Some of the articles in the recent special issue of *Women's Studies Quarterly* on Teaching about Peace, War and Women in the Military,[41] do touch briefly on the theoretical questions, but none presents an extended analysis.

I would like to conclude here with a brief sketch of several lines of reasoning on which to found the linkage between feminism and pacifism as political ideologies. I will focus here mainly on the theoretical lines that lead *from feminism to pacifism*, rather than from pacifism to feminism. This is in part because the arguments from pacifism to feminism are somewhat better understood on a theoretical level today, though not necessarily well practised in the peace movement. For example, it has been widely understood as one ground for pacifists to adopt feminism that a major underlying cause of war is the sex role socialization of males to acceptance or practice of violence. Thus many pacifists today accept that feminist demands for changes in sex roles are a significant aspect of the struggle to overcome violence at all levels in human life.[42]

But the arguments from feminism to pacifism seem more problematic. Some writers still base the linkage on women's nurturant roles, and their corresponding potential contribution to peace. Jean Elshtain, in an essay on "Women, War, and Feminism," argues correctly that "the real need of the moment is for the securing of a conceptual foundation rather than a series of ad hoc responses to crises."[43] But Elshtain, citing Sara Ruddick's analysis of "Maternal Thinking,"[44] suggests that we pursue "a feminist rethinking of the possibility that women as a group do indeed tend to have a set of interests in . . . the preservation and growth of vulnerable human life." Ruddick herself is more careful to distinguish *maternal* thought from *women's* thought, and her position warrants separate consideration. But any argument that relies primarily on the maternality and nurturance of "women as a group" as the ground for a feminist pacifism founders on the realities of women's multifarious non-maternal, non-nurturant behaviours.

I suggest, rather, that it is possible to discern a number of lines of argument that lead from underlying premises of feminism to the logical necessity of pacifism. The fact that many feminists have not followed-- and will not follow--through this logic to adopt a pacifist position does not prove that there is no such logical connection. Nor does their failure or refusal to do so invalidate their feminism. But I believe that the growing number of feminists who do seek to integrate feminism with pacifism today reflects a development based upon this logic. Like Zillah Eisenstein, who has argued that the logic of both history and theory drives liberal feminism towards a radical future,[45] I would argue that both liberal and radical feminism have a radical pacifist future (and, by a different but similar route, that both liberal and radical pacifism have a radical feminist future).

I can only sketch here very briefly some possible lines of connection. The analysis requires more extended consideration, and these suggestions are put forward in hopes of advancing discussion, rather than as definitive propositions. In particular, there appear to be five main lines of connection from premises of feminism to a position of pacifism: (1) first, and most widely recognized, is an argument based on the interconnections among *patriarchy*, domination, and war; (2) second, also fairly widespread, is an argument based on shared concern with the elimination of *violence* in both "private" and "public" spheres; (3) third is an argument from the premise of *equality*; (4) fourth is an argument derived from the premise of *inalienable rights*; and (5) fifth is an argument from the premise of *sisterhood*. I will limit myself here to further comment on the first and the fourth.

The argument that has been used most frequently to establish a linkage between feminism and pacifism is that patriarchy, dominance, and war are inextricably connected.

"Reflect on the patriarchs," wrote Virginia Woolf, in *A Room of One's Own* (1929):

19

True, they had money and power, but only at the cost of harbouring in their breasts an eagle, a vulture, for ever tearing the liver out and plucking at the lungs--the instinct for possession, the rage for acquisition which drives them to desire other people's fields and goods perpetually; to make frontiers and flags; battleships and poison gas; to offer up their own lives and their children's lives.[46]

Fifty years later, Mary Daly wrote in *Gyn/Ecology*: "Patriarchy *is* the State of War." Daly intends more by this remark than the usual association between masculinity and violence. Patriarchal war, she argues, is essentially directed against women and what women represent to men: life and creativity.

The male sense of barrenness . . . breeds hierarchical structures of violence, epitomized in war . . . . The rulers of patriarchy--males with power--wage an unceasing war against life itself. Since female energy is essentially biophilic, the female spirit/body is the primary target in this perpetual war of aggression against life.[47]

Patriarchy is necrophilic, Daly argues, and "Woman hating is at the core of necrophilia." In sum, ". . .women are the objects of male terror, the projected personifications of the Enemy, the real objects under attack in all the wars of patriarchy."[48]

Similarly Pam McAllister, in *Reweaving the Web of Life*, asserts that "War is inherent in the patriarchal structure." But despite the frequent appearance of such remarks, we do not yet have a full and careful analysis of the structural and ideological links between patriarchy and war.

Piecing together points noted by different authors, I would suggest that such an analysis would examine at least the following connections: (a) the emergence of patriarchy and war together in the history of "civilization" (coinciding also with the emergence of class or caste societies, slavery and racism); (b) the male monopoly of "legitimate" or state violence and its functions in maintaining the powerlessness and subordination of women; (c) the patriarchal character of military institutions and their prevailing misogynist propaganda; (d) the military exploitation of women in service roles and prostitution; (e) the role of mass rape in warfare; and (f) the promotion of war and battle "heroism" as proofs of "masculinity" in patriarchal propaganda. These points underlie the argument that war and military institutions are essential and integral to patriarchy, and must be eliminated if patriarchy is to be overcome. Given the interconnectedness and interdependence of patriarchy and war in all these respects, the argument seems clear that feminists must challenge the war system.

The argument from the premise of inalienable rights is of a

somewhat different nature, resting more in political philosophy than in the examination of history and institutions. That the premise is long-standing in the ideas of feminism is clear from the words of the Declaration of Sentiments adopted by the women assembled at the Seneca Falls Conference of 1848. These early feminists had recourse to wording drawn from the US Declaration of Independence. They declared:

> . . . that *all* men and women are created equal; that they are endowed . . . with certain inalienable rights, that among these are life, liberty and the pursuit of happiness.[49]

Now the source of this statement was a document designed to justify a revolutionary war--why then do I cite it as an argument leading to pacifism?

The connection is suggested in an argument offered by Barbara Deming in 1971:

> What is it that those who advocate nonviolent revolution believe most essentially? They believe, in the first place, what most Americans supposedly believe--solemnly recite in school, from the Declaration of Independence: that all of us are born with certain inalienable rights . . . . Rights, that is, not to be taken from us under any circumstances. Among these rights the right to life, the right to liberty, the right to the pursuit of happiness.[50]

Deming in this essay is not arguing the connection between feminism and pacifism; she is pointing to the grounding of nonviolence in the notion of "inalienable rights," rights "not to be taken from us under any circumstances." If we accept seriously this idea, Deming maintains, it follows that we must respect these rights even in our adversaries:

> For it is not possible to affirm our own rights as inalienable simply by acting out: they are *mine*. We can affirm this only by acting out: they are *ours*--yours, and therefore mine; mine, and therefore yours.[51]

Moreover, this is true even of those adversaries who would deny these rights to ourselves and to others:

> We believe that one does not have to injure or destroy even the people who are usually termed "the real enemy"--those who hold, and abuse, real power. . . .We refuse to call even those people "enemy" in the sense of: those to be destroyed.

Deming notes the connection between this idea and the Christian distinction between "the sinner" and "the sin"--but her argument is not one of religion, but one based on the logic of commitment to the principle of *inalienable* rights. If we deprive others of life or liberty by force of arms, how can we claim that our own rights to life and liberty are "inalienable"?

There are those who ask: But how else can we secure our own rights to life and liberty, and the rights of others, from those who have denied both, and have oppressed, exploited, raped and even exterminated many millions of us through the ages? This is clearly the question posed to us from those who advocate and support women's participation in revolutionary armed struggles. To this Deming and others reply: by the methods of nonviolent action. These methods have been described and argued by Deming and many other contemporary writers including Joan Bondurant, April Carter, Gene Sharp,[52] and most recently many books and pamphlets on feminism and nonviolence. Whether this response is adequate is a question that remains open.

While contemporary feminism no longer dwells so much on the notion of "inalienable rights" as did the nineteenth-century women's movement, I would argue that it does remain a fundamental premise of feminism, underlying all feminist rejection of efforts to deny rights to women on any grounds of nature or tradition. The very groundwork of feminism is the notion that women, despite their genetically inherited differences from men (however great or small), are human beings endowed with rights, not to be taken from us--i.e., inalienable. But if "women" as a class of human beings have inalienable rights to be spared deprivation of life and liberty, so do all human beings. And just as men have no ground on which to arrogate to themselves the privilege and authority of removing such rights from women, neither do women or men have the ground or authority to remove such rights from any others. The contradiction between the notion of *inalienable* rights to life and liberty on the one hand, and the *powers of life and death* exercised by governments and armies on the other hand, is nearly absolute. And on this ground, it follows that feminists committed to securing the rights of women as human beings, must question any right claimed by governments or armies or parties or individuals to enforce their will on others by force of arms and deprivation of their lives or liberty.

Much careful thought remains to be given to developing these and other lines of analysis for those who are concerned with the theoretical foundations of integrating feminism and pacifism. In this pursuit, I believe we may appropriately restate the passage quoted from Beverly Woodward at the outset:

> [Feminist] studies is a discipline rooted in our passions--in fear, in revulsion, in love, in hope, in stubbornness: in the fear of what humankind may yet do to itself, in revulsion at the cruel destruction that has already been wrought, in the love of life and the potentialities it bears, in the hope that we may still affect our common human future, in the stubborn refusal

to give up in the face of the seemingly insuperable obstacles to the creation of a peaceful and just world order.

Comments

Barbara Roberts

I want to comment on two things that you said. I hate to throw the baby out with the bathwater and I'm into the whole feminine motherhood thing now. It seems to me that we need to claim those traditional female or even feminine values because that's one of the major sources of our strength as feminists. I think maybe a way we can do that is to make sure that our demands for reproductive choice are always present in the discourse because that's the link between the definition that you were using of feminism today and the not explicitly feminist women's movement, which I think in fact starts from some unarticulated feminist premises. Secondly, I have some profound qualms about some of your premises. First I want to say that I don't believe that women are naturally more peaceful than men but I don't think I can accept your assumption that we are in fact no less violent than men. We all, I think, know the statistics on violence against women and something that I began to do a couple of years ago is to figure that, OK, if we assume one victim equals one assailant, let's add it up and see what percentage of North American men seem to be doing this.[53] I think a simple glance at the statistics shows that a majority of North American men are very likely involved in direct physical violence against women to say nothing at all of the forms of structural violence. Some of the things I did to my kids I'm so ashamed about and I think most of us who have kids can say that. But in terms of responsibility in perpetrating direct physical violence against kids, I want to refer to something that Linda Gordon and Wini Breines pointed out in their 1983 *Signs* article.[54] They said first of all that we don't have any data-- even estimates--on what percentage of assaults against kids (I mean hitting and stuff like that) are made by women. But even if we assume, and we have no empirical reason to do so, that it's 50 percent, when we consider that women do over 95 percent of the childcare, then our level of violence would be disproportionately low rather than disproportionately high. I think whatever tentative ideas we come to we need to take these kinds of data into account.

Berenice Carroll

The points you are making are very important and need to be dealt with much better than they have been in terms of producing data.

Ursula Franklin

A little while ago I wrote a piece in *The Status of Women News*[55] on feminism and pacifism. I think that one of the linkages is our response to power, and there are a couple of things that I just now want to say again in the same spirit as Barbara because I think that first of all one should not confuse pacifism with being against war. Pacifism is not anti-war, pacifism is the advocacy of a way of life in which the roots of war are attacked and war is unnecessary. And I think in that sense women as feminists see that what produces war, and not only war on the battlefield but war in the work place and everywhere else, is a system of threats. It's saying you do as I do or else. And it doesn't matter whether that's done to women, to kids, or to people who have no economic power. Pacifism is the wish to eliminate the condition of people being threatened, people being without choice. In another place[56] I have said that violence is in many ways resourcelessness and consequently non-violence is resourcefulness. It is the lack of humanity and imagination that makes people start to hit somebody over the head if they don't seem to do what is required of them, whether that is the organized violence of the state or the teacher thundering down on the kids. Basically what I think is that as feminists we know from our own bodies and our history and women's lives what a threat system does to people. And so if you understand that pacifism is not being against war but being against a threat system then you can see that women as feminists have to deal with power. Are they going to use power the way men abuse power or will they find ways in which they can use power unthreateningly? Like Barbara, I think one should not discount the experience of women either in the family or at the paid work place where, not necessarily by choice, they've found many ways of dealing with conflict without the use of the threat of force. And so I think the linkage is power and I think if feminists don't understand that the feminist vision requires the pacifist use of power, then feminism is nothing more than a changing of the guards.

Notes

[1]Peace and Change 3, 4 (Spring 1976): 3.
[2]For further discussion of these points, see: Berenice A. Carroll, "The Outsiders: Comments on Fukuda Hideko, Catherine Marshall and Dorothy Detzer," Peace and Change 4, 3 (Fall 1977): 23-26, and "Feminist Politics and Peace," in Dorothy McGuigan, ed., The Role of Women in Conflict and Peace: An Interdisciplinary Symposium (Ann Arbor: Center for Continuing Education, University of Michigan, 1977). On the exclusion of women from the peace movement or its leadership, see also for example: Devere Allen, The Fight for Peace (New York: Macmillan, 1980), chapter 13; Barrie Thorne, "Gender Imagery and Issues of War and Peace: The Case of the Draft Movement in the 1960's," in McGuigan; and Richard L. Johnson, "The New West German Peace Movement: Male Dominance or Feminist Nonviolence," in Marianne Burkhard and Edith Waldstein, eds., Women in German Yearbook 1 (Lanham, Maryland: University Press of America, 1985), pp. 135-62.
[3]See, for example, Women's Equity Action League, WEAL Washington Report 13, 3 (June/July 1984), and the publications of WEAL's Women and the Military Project.
[4]Polity 10, 2 (Winter 1977): 192-217.
[5]Judith Stiehm, "Women, Men, and Military Science: Is Protection Necessarily a Racket?" in Ellen Boneparth, ed., Women, Power, and Policy (New York: Pergamon Press, 1982), p. 291.

Some historians have argued that women's rights have been advanced by periods of war and armed revolution, in which women are called upon to shoulder tasks and burdens similar or identical to those of men. See essays by Joan W. Scott and Persis Charles in the special issue on "Teaching About Peace, War, and Women in the Military," Women's Studies Quarterly 12, 2 (Summer 1984): 2-6, 7, and the references on pp. 49-50; also Carol R. Berkin and Clara M. Lovett, eds., Women, War, and Revolution (New York: Holmes and Meier, 1980). While one might derive from this an argument that feminists should favour both war and armed revolution, I have not seen any explicit argument to this effect. The debates on this subject among historians have not concerned policy prescriptions, but assessment of the historical facts and the political contexts and implications of women's relationships to war and revolution. See also Cynthia Enloe, Does Khaki Become You? The Militarization of Women's Lives (Boston: South End Press and London: Pluto Press, 1983) for a critical assessment of the uses to which women have been put by military forces.

[6]Elizabeth Janeway, The Powers of the Weak (New York: Morrow, 1980), p. 300.

[7]Feminism and Nonviolence Study Group, Piecing it Together: Feminism and Nonviolence (Devon, England: By the Authors, 1983), ch. 5, pp. 34-5.

[8]Onlywomen Collective, Breaching the Peace (London: Onlywomen Press, 1983), p. 5 and passim. Cartoon from Breaching the Peace.

[9]Peace Links: Women Against Nuclear War (Washington, D. C.: n.d.).

[10]See Carroll, "The Outsiders."

[11]Sandi E. Cooper, "The Work of Women in Nineteenth Century Continental European Peace Movements," Peace and Change 9, 4 (Winter 1984): 18-19.

[12]Sandi E. Cooper, "Women and the Continental Peace Movements: The Effort to Prevent World War One," paper given at the 6th Berkshire Conference on the History of Women, June 2, 1984, p. 17.

[13]Carolyn Stephenson, "Pacifism and the Roots of Feminism," unpublished MS, 1982, p. 7.

[14]Alice S. Rossi, ed., The Feminist Papers (New York: Bantam Books, 1974), p. 304.

[15]Ellen Key, War, Peace, and the Future [1916] (New York: Garland Publishing, 1972), p. 199.

[16]Marie Louise Degen, The History of the Woman's Peace Party [1939] (New York: Garland Publishing, 1972), p. 40.

[17]Jane Addams, Peace and Bread in Time of War [1922] (New York: Garland Publishing, 1972), pp. 82-3.

[18]Mari Jo Buhle and Paul Buhle, eds., The Concise History of Woman Suffrage (Urbana, IL: University of Illinois Press, 1978), p. 195.

[19]See Stephenson, "Pacifism and the Roots of Feminism," pp. 6, 30; also Blanche W. Cook, "The Woman's Peace Party: Collaboration and Non-Cooperation," Peace and Change 1, 1 (Fall 1972): 36-42.

[20]Susan Groag Bell and Karen Offen, eds., Women, The Family, and Freedom: The Debate in Documents (Stanford, CA: Stanford University Press, 1983), vol. 2, p. 260.

[21]Ibid., p. 261.

[22]Midge Mackenzie, Shoulder to Shoulder: A Documentary (New York: Knopf, 1975), pp. 280, 286, 293-4.

[23]Quoted by Judith Wishnia, "Pacifism and Feminism: The French Connection," in this volume, p. 110.

[24]See, for example, Blanche W. Cook, Crystal Eastman on Women and Revolution (Oxford and New York: Oxford University Press, 1978); Cook, "The Woman's Peace Party"; Jo Vellacott Newberry, "Women and War in England: The Case of Catherine E. Marshall and World War I," Peace and Change 4, 3 (Fall 1977): 13-17; Mackenzie, Shoulder to Shoulder: A Documentary; and Wishnia, "Pacifism and Feminism: The French Connection," in this volume, pp. 103-13.

[25]See, for example, on the peaceful character of neolithic

settlements, Jacquetta Hawkes, Prehistory, Vol. 1, Part I, of the
UNESCO History of Mankind: Cultural and Scientific Development
[1963], (New York: New American Library/Mentor, 1965), p. 358.

[26]Elise Boulding, Women in the Twentieth Century World (New
York: Halsted Press, 1977), p. 227; see also Boulding, The Underside of
History: A View of Women Through Time (Boulder, Colorado:
Westview Press, 1976), pp. 35-68, 769-91, 674-5.

[27]Pam McAllister, Introduction to Reweaving the Web of Life:
Feminism and Nonviolence (Philadelphia: New Society Publishers,
1982), pp. ii-iii.

[28]Sally Miller Gearhart, "The Future--If There Is One--Is
Female," in McAllister, ed., Reweaving the Web of Life, p. 280.

[29]Charlotte Perkins Gilman, Herland (New York: Pantheon
Books, 1979).

[30]Monique Wittig, Les Guérillères [1969] (New York: Avon,
1973), p. 130.

[31]Ibid., frontispiece.

[32]WEAL Washington Report, p. 11.

[33]The Journal Staff, Women: A Journal of Liberation, special
issue on Peace and War, 8, 1 (1981): 6. The introductory remarks in this
article bear a striking resemblance to the remarks of Matilda Joslyn
Gage (above) on women's participation in the U.S. Civil war: "Women,
who made up 30% of the Sandinistas, played a crucial role in this
resistance. They fought, delivered messages, arranged transportation,
stored food and medicine, hid arms, built barricades, led military
attacks and bank expropriations, healed the wounded, and buried the
dead."

[34]Ellen Musialela, "Women in Namibia: The Only Way to Free
Ourselves . . . ," in Miranda Davies, ed., Third World--Second Sex
(London: Zed books, 1983), p. 85.

[35]Barbara Roberts argues that men who engage in acts of violence
against women (rape, assault, wife battering, etc.) may be in the
majority, though she acknowledges that the conclusion is speculative.
"The Death of Machothink," Women's Studies International Forum 7, 4
(1984): 195. I am not convinced that the figures she cites warrant this
conclusion, and I believe there are some dangers in overstating the
prevalence of male violence, as there are also in ignoring the existence
of violent behaviour by women (especially against children). This is in
no way to deny that the unacceptably high rates of male violence
against women are extremely serious and significantly related to the
perpetuation of the war system.

[36]Niccolo Machiavelli, The Prince [ca. 1513/14] (New York: New
American Library/Mentor Books, 1952), p. 49.

[37]"Address to the judges at the Second Criminal Court, Frankfurt
. . . 20 February 1914," Vorwaerts, 22 February 1914, reprinted in
translation in J. P. Nettl, Rosa Luxemburg (London: Oxford University
Press, 1966), vol. II, pp. 488-92.

[38]See Bella Abzug with Mim Kelber, Gender Gap (Boston:

Houghton Mifflin, 1984); and Sandra Baxter and Marjorie Lansing, Women and Politics (Ann Arbor: University of Michigan Press, 1980).

[39]Virginia Woolf, Three Guineas [1938] (New York: Harcourt, Brace, Jovanovich, 1966), p. 83.

[40]Nannerl O. Keohane, Michelle Z. Rosaldo and Barbara C. Gelpi, eds., Feminist Theory: A Critique of Ideology (Chicago: University of Chicago Press, 1981); Carol Gould, Beyond Domination: New Perspectives on Women and Philosophy (New Jersey: Rowman and Alanheld, 1983); Liz Stanley and Sue Wise, Breaking Out: Feminist Consciousness and Feminist Research (London: Routledge and Kegan Paul, 1983).

[41]Women's Studies Quarterly 11, 2 (Summer 1984).

[42]See for example Johnson, "The New West German Peace Movement: Male Dominance or Feminist Nonviolence"; Brian Easlea, Fathering the Unthinkable: Masculinity, Scientists and the Nuclear Arms Race (London: Pluto Press, 1983); Betty Reardon, "A gender analysis of militarism and sexist repression: a suggested research agenda," International Peace Research Association Newsletter, Summer 1984; and Barbara Roberts, "The Death of Machothink: Feminist Research and the Transformation of Peace Studies," Women's Studies International Forum 7, 4 (1984): 195-200.

[43]The Nation, June 14, 1980, p. 724.

[44]Feminist Studies 6, 2 (Summer 1980): 342-67.

[45]Zillah Eisenstein, The Radical Future of Liberal Feminism (New York and London: Longman, 1981).

[46]Virginia Woolf, A Room of One's Own [1929] (New York: Harcourt, Brace, World, 1957), pp. 38-9.

[47]Mary Daly, Gyn/Ecology (Boston: Beacon Press, 1978), pp. 361, 355.

[48]Ibid., pp. 62, 39.

[49]Alice Rossi, ed., The Feminist Papers (New York: Bantam, 1974), p. 416.

[50]Barbara Deming, We Cannot Live Without Our Lives (New York: Grossman, 1974), p. 3.

[51]Ibid., p. 9.

[52]Joan Bondurant, Conquest of Violence (Berkeley and Los Angeles: University of California Press, 1967); April Carter, Direct Action and Liberal Democracy (New York: Harper and Row, 1973); Gene Sharp, The Politics of Nonviolent Action (Boston: Porter Sargent, 1973).

[53]Barbara Roberts, "The Death of Machothink."

[54]Wini Breines and Linda Gordon, "The New Scholarship on Family Violence," Signs: Journal of Women in Culture and Society 8, 3 (Spring 1983): 490-531.

[55]Ursula Franklin, "Women and Militarism," Status of Women News 8, 1 (February 1983): 8.

[56]Ursula Franklin, "The 1979 Sunderland P. Gardner Lecture," Canadian Quaker Pamphlet No. 8 (Argenta, B.C.: Argenta Friends School Press, 1979), p. 3.

WOMEN, PEACE AND HISTORY: NOTES FOR AN HISTORICAL OVERVIEW

Dorothy Thompson

In common, I imagine, with many of the other contributors to this volume, I have been occupied with three concerns for most of my life-- the study of history, the attempt to avert world war and to create an atmosphere in which peace might be established, and the attempt to understand and to change the relative status of women and men in my own society. In all three concerns I have been one among many contemporaries, but also part of a movement or tradition stretching back into the past. In this paper for the first time I am going to try and bring these three things together, to make connections not only in contemporary politics, but also in the dimension of history. I want to look historically at some of our current preoccupations, though I am well aware that the question, for example, of the relationship between gender and war is one on which there is little agreement but a great deal of feeling. However, perhaps raising some of these questions in this way may help to clarify, if not to answer them.

To attempt any sort of historical survey of war and peace is, in effect, to tackle the whole of recorded history. Indeed, pre-history produces myths and legends involving tales and images of conflict, conquest, pillage and destruction. The vocabulary of historians is that of peace and war. The years in which I grew up, for example, are referred to in all standard text-books as "the inter-war years," and looking back on them, I think it is probably true to say that this was how they seemed even at the time. Today we in Europe and North America already feel that we are living in a "pre-war" atmosphere rather than one of peace, while for many millions throughout the world a state of "peace," of total non-conflict and stability, must seem as far away as the primeval paradise of myth. One dictionary defines "peace" as the "period between wars," and even the O.E.D. defines it in terms of war--"peace-time--period when country is not at war." Perhaps one thing we should ask of our historians is a re-examination of the positive definitions of peace. One way in which this question is being put in our own times is the polarization of peaceful--feminine qualities and masculine--warlike ones. In his oratorio *Or Shall We Die*, Ian McEwan puts into the woman's voice the lines:

Our science mocks magic and the human heart
our knowledge is the brutal mastery of the unknown
. . . .
Shall there be womanly times, or shall we die?
Are there men unafraid of gentleness?
Can we have strength without aggression,
without disgust,
strength to bind feeling to the intellect?[1]

As a poetic image this polarization is powerful. Inevitably, however, when such an idea becomes too literally accepted there are problems. What I want to do in this paper is to look at two questions. The first is the historical concept of a "peace movement," the view that there has been throughout history a conflict between "peaceful" and "warlike" elements in society, and that the contemporary peace movement is the heir to the continuous and persistent opposition to war. The second is that women have been invariably, or even generally, the bearers and transmitters of this tradition of peace, with men as the instigators of conflict, the aggressive elements within human culture. Both these questions are complex ones, and I have to start by saying that history is not going to provide a simple answer to either. Example and counter-example may, however, take the discussion forward, although the terms of the discussion can never be purely historical. We are in the fields of psychology, anthropology and creative imagery, and can hardly hope to establish points with any degree of certainty.

Is there, then, a history of the peace movement? For many of my generation it seemed a historically and theoretically established "fact" that capitalism caused wars. We found in the socialist and anti-capitalist traditions of industrial society a strong and sympathetic historical precedent for our own activities. However, problems soon emerged from this analysis. Not the least of these was that many of the longest and cruelest wars in human terms took place in pre-capitalist societies, and that many simple, tribally-organized societies have lived, and still live, in conditions of continual inter-group warfare in which the proportion of the population to die by violence compares with that in high technology wars. In other words, although the destructive potential of modern fighting forces is greater and more horrific than anything in the past, the actual proclivity of states for war-making does not seem to be greater. In the search for deeper "causes" of war, we seem to be driven to factors in the very nature of human society or of individual human beings. Such conclusions inevitably breed pessimism, so that to locate the evil in the nature of only one half of the species may be a source of encouragement, at least given the only apparent alternative. But is the search for a single causative factor justified?

In our own times there can be no greater disaster imaginable than the outbreak of war between the great powers. One of the constant themes of all peace writing is to remind the world of the nature of nuclear weapons and their destructive potential. But in past ages, war was not necessarily the greatest threat which people faced. Humanity was threatened throughout the centuries by famine and by plagues. Death in battle was only one way in which life might end violently, or mutilation or physical crippling occur. Some civilian occupations, like underground mining, were at least as dangerous as soldiering, while the everyday lot of the common soldier, even in wartime, might be preferable to that of the poor cultivator and his family. Where death from disease, famine or slow starvation faced whole populations, the line between peace and war may not have been as sharp, as indeed it may still not seem in some parts of the world in which nuclear conflict does not appear to threaten.

We need also, perhaps, to remember that the involvement of whole populations or even of all a nation's young men in wars is a comparatively recent development. For centuries in medieval and early modern Europe and Asia wars were fought by mercenaries or by professional military castes whose training and values may have been far removed from those of the rest of the population, male as well as female. The non-military parts of a nation could be victims of sack or pillage, or could be driven out by conflicting armies, but such disasters may well have seemed on a par with famine, plague or disasters of nature, and not as anything over which they had the remotest control. In a poem calling for peace, a nineteenth century radical poet could write that:

> There is peace that more has slain
> Than ever died in red campaign.[2]

and this reminds us that there have been many occasions in the past when arms have been taken up very consciously as the lesser among evils. The dominion of a class or a foreign power may have seemed a greater burden than the dangers of armed resistance. It was a woman leader who urged, in the resistance to Fascism in Spain, that "It is better to die on our feet than to live on our knees."

This is a very obvious point. But it has to be stressed that as far as proximate causes go, wars have had very many different ones. Men and women have been involved willingly as well as unwillingly, and have not always been pawns or dupes. Wars have been "caused" by the desire of rulers for wealth, territory, slave labour, glory, status or power. They have also been fought in resistance to such moves, or to overthrow oppressive governments or foreign dominion. They have been fought to spread religion or in furtherance of private feuds. They have been fought by soldiers willingly engaged in a cause in which they believed, or by poor men forced to bear arms in a cause from which they had no possibility of gain. They have been fought by volunteers, by mercenaries, by conscripts, and on occasion by women as well as men.

Perhaps the greatest hope for our generation is precisely that modern superpower conflict is *not* the heir to all conflicts in the past.

Apart from a small nonviolent pacifist tradition, to which I will return in a moment, most people would distinguish in past conflicts between differing wars. And just as wars have differed and have had specific causes, so have peace movements and movements to resist and to put an end to wars. It seems to me that in the modern world those who see wars as recurrent and a necessary part of international relations, and who try to use the vocabulary of past conflicts to justify great power confrontation in the present are doing the gravest disservice to rationality. In a recent play on BBC radio the hero (an American of course) in a speech defending the US bases in Britain, spoke of the peace supporters as idealists who believed that peace could be achieved by "laying down the sword--including the missiles on the base." This description of a weapon which can kill hundreds of thousands of people and lay waste whole stretches of country for generations ahead as a "sword" is an example of the most dangerous kind of deception. Whether we draw the line in 1914 or with the invention of nuclear weapons, we have to insist that modern warfare is different in quality as well as scale from anything that has gone before.

Even in the modern world, when most people would claim, whether through disarmament or through rearmament, to be trying to prevent war, there are questions of causality and choice which are far from simple. Many supporters of the peace movement would not condemn national liberation movements which initiate armed risings against colonial or neo-colonial governments, and many more would maintain that the last war had to be fought, once the attempts to restrain German aggression and expansion by diplomatic means had failed. Looking back to the pre-war years, blame can be apportioned for that failure, and it may well be argued that a war could have been prevented. In the actual situation which existed in 1939, however, armed conflict seemed to many, and still seems in retrospect, to have been the only course of action.

There is, as I have said already, a tradition of absolute refusal of violence within the peace movement. In Europe it has mainly been associated in the past with some of the small Christian groups, although now it also has supporters from other religious teaching. The main Christian churches accept in one form or another the doctrine of the just war, and there have been few wars in recent times which have not had priests in plenty to bless them. A minority of Christians have, however, at least since the seventeenth century or so, eschewed violence and the bearing of arms totally. This is certainly a tradition with a continuous history in Britain, and one could point to a number of courageous proponents of it. In the nineteenth century members of the Society of Friends opposed colonial wars and urged peace and conciliation in international affairs generally. Individuals in the present century have refused to be conscripted and have established the right to conscientious objection to military service. There was also a strong tradition of absolute pacifism in the early socialist movement. Objectors who refused to fight in the 1914-18 war on political rather than religious grounds were more likely to be imprisoned rather than allowed to do non-combatant duties.

The pacifist tradition, political and religious, was probably at its strongest in Britain during the nineteen twenties and thirties. The Peace Pledge Union which called on its members to pledge themselves never to take part in war and the strong pacifist tendency within the Labour Party caught the imagination of the generation which grew up in the traumatic aftermath of the 1914-18 war. It seems a logical idea that such a pledge, internationally honoured, must restrain the world's rulers. It has become a propaganda myth of some circles in Britain that this movement, epitomized for many by the famous debate in the Oxford Union in which the motion was carried "That this house would not fight for King and Country" encouraged Hitler's expansionism and so led directly to the Second World War. In fact, as recently-released British cabinet papers show, Hitler was receiving encouragement of a more specific nature from much higher levels of government in these years. And when the war did break out, many of those who signed the peace pledge in fact joined the forces. Some had changed their views even earlier and supported the Spanish republican forces, or even volunteered to fight against Fascism in Spain.

The peace movement before 1939 had several facets. The pacifist was one, another was the search for collective security, at first through the League of Nations and later through a system of alliances aimed to prevent aggression by Germany. It should also be remembered that there were warning voices at the time of the First World War and the peace treaties that followed it against the imposition of humiliating terms on the defeated nations. This was a strong element in the politics of the socialist and Labour movements, as I remember from my own family. In fact, it may well be that many people, like the Labour leader George Lansbury, were so keenly aware of the culpability of the allies in imposing draconian peace terms on Germany, that they failed to realize the way in which the most reactionary forces were exploiting the grievances to overthrow democratic institutions and replace them with militaristic and expansionist elements which were to tear the continent apart.

Like the causes of war, resistance to them has usually been very specific to the actual situation. A rhetoric of hostility to warfare and a desire for "the piping days of peace" is by no means confined to pacifists or anti-militarists. For it has to be remembered, and it is very relevant to the problems of the modern peace movement, that the great military powers themselves have often claimed to be the protectors of world peace. They have indeed justified the maintenance of great armies and navies in the name of the preservation of peace. The armies of Rome subdued the warring tribes and established the Pax Romana. Centuries later the British Empire imposed the Pax Britannica by force, and kept open trade routes and Imperial connections by land and sea. Past empires have gained and maintained hegemony over large parts of the world by the mere threat of force and the presence of massive armed strength. Over the centuries the cast list of the great powers has changed, one declining or being eliminated as another, newer and brasher, has arisen. But the ones on the top of the heap have always called for peace and the preservation of the status quo.

At least since Roman times the game of deterrence has been played under the same slogan--*Si vis pacem, para bellum*--if you wish for peace, prepare for war. Alas, such heavy-handed peace keeping has never produced stability. The one great empire with no rivals to fear has never emerged. Massive war preparations have always provoked counter-measures by rival powers which have eventually led to clashes and to war.

Opposition to war has, in terms of speech and action, been either on a high moral plane or very specific to particular conflicts. We do not know the responses of the great majority of the people, of both sexes, who kept their heads down and struggled for their livelihoods throughout the centuries. We know that in societies that enforced conscription, census lists tend to have surprising gaps in the conscriptable age groups. Young men of military age sloped off or kept out of the way of the census-takers in Italian towns in the eighteenth century, as they did in the United States during the Viet Nam war. In Britain the press gang was needed to "recruit" seamen for the navy in the eighteenth and nineteenth centuries, and its operations were opposed by men and women in the coastal districts. The tricks reported in the nineteenth century to persuade young men to take the King's shilling and thereby to commit themselves to service in the army suggest that Her Majesty's recruiting sergeants were not overwhelmed by willing recruits. There are few rural or seafaring communities which do not have stories of resistance to recruiting. For example, at the end of the eighteenth century when the Earl of Seaforth agreed to raise a regiment of 1000 soldiers to fight in the French wars, the men on his estate in the Island of Lewis resisted enlistment very strongly. A local historian described the incident:

> When Seaforth arrived in Lewis on his recruiting campaign, the men of Uig took to the hills, and set up a camp near Uig Lodge. A boat, manned by women, was sent to Calanish to ferry Seaforth across. He was far from pleased at this unexpected reception, but the parish minister of Uig, Mr. Munro, managed to cool his temper, and assured him the people would soon tire of the cold hill-tops.
> The next day, Seaforth and the minister set off for *Cnoc a' Camp*, Camp Hill, where the latter remonstrated with his suspicious flock for their unpatriotic conduct. After a good deal of discussion, an assurance was given that wherever a man had only one son, that son would not be taken, but where there was a large family, two might be taken.
> . . .
> The need to recruit more men was probably what caused

Seaforth to send a press-gang to the island. When the factor heard what was being planned, he wrote to Seaforth, asserting that such an action would be fatal, as not a soul in either the town or the country would remain at home. This news was most unwelcome, as the country people had already given more than their complement of men, especially in the Point area, where there was likely to be land left untilled, as the wives of the enlisted men refused to work it.

It was probably at this time that a press-gang came to the village of Knockard in Ness. All the fit males between sixteen and thirty were marched away in spite of the repeated attempts by their women-folk to free them, attempts which were foiled by bayonets held at their breasts.[3]

We might also recall the episode in Elizabeth Gaskell's novel *Sylvia's Lovers* in which the local people demolish the inn from which the press gang operated, an episode based on an actual event. But these are fragments. Our knowledge of conscious opposition to war by the ordinary people, like so much else of their history, has to be based on elusive and fragmentary evidence, or on behaviour at times of great national drama or crisis.

I have suggested that the modern peace movement is not heir to a continuous tradition of opposition to war, certainly not to one of opposition to the bearing of arms. This is not to say that it *ought not* to be so. There are many people today who would say that no problem in the past has ever been solved by resort to arms. The fact is, however, that people of many different classes and nations have resorted to war and to arms to attempt a solution.

How far has the opposition to the use of force been a female concern? Have peace movements in the past been led, inspired and supported more by women than by men? As many of the papers in the present volume show, there have been organizations and movements, in the recent past at least, in which a very specific appeal has been made to women, and in which a feminist rhetoric has been invoked. Women as the bearers of life have been urged to take a stand against the senseless destruction and waste of young life that war involves. But it is disingenuous to present this pacifist opposition to the war as more powerful or more important than that organized by men of the same persuasions. A recent biography of the pacifist Mary Sheepshanks puts the position in 1914 in this way:

> Whereas the English war poets, among countless articulate men, had to endure the gas, the trenches, the barbed wire and the putrescent corpses in the mud before coming to the conclusion that the whole debacle was murderous futility, women like Mary Sheepshanks and her friends recognised that the 'Great War' was tragic wickedness from the very second it began.[4]

This is, of course, quite amazing special pleading, and in no way compares like with like. Of course the most moving of the war poets move us precisely because they do speak from the bitter experience of actual war, but the parallel with Mary Sheepshanks is not the war poets but the very many men pacifists, many of them from the socialist and labour traditions, who also fought against the outbreak of war and opposed it from its outbreak. Many of these lost their jobs, lost their following and served periods in gaol for their principled opposition to war; one could mention figures as dissimilar as Tom Mann and Herbert Morrison as examples. It is no service to the women's movement to make this kind of slick comparison. As historians we would like to know a lot more in qualitative terms than we do, or perhaps than we ever shall, about responses to that war. We all know that not only the labour movement in the major European powers, but also the women's movements in the same countries, split when the war actually broke out, with a minority in both movements sticking to their professions of internationalism. We also know that the absurd and, in retrospect, pathetic patriotism of the early volunteers, described by Mary Sheepshanks vividly in her correspondence with Bertrand Russell, but also by many other contemporaries, faded with the experience of trench warfare. We know that eventually conscription was introduced in Britain, and that the battles of the last years of the war traumatized a whole generation. We are beginning to know more about the actions of a small number of women who set up international organizations, even when war was still being waged, to outlaw war. But do we have any evidence that pacifism of this kind was stronger among women than among men, or, much more difficult, that the majority of ordinary women were less taken in than men by the rhetoric of patriotism and war? As I have said, many of the pre-war women's leaders took part in recruiting drives and patriotic demonstrations. Men writing in the aftermath of war about the experience of battle spoke of the impossibility of conveying any idea of that experience to the women who had remained at home, and who often clung to a romantic and simplistically patriotic view of war. All we can say, surely, is that a small number of men and a smaller number of women protested publicly about the resort to arms in 1914. As the war progressed, intelligent and sensitive people of both sexes experienced its horrors, in battle or in the many auxiliary services that women performed, and many of these determined to do all they could to prevent another war.

We can certainly say that men must, in historical terms, take the responsibility for the political events leading up to the war, for women had no political voice at that time. Many women pacifists believed that the women's vote would be given for peace and against war, and would be a powerful instrument in national politics. The fact that there is no evidence that this happened (I think we *do* have evidence that the women's vote influenced some aspects of the policies of all governments during the twenties and thirties) reinforces the complexity of the question.

Opposition to specific wars, during the nineteenth century at least, seems always to have been determined by the actual situation rather than by the gender of the opponents. Mary Wollstonecraft, like most of her fellow-radicals, was opposed to the war between Britain and revolutionary France and, as the wars dragged on, the crowds who rioted against food shortages and profiteering by middlemen from the wartime conditions included men and women. The Chartists, men and women, continually protested against British military actions in Ireland and in other parts of the Empire. They protested against the British invasions of Afghanistan in 1844--then, as now, it was a sensitive area--and against the suppression of the Canadian uprisings of 1837. The women also complained about the activities of the press gang and the violence of police and troops against demonstrators in Britain and Ireland. But these protests do not seem to have been gender-specific, and when we come to what is often seen as the first modern peace movement, that against the Crimean War of 1853-55, the situation is complex. In the whole series of skirmishes in Europe which accompanied the break-up of the Ottoman Empire, level-headed people in Britain tried to prevent the eruption of a major European war. It was to prevent this that the Eastern Question Association, forerunner of much of the modern socialist movement, was formed. The excellent *Englishwomen's Review* in 1878 used the continuing danger of European war in the south-east of the continent to press the case for women's suffrage:

> The Peace party in the country would have received a larger augmentation of force if women equally with men possessed the authority of citizens to elect their governor.[5]

In 1853, however, the peace movement was led by politicians of the Manchester school who urged free trade and unrestricted competition as the answer to all the world's problems. They were attacked by the hysterical patriotism of the poet laureate, Tennyson, in the famous lines:

> Though niggard throats of Manchester may bawl
> What England was shall England's sons forget?
> We are not cotton-spinners all,
> And some love England and her honour yet.

They were also attacked by the Queen, who wrote to Disraeli:

> The Queen is really distressed at the low tone which this country is inclined to hold . . . Oh if the Queen were a man, she would like to go and give those Russians such a beating![6]

In the early stages of the Crimean War, they were also attacked by the

Chartists. These working-class radicals had always compared Poland and Ireland, had always seen Russia as the bastion of reaction in Europe, and could not bear the thought that Russian influence in Europe should go unresisted. Women as well as men joined in breaking up the meetings of the "peacemongers," just as women as well as men had objected in 1850 to the official visit of the Austrian general Heynau, suppressor of the 1848 Hungarian revolution. At Barclay and Perkins' brewery the general had been set upon physically by the workers, including

> a large portion of the females [who] took part in this glorious manifestation, and tore the fellow's grisly moustachios until he roared again and again with pain and fury.[7]

Historically speaking, then, we have to see that support for war and opposition to it, as far as these have been publicly expressed, have been the province of both sexes. If fighting has been mainly a masculine occupation, the encouragement to do so and the appeal to physical force as a means of solving world problems have been significantly masculine only insofar as nearly all public political speech and action have been masculine. The reigns of the queens in England, in particular those of the two longest-reigning, Elizabeth I and Victoria, have not been periods of peace, but of continuous expansion and colonial wars.

An important part of the programme of the modern women's movement has been to defend and stress the importance of the values which Ian McEwan describes as "womanly." When women have fought their way into public life in past ages, they often, of necessity, left behind in the home and the nursery the caring and nurturing aspects of their lives, and those parts of their mind which responded directly to experience and took little notice of pseudo-rationality and the dictatorship of the clock and the timetable. A powerful image of the modern polarization can be seen in the picture presented by the US air base at Greenham Common. Nothing could illustrate more vividly the phrase of Antonio Gramsci, "pessimism of the intellect, optimism of the will." On the one hand can be seen barbed wire snarled in stiff coils around wire mesh fences and concrete structures. Armed guards in identical drab uniforms parade around the inside of the fence, guarding the emplacements and the huge motorized transporters. Overhead helicopters growl menacingly. Outside the fence, in small groups around the gates, women in all colours and shapes of clothes, housed in improvised shelters made from living wood and coloured cloth, come and go in unstructured groups, exchanging views, constantly improvising, governed not by orders or by rule books, but by a common agreement and purpose. The women represent life and a determined hope of future life, in the face of the dead intellectual equation of the machine, claiming to preserve peace by destroying all life--surely the ultimate intellectual abstraction. And in this particular instance the polarization is dramatically made between male and female, in persons and in images.

38

The Greenham image is, however, a dramatic and political statement. Hostility to it can be found among women as among men who do not accept the analysis on which it is based. If wars in the past have been 'caused' in a deep sense by the encouragement of aggressive elements in the human psyche, we have to beware of seeing such elements as being a part of the make-up of only one sex. There is a temptation in such an analysis. Historically it is true that, like all public and political activity, wars have in the main been fought and engineered by men. But where women have been rulers, they have been as bloodthirsty as their male counterparts, and indeed history is not without its female warriors in certain ages.

The clan conflicts of ancient Europe abound with stories of women's part in battles. Irish epic tradition contains more than one warrior queen, including the warlike Queen Maeve who

> herself took supreme command and went before her troops, a "woman comely, white-faced, long-cheeked and large" with golden yellow hair and bearing in her hand a straight spear . . .

She led her troops against the warriors of Ulster and personally supervised the single combat between champions which was to determine the outcome of the battle.[8]

Tomyris, Queen of the Celts, was credited by Herodotus with the personal destruction of Cyrus the Great. She led her troops against those of the Persian leader who had captured her son and refused to give him up. Herodotus described the battle:

> The Massagetae, under the personal generalship of Tomyris, at length prevailed. The greater part of the army of the Medes and Persians was destroyed; and Cyrus himself fell . . . On learning that her son was dead, Tomyris took the body of Cyrus, and dipping his head in a skinful of gore, she thus addressed the corpse: "I have conquered thee in battle, yet am I destroyed, for thou hast taken my son by guile. But thus I make good my threat, and give thee thy fill of blood."[9]

English school children all know the name of Boudicca, the Celtic queen who, six hundred years after Queen Tomyris, was credited with having dispatched seventy thousand of the invading Romans. A Roman historian set down her speech to her followers:

> It is not as a queen descended from noble ancestry, but as one of the people that I avenge our lost freedom. Roman lust has gone so far that not even our very persons are left unpolluted. If you weigh well the strengths of our armies you will see that in this battle we must conquer or die. This is a *woman's* resolve. As for *men*, they may live and be slaves.

When, after a series of victories, she was finally defeated by the Roman invaders, she took her own life rather than be made part of a Roman triumph.

Many other writers speak of women warriors amongst the Celtic and other North European tribes during the Roman period, including Tacitus who spoke of women among the barbarians who dressed like men and were skilled in the use of weapons. In *Germania* he described the part taken by the women in the resistance of the tribes who fought against the invading Romans:

> It is a principal incentive to their courage that these squadrons and battalions are not formed of randomly recruited men but are assembled from families and clans. The hostages for their courage, therefore, are near at hand; they have within earshot the shouts of their women and the cries of their children. These too are the most valued witnesses of each man's conduct, his most enthusiastic applauders. . .Their traditions record that armies beginning to give way have been rallied by the females, thrusting their bodies forward, urging on the men and asserting the horrors of impending slavery . . .[10]

Very similar stories occur in Irish mythology, of women accompanying soldiers to battle and urging them on with cries and shouts during the fighting.

These are examples from very long ago; their authenticity may be questioned and certainly the extent to which they represent history as opposed to myth. And yet, we know that the essential story they contain is historically true. If the male image of the soldier is held to legitimate war, to encourage the young man in the creation of a glamourous persona, gallant, honourable, clothed in a uniform which shows off his manly figure, armed with sword and gun, phallic symbols par excellence, at once the protector and the conqueror of women, if this image helps to perpetuate the great swindle by which the young men are enticed into slaughter, death and mutilation, can we honestly say that it is an illusion fostered only, or even mainly, by the men themselves? If women protest, and reasonably, against the sex-object presentation of women, is not the idealization of the soldier a fantasy of a similar order? In most societies women are the child-rearers and the educators of the child in its earliest most impressionable years. A society which puts a high premium on the military virtues, as well as on nationalism or racism, does so by instilling these ideas at all levels, starting in the nursery.

Women, as a sex, cannot shrug off their complicity in militarism. The handers-out of white feathers, the glamourizers of a bogus military image, the instillers into little boys of the soldierly virtues have played their part, and there is no evidence to suggest that they have been in a minority. If the humane qualities are not held in respect in public life, we may assume that women who emerge into public life may well do so with as little regard for these qualities as their male counterparts. Indeed, we can look around the political world today and see many statespersons whose gender seems to have little effect on the bellicosity of their behaviour.

Most of what I have said is obvious and hardly very controversial. But there is a danger of creating false polarities within the peace movement, at a time when the maximum of unity is necessary if any degree of success is to be achieved. If there are elements in our natures and in our response to challenge which make us too easy victims of the propaganda of bogus nationalism or the romantic belief in the possibility of protecting the things we value by force of arms, I think an historian would say that these things exist in both genders. Aggression may take different forms in different people, different groups and different classes. But the need to control aggressive impulses, to work at the solution of differences over long periods of time, and above all to compromise and to respect the views of others is one which all people share, and there is little to be gained by playing the age-old game of nationalist and sectarian politicians of shifting the burden of guilt for the world's predicament onto one nation, one class or even one sex.

Comments

Jo Vellacott

I think that your main argument is important: we need to avoid polarization in the peace movement. This is something that I also argue. But there's one thing that I really take issue with, and that is, and I'm quoting here from the typed version of your paper, "If fighting has been mainly a masculine occupation, the encouragement to do so and the appeal to physical force as a means of solving world problems have been significantly masculine only insofar as nearly all public and political speech and action have been masculine." I think that's a very circular kind of argument; the point is why have all public, political speech and action been masculine, and what is the significance of that. I think that we could go too far in saying that we are equally complicit; we are complicit within a system that has grown up as a male-dominated system and we must expect to challenge that whole system and change it. Many of the examples you give are ones of women who have, in fact, entered that system without changing it and, therefore, have been part of the militaristic system. I agree with you that we cannot assume that women will change it because they are women, but I think we must look for that kind of major change rather than accepting that the system will be the same however we go about it.

Dorothy Thompson

I do very much take this point, but I would also say that, of course, as a great majority of ordinary working people haven't been in the business of making public statements either, it's not totally a sex division. The fact is that when women do come into this public domain they very often leave femininity or whatever womanliness behind, so that the changes that have to be brought about are not simply gender changes, but I wouldn't really query your main point. I'm sure you're right.

Notes

[1]Ian McEwan, Or Shall We Die? (London: Jonathan Cape, 1983), pp. 31-2.

[2]Ernest Jones, "God of Battles, Give us Peace," (1851).

[3]Donald Macdonald, Lewis, a History of the Island (Edinburgh: Wright Publishing, 1978), pp. 117-18.

[4]Sybil Oldfield, Spinsters of this Parish (London: Virago, 1984), p. 176.

[5]Englishwoman's Review 1878, cited in Chronology to My Country is the Whole World: An Anthology of Women's Work on Peace and War, comp. by Cambridge Women's Peace Collective (London: Pandora Press, 1984), p. 274.

[6]Cited in G. E. Buckle, Life of Disraeli (London: 1920), Vol. VI, p. 217.

[7]Reynolds' Weekly Newspaper, September 8, 1850.

[8]J. M. Flood, Ireland: Its Myths and Legends (Dublin: Talbot Press, 1916), p. 72.

[9]Cited in Elizabeth Gould Davis, The First Sex (London: Vintage Books, Random House, 1975), p. 213.

[10]Tacitus, Germania, 7.(3), 8.(1), and passim.

FEMINISM AND PACIFISM, OR, THE ART OF TRANQUILLY PLAYING RUSSIAN ROULETTE

Micheline de Sève

The relationship between women and peace is relatively simple to establish. Being without weapons, women have everything to fear from off-duty, drunken soldiers and marauding victorious troops. As spouses and mothers, they fear for the lives of their sons and husbands away at war. Women and their children remain behind; for them war means privation, absence, anxiety and additional labour. Under conditions more stressful than in "peacetime," women replace the traditional male labour force in addition to acting as sole caretakers of children, the sick and the elderly, those non-combatant members of society dependent on women. Yet the position of women has worsened now that the techniques of modern warfare have eliminated the distinction between front and civilian battle zones. Female civilians live with the horror of incinerated cities and the massive carnage caused by bombings against which we are defenceless.

As soldiers, men at least have the illusion of number and physical force. Shoulder to shoulder with their comrades-in-arms, they often become intoxicated with the exaltation of combat, perishing or conquering as heroes. No such exaltation or heroism exists for the female non-combatant; her death is a victim's glory-less death. Women are condemned to the everyday dull drudgery of fighting rationing and obtaining a space in the closest shelter. It is not surprising that women hate war more than ever, now that it surrounds us to the point of obliterating the classical distinction between military and civilian populations. The patriarchal principle of the rigid separation between the private sphere, considered women's domain, subordinate, certainly, but relatively protected, and the public sphere, the world of politics and war, is no longer valid. The logic of the isolation of women in an environment protected from the harsh confrontation between "real men", a logic which pretended to guarantee women's and children's physical safety in exchange for female freedom, has no meaning in the face of contemporary reality. The lives of women as mothers and spouses no longer have that sacrosanct character; their exclusion from the public sphere can no longer be explained by their exemption from its least enviable expression: war.

44

*   *   *

Traditionally pacifist, as a result of the functions they assume (lugging a gun and a child at the same time is, to say the least, arduous), women respond to the ever increasing threat of global war and total destruction through their massive adherence to peace movements. Tens of thousands of women manifest their objections to the storage of radioactive material and the location of nuclear power plants on the outskirts of their cities. Unlike men, women are not socialized to value an "esprit de combat." They can respond without self-restraint to a spontaneous survival reflex. The problem, then, is not the awakening of women's consciousness. As strangers to the experience of war, they have become squarely opposed to it. But even if all women rose up in dissent against the authorities and the ministries of defence in their respective countries, they would lack the necessary power to mobilize public opinion and impose demilitarization.

The images of life during wartime which we have briefly evoked, however, belong to another era. In effect, the threat of nuclear war reduces aspirations of heroism to nothing, as is true of all projects which claim justice through the force of arms. How many men will still be able to boast of targets "neutralized" from a distance, or record figures of persons napalmed in an attack? Perhaps children brought up in the micro-computer age, familiar with video war games and viewing approximately 10,000 murders a year on the family television screen, could attain the necessary degree of insensitivity to set off the hecatomb? Of course, it is still hardly possible to conceive of this type of "total war" unless one lives in a mode of abstraction completely alienated from humanity and concrete reality. Otherwise, how can we imagine that an individual of sane mind could consciously push the button releasing heat-guided missiles capable of annihilating millions of his own kind?

*   *   *

Beyond the real threat of annihilation that weighs heavily on all of us, a new element has entered the picture: armed violence, for a long time alien to women's spirit, has now become opposed to the humanity of men themselves. Far from being a figment of our imaginations, the total destruction of the enemy is now possible; a thorny problem, however, is that it risks the total annihilation not only of the conquered but of the conquerors. For the first time in history, men of war are forced to envisage conjointly the disappearance of all combatants as a result of their quest for the ultimate weapon. Thus, they are constrained to think of their relationship to arms negatively, as a form of violence which threatens to go beyond their intentions and annihilate both parties. This is the source of continuing negotiations, accords on arms limitations, and even prohibition of nuclear armaments. It is crucial to halt the arms race and move back the "clock" or the planet itself will bear the costs of a confrontation between world powers. Everyone is agreed on this latter point, but the problem is essentially this: to limit war is to dream of civilizing death itself, of normalizing a confrontation which by its very definition marks the failure of all reasonable means of conflict resolution.

*   *   *

We are embarked on a dead end: war is not inevitable, but it is a foreseeable consequence of relationships based on force which form the web of power in our societies. Every act of domination runs the risk of ultimately unleashing a chain reaction of episodes of escalating violence.

To propose the self-regulation of armaments under such conditions is absurd, for what will occur if the warring elements are backed into a corner, faced with the inevitable prospect of surrendering? Rather than perish, will they not be tempted to sweep the enemy away with them, pushing the button in a final gesture of defiance? Faced with conventional weapons, which bring death to their own camps in any case, would not the warring states sacrifice their last card, even if it were the threat of apocalypse?

Even assuming that all the powers agreed to give up their nuclear arsenals, on what basis could trust--and this is a key word--be established between irreconcilable enemies? Would not the inclination always remain to protect oneself with research for ever more efficient warheads, and, if necessary, to ensure deterrence by threatening to use an ultimate weapon?

Patriarchal hierarchy does not rest on the consent of the dominated but on their subordination by force. Historically, violence has always been the instrument of domination par excellence, and it is this which must be abolished if we intend to eradicate the risk of generalized armed confrontation. However, a number of pacifists hesitate at the magnitude of the problem and consider non-violence as utopian in the absence of social change. These "realists" define their movement as anti-nuclear but do not reject support for the liberation struggles of oppressed peoples. Indeed, revolutionary violence is legitimate, but the civil wars and conflicts raging in Central America, the Middle East, in Africa and elsewhere do not pose any less of a threat in terms of unleashing an East-West confrontation which could lead to total devastation:

" . . . and there shall no longer be any death; there shall no longer be any mourning, or crying, or pain; the first things have passed away." (Apocalypse, 21: 4)

46

*   *   *

Since we cannot in good conscience preach disarmament to peoples in revolt against tyranny, it is important that we confront the problem at home, where war is already virtually indistinguishable from the total destruction of humanity. If we choose otherwise, the mechanism set to explode will do so sooner or later. All civilizations are mortal, including our own patriarchal society.

Essentially, this means that both men and women must learn to eradicate the elements of violence in their relationships, as well as their indifference to the fate of other human beings. Pacifism cannot merely limit itself to a call for arms limitation any more than feminism can be satisfied with a model of socio-economic equality that is based on the erosion of the socio-cultural identity of women, rather than grounded in the recognition of the universal value of their specific human experience. Both of these movements necessitate radical social change, directed towards a feminization of society. In fact, women's identity is built on their capacity to base relationships with dependents entrusted to their care on principles of a gradual teaching of autonomy and an attention to diverse individual needs. This understanding and sympathetic attitude, resulting from women's daily experience of interpersonal relationships, becomes a handicap in the public sphere where women's affectivity and tolerance are made to work systematically against them. It is, however, exactly this type of orientation which can establish relationships of trust based on sensitivity to the needs of others and a sense of solidarity with members of one's own species. It is a question of ethics; it is also a necessity if we intend to survive.

*   *   *

No dream of peace can endure in a world where differences and social inequalities at all levels constantly set off cycles of violence and repression. Peace implies mutually satisfying relations which can only be established between equals, otherwise injustice feeds power and the will to resistance.

Pacifists are, in a sense, trapped. War is the logical consequence of relations of force, yet at the same time, servitude is intolerable to both individuals and nations. The problem demands a more comprehensive analysis than the call for the rejection of nuclear armaments. There can be no solution if we ignore all of the conventional wars which ravage entire nations, the episodes of violence which systematically mutilate the personality of women in all contemporary societies, and the model of adulthood based on a glorification of revenge and assimilation to the dominant power elite. For their part, feminists cannot ignore the dangers posed by militarism, nor be satisfied with a mitigated form of pacifism which pretends to reduce the panoply of weapons which are lethal in any number. It is precisely this which I call "tranquilly playing Russian Roulette," with or without nuclear missiles.

*   *   *

So, then, what are our chances? We must actively work to remove the most glaring inequalities between nations, which produce the most murderous wars. Yet we have not even abolished the roots of violence in our own daily lives. Women, we know, are battered by their husbands, children are sexually molested more often by their male parents than by strangers. Should not a certain empathy inspire both pacifists and feminists to actively intervene against this type of behaviour in every instance where they can act effectively? Similarly, should not pacifists automatically oppose flagrant social inequalities deriving from racism (the exploitation of the immigrant labour force); sexism (pornography, the economic or sexual exploitation of women); contempt for the young (the condemnation of this segment of society to poverty or dependence); indifference to the vagaries of old age (extreme poverty, drugging and dumping of the aged in overcrowded nursing homes)?

Would not the credibility of pacifism as a social movement be enhanced if those who supported it concretely acted on their capacity to undermine the basis of violence wherever it is manifested? Thus, concerted mass action could overcome repression by starting with these lesser but linked injustices in everyday life. Pacifism, defined as the practice of non-violence, would mean active intervention to change the world, opening an immense field of activity which is not utopian.

Many feminists, active in the pacifist movement, discovered relatively early the same sexism and authoritarianism there that they had rejected and left behind in other social and political organizations. Cannot the temporary nature of women's involvement within the central core of peace organizations and the gulf between these groups and the thousands of female and young sympathizers who come out for mass peace demonstrations, be linked to the reluctance to extend the boundaries of activism to embrace the totality of interpersonal relationships which are also political? Is it not the refusal to push the analysis to its ultimate consequences, rather than the poverty of its inspiration, which limits the impact of a peace movement, vital for the survival of both men and women?

References

Carroll, Berenice A. "Feminist Politics and Peace." In Dorothy G. McGuigan, ed. The Role of Women in Conflict and Peace. Ann Arbor: The University of Michigan Center for Continuing Education of Women, 1977.

D'Eaubonne, François. Le Féminisme ou la mort. Paris: Pierre Horay, 1973.

Dossier: "Demain la guerre," La vie en rose 15 (janvier 1984).

McAllister, Pam, ed. Reweaving the Web of Life: Feminism and Non-violence. Philadelphia: New Society Press, 1982.

Roberts, Barbara. "The Death of Machothink: Feminist Research and the Transformation of Peace Studies." Women's Studies International Forum 7, 4 (1984): 195-200.

Ruddick, Sara. "Preservative Love and Military Destruction: Reflections on Mothering and Peace." In Joyce Trebilcot, ed. Mothering: Essays in Feminist Theory. Totowa, New Jersey: Rowman and Allanhead, 1983.

Woolf, Virginia. Three Guineas. London: Hogarth Press, 1938.

PART II

HISTORICAL CASE STUDIES

Käthe Kollwitz: *Gefallen* (Killed in action), Lithograph 1921, Kunsthalle, Hamburg
Source: Mina C. Klein and H. Arthur Klein; *Kaethe Kollwitz; life in art* (New York: Holt, Rinehart and Winston, 1972)

WOMEN'S PARTICIPATION IN EUROPEAN PEACE MOVEMENTS: THE STRUGGLE TO PREVENT WORLD WAR I

Sandi E. Cooper

Late in April, 1915, eight months after the First World War broke out, approximately 1,200 women from neutral and belligerent nations assembled at The Hague for a congress that had been called by women leaders of various suffrage and social reform movements. After four days of meeting, a series of resolutions passed which protested the unprecedented human suffering caused by the war; condemned territorial transfers without consent of the governed; demanded permanent arbitration and mediation to resolve future international conflicts; insisted on democratic control of foreign policy and on women's right to vote. The congress also advocated universal disarmament, free trade on land and sea, changes in the education of youth and a voice for women in the peace settlement.[1] From this congress and its follow-up meeting in Zurich in 1919, came the establishment of the Women's International League for Peace and Freedom, often called the first woman's association organized across national boundaries devoted to ending man's oldest profession.

Celebrants of the 1915 meeting--both participants and its future chroniclers--hailed it as a remarkable event demonstrating cross-class, cross-national solidarity that only women could attain. To Emily Hobhouse, an English organizer, the meeting was the occasion when "peace appeared again upon earth . . . nurtured by womanly love and wisdom."[2] A recent description claims that "for the first time in history, women of different nations met together at a time of war to express their opposition and consider ways of ending the conflict."[3] As a way of illuminating the women's achievement in 1915, yet another author has argued:

> Prior to 1900 the peace movement reflected primarily the interests and attention of men. Indeed, women were generally denied entrance into public life. Those who persisted usually worked within established peace organizations that were reluctant to give responsible positions to women. Of course, many women were not interested, or else believed that they

51

had no power to make a contribution to peace. There were notable exceptions.[4]

In an effort to demonstrate the general superiority of women's anti-war activism, in 1914 the English feminist pacifist Emmeline Pethick-Lawrence condemned the entire pre-war peace movement as "passive and negative."[5]

A close examination of the actual record of the 1915 Hague congress reveals something less than unanimity among its participants.[6] Secondly, the content of the action resolutions in favour of international organization differed little from demands made by European and American peace activists for the preceding quarter century--if not longer. Thirdly, much of the evaluation of the women's congress suggests a fundamental problem which has plagued peace and women's movements down to the present. Both suffer from historical amnesia, a product of discontinuity. Movements lacking two to three generations of continuous ideology and membership might avoid the pitfall of hardening of the bureaucratic arteries, but they suffer from the absence of oral traditions. With the recent explosion of women's history in the last fifteen years, solid correctives to that amnesia have taken shape--for those willing to do the reading and studying. But peace activists and scholars alike must often re-invent the wheel each time an upsurge in peace activism occurs. Peace movements have not received the kind of attention from either establishment or radical scholars as have, for instance, diplomatic crises or working-class experiences. In this paper, an effort will be made to redress that imbalance.

To focus on continental European peace and women's activism in the last century will also provide a corrective to the mistaken Anglo-American tendency to take Anglo-American experience as a model for that of the rest of the world.[7] It is true that peace and women's movements were both born in the English- speaking nations astride the Atlantic in the first half of the last century.[8] The first peace societies saw light as small citizen groups mainly inspired with religious indignation and fervour, catalyzed by the horrors reported from the Napoleonic Wars (particularly the Russian campaign). In London, New York, Massachusetts and Ohio, Quakers and dissident Protestants joined in parlours and churches to mount propaganda against war as unChristian. By the 1820s, the societies were sufficiently bold to create national organizations in Britain and the United States. Their ambition was to seed like-minded groups of "friends of peace," particularly in western Europe. It was these Anglo-American groups, first organized in countries which were already unified and which enjoyed limited measures of parliamentary and democratic practices, that produced the first associations of private citizens who lobbied to transform foreign policies. The Anglo-American peace movement was responsible for calling the mid-century international peace congresses, three of which met on the continent--in Brussels in 1848; in Paris in 1849 and in Frankfurt a. Main in 1850. However, on the continent, the fundamentally religious impulse--some have even called it "messianic"[9] -- of the British peace society was submerged in the message of the Manchester liberal economists, 'Free Trade means Peace'. By mid-century, Anglo-American peace groups had survived and prospered for over thirty years, mounting numerous campaigns against aggressive foreign policies and military expenditures, publishing newspapers and pamphlets, sending agents to lecture throughout the northern United States and all over England. What they could not do was persuade European liberals to adopt their ideals of peace. A continent breeding revolution for social or national causes, which, in turn, bred counter-revolution, militarism and assertions of monarchical authority, did not provide fertile ground for the generous vision of pious pacifists, many of whom would not condone violence even in self-defence.[10] The ideal of pacifism as absolute non-resistance to evil remained an unreal vision. The French feminist-pacifist, Eugénie Niboyet, who took up the peace cause in 1844 by publishing a weekly, *La Paix des Deux Mondes*, rejected the Quaker ideal of peace, insisting that some wars were justified. Further, Niboyet saw that international peace flowed from domestic justice and the religious pacifists were silent on any question of domestic politics.[11] Religious pacifism appealed neither to those Chartists who took up the question in the 1840s nor to those Americans during the Civil War who wanted an end to slavery.[12] For Europe, the Anglo-American peace message was inappropriate.

In Europe, organized peace societies finally took root during the 1860s, particularly during the 1867 Luxembourg crisis, without the agency of British mid-wifery. Three types of peace organizations developed. The first advocated programs which are best described as "liberal internationalist." Of these, the earliest example was founded in Paris by economists, businessmen, bankers and journalists, and called the *Ligue internationale et permanente de la paix*. Its main spokesman became Frédéric Passy, a student of the economist, Bastiat, and a firm believer in free enterprise and free trade.[13] Passy argued for the preservation of peace through the formation of international institutions to contain conflict. Such institutions would benefit all Europe--republican or monarchical--argued Passy. An organized peace where arbitration defused conflict would eventually permit the reduction of arms costs. In the assessment of liberal internationalists, it was the arms race (not the class or economic structure) which fueled the social question and caused poverty. Arms expenses drew away capital needed for investment and development, and thus eliminated useful employment, prevented needed public services and utilities from developing and, if not curbed, would eventually bankrupt Europe. The overall analysis made by liberal internationalists fused a devout faith in private property, free trade, and law with a belief in progress (meaning the extension of education and political democracy). The right of the nation-state to exist was a *sine qua non*. Passy's Parisian league, operating under the constraints of Napoleon III's domestic surveillance, chose to lobby the elites, hold few public meetings and charge high membership dues. Women were welcome in the audience of public lectures.

Also in 1867, a second peace society, called the *Ligue internationale de la paix et de la liberté*, was born in Geneva. This group also advocated arbitration and international mechanisms for solving conflicts but went considerably further in its programme. Its members, a combination of exiled republicans from 1849 counter-revolutions and anti-Napoleonic Frenchmen, insisted that war was the result of dynastic ambition and the denial of human rights. Peace, therefore, had to result from domestic and national justice. In September, 1867, its founding congress was led by Garibaldi and the meeting was supported by liberals such as John Stuart Mill, Freemasons, socialists and Saint-Simonians, the exiled Victor Hugo and a number of Swiss progressive politicians. Members demanded separation of church and state; mass compulsory secular education; an end to standing armies and the creation of national militias; republics where monarchies existed; national liberation for oppressed peoples; freedom of speech and press; and universal manhood suffrage. Implicitly, wars of national liberation were regarded as sacred, but wars of expansion were denounced as deplorable.[14] It was this peace league which embraced women's emancipation as part of its programme one year after it was founded.

The addition of women's rights and, indeed, of women's participation in the work of the peace society was the result of a campaign led by a Genevan woman, Marie Pouchoulin-Goegg. In the spring of 1868, Goegg founded the first women's peace society on the continent--the *Association Internationale des Femmes*.[15] Her intention was to organize "women of all social classes" and "obtain for women all the same rights which men enjoy in the State as well as the same work and vocations as men."[16] In a speech delivered to the second congress of the Genevan peace league, she stated flatly that the leaders of the French Revolution had undermined their own objectives by proclaiming the rights of man but ignoring "those no less imprescriptable rights of women." Men, she noted,

> have paid dearly for their mistake and their descendents still suffer. By denying women as their equal, arrogant men have demeaned their own stature. If women had been called from 1789 to develop their own abilities . . . society . . . would have progressed.[17]

Goegg's group worked separately from the Ligue to educate women on war and peace questions through public meetings and lectures. Following the Franco-Prussian War, she turned her energies to Swiss feminist causes but remained on the board of the *Ligue internationale de la paix et de la liberté*.

The third 1860s organization concerned with international peace was not primarily a peace society. This was the International Working Men's Association--the first socialist International. As the

International fell increasingly under Marx's influence, its members, who had been willing to collaborate with the Genevan peace league originally, began to depart.[18] Besides Marx, Cesar de Paepe and other socialist spokesmen distrusted collaboration with any middle-class organization, even on the cross-class issue of peace. The International took the position that war resulted from capitalist exploitation and, therefore, peace would be the natural product of the socialist revolution. It also refused to permit women participants and ignored Marie Goegg's request to present her programme in 1869.[19]

Hence, apart from the unique instance of Eugénie Niboyet's newspaper in Paris, women's peace activism on the continent in the first three-quarters of the century was confined to Marie Goegg's association. Only the radical republicans in the *Ligue internationale de la paix et de la liberté* demonstrated any willingness to include women's rights in their broad conception of democracy and peace. Women activists in the peace cause elsewhere in Europe up to the *fin de siècle* were usually to be found in peace societies with similar orientations. Another example was the short-lived Milanese society, *Libertà, Fratellanza e Pace*, which added two feminists, Paolina Schiff and Christina Lazzati, to its central committee in 1879. In the years after the Franco-Prussian War, continental peace societies were very difficult to sustain. The wave of membership which the crisis of 1867 had generated slipped from thousands to dozens. Meetings in Paris, particularly, often attracted only five to ten of the most committed. In Germany, organized societies totally disappeared for two decades at least. Under these conditions, anyone who wanted to participate was more than welcome. By the 1890s when continental peace societies began to grow and revive, absolutely none of the organizations placed restrictions on women.

The impact of the Franco-Prussian War and the evolution of parliamentary institutions in Europe also minimized the differences between liberal internationalism and republican or radical internationalism. On the other hand, the establishment of the Second International in 1889 had the effect of exacerbating differences between middle-class and socialist peace prescriptions, although parliamentary collaboration often occurred between representatives of the two positions. What galvanized the growth of the peace movement as the century wore to a close was the frightening progress of the arms race. The cost of armaments, which promised to bankrupt Europe, contrasted with the cheapness of arbitration procedures, which proved able to defuse certain conflicts, as in the *Alabama* case of 1872, mobilized considerable peace propaganda. In 1889, peace societies from France, Britain and Switzerland called another international congress in Paris which was a great success. From 1889 to 1914, the private peace societies managed to convene annual international congresses nearly every year. Two to four hundred delegates and sometimes 1000 or more spectators gathered to discuss, debate and vote resolutions on arbitration, international law, arms control, education, contemporary crises, freedom of the seas, freedom of commerce, tariff reform, relations with women's and socialist organizations, a possible federation of Europe, a permanent court of arbitration, obligatory arbitration and the rights of neutrals--among other topics. Besides the annual congresses, peace societies organized national peace associations which also held congresses in France, Britain, Italy, Germany, Austria, the Scandinavian nations, the Netherlands, Belgium and, after 1906, Tsarist Russia. Peace journals appeared in almost every language along with an outpouring of scholarly and popular books. In 1892, the movement created a central headquarters, the *Bureau internationale de la paix* in Berne, which also published journals and organized international congresses. At no time before or since has an international network of peace activists functioned so consistently or so regularly.[20] Its membership, mainly educated middle class from various liberal professions, obviously failed in its primary object--to prevent the great war which they both feared and predicted.[21] The existence of this movement testifies to the fact that not everyone in pre-1914 Europe was engaged in manufacturing the five long-range and four short-range causes of World War I. As early as 1892, the International Peace Bureau issued a special appeal to women's associations to affiliate with the movement and attend peace congresses.[22] A few years later one French peace activist went so far as to argue that the only way to insure international peace would be "to give women the posts of ministers of foreign affairs and war" in every government.[23]

Women participated in the peace movement from the 1890s to 1914 in all possible ways. Some joined or backed older organizations. In the Swiss Romande, for instance, the membership of the *Ligue internationale de la paix et de la liberté* by 1905 was approximately one-third female.[24] During the 1890s, the approach that Marie Goegg had used--separate women's peace societies--also reappeared. In the International Council of Women, a separate committee for International Peace and Arbitration was created with membership from a dozen nations.[25] In Britain and France, women's peace societies were either created or separated from older peace groups. The Liverpool and Birkenhead Women's Peace and Arbitration Society claimed over 300 dues-paying members in 1894. Entirely staffed by women, its program denounced the "high-handed and unjustifiable manner" in which the British government treated the peoples of Matabele (now Zimbabwe) in 1893-4; attacked increased naval expenditure and deplored the creation of Boys' Brigades for military training in the schools. For resolving European tensions it favoured arbitration which, the women argued, could be instituted the moment that governments were willing.[26] This society existed quite separately from the Women's Auxiliary of the British Peace Society which was headed after 1882 by the well-to-do Quaker, Priscilla H. Peckover.[27]

In France women's peace societies began to multiply in the 1890s. The first was established by the radical feminist Eugénie Potonié-Pierre in 1895 and called the *Union Internationale des Femmes*. It was created after a visit by the English pacifist, Ellen Robinson, secretary of the British Peace Society. The Union promised to coordinate women's rights organizations in a struggle against "military glory [which is] pure chimera" and to oppose "the destruction of man by man."[28] Little remains to indicate what the organization actually did beyond issue manifestos which Potonié-Pierre circulated among feminists in Italy, Greece, Germany and Austria.[29] The twenty-one English women who signed the initial appeal that Robinson brought to Paris in 1895 had hoped for an improvement in Anglo-French relationships as a model to "influence the actual condition of Europe."[30] The idea of close Anglo-French relationships was an old dream among European peace activists, found as early as 1814 in Saint-Simon's plan for the re-organization of Europe. By 1897 Robinson admitted that, while the Union had not grown very much, it had remained an informal network of "women from several nations who meet to advance the peace cause."[31] Its membership was mainly involved in other causes--from temperance to reform of laws about prostitution. For Potonié-Pierre, no international peace program could stand alone and apart from issues of domestic reform. Her twenty-year commitment to feminism had begun with the *Ligue de Droit des Femmes*. She had toiled as well for trade union and labour causes. Both women's and working people's rights were inseparable from peace to her. *L'Union internationale* also insisted on universal suffrage as a requirement for international peace.[32] Potonié-Pierre had never been one to mince words in order to please the powerful. In the name of the Union, she sent, for instance, a sharply worded attack on Crispi's government for its policies in Africa in 1895-6.[33] Her death in 1898 removed the Union's most energetic voice.

Two other peace societies organized by and for women were also established in Paris in the 1890s. In 1896 a socially prominent woman, the Princess Gabrielle Wiesniewska, organized the *Ligue des femmes pour le désarmement* which changed its name to *Alliance des Femmes pour la Paix* in 1899. Wiesniewska, who had no previous record of any political activism, traded on her numerous personal connections among well-to-do women throughout Europe to launch the league. Letters and manifestos were sent to foreign "sisters" all over Europe. In the Netherlands, a coordinate society was established by another aristocratic lady, Johanna Waszklewicz-Van Schilfgaarde, which broke from Wiesniewska's group within a few years. The Dutch women's peace organization began publication of a serious journal, *Vrede door Recht* and merged with the older general peace society in Holland which had not functioned for decades. Waszklewicz-Van Schilfgaarde's group thoroughly re-energized the movement in the Netherlands.[34]

Both the Parisian princess and the Dutch aristocrat approached the question of peace by a strategy based on personal contacts in high places and appeals to elite women to influence powerful men. While their method of operating was immensely conservative, their arguments--at least initially--were not. Wiesniewska, in particular, focused directly on arms control, the dangers of the arms race and the need to reduce armaments. In her appeals sent abroad, she proposed that the main purpose of the league was to spread "the idea of international disarmament, to bring an end to fratricidal warfare and inaugurate the desired age of justice and harmony."[35] If women in all countries worked to teach their sons to hate war, then none could be charged with undermining its nation's defence.[36] In contrast, the international peace movement had avoided the subject of disarmament during the nineties and emphasized the organization of international institutions. Wiesniewska's propaganda, in that context, was far more "radical." She claimed that several thousand supporters applauded her effort within one year.[37]

Actually, not all women reacted as favourably as she claimed. The leading Portuguese feminist-pacifist, known by the pseudonym Caiel, commented:

> in the current state of the question [of world peace] it could be dangerous to suggest general immediate disarmament to an international congress [of diplomats]. War itself . . . might result from this well-intentioned initiative towards the ideal pacific state.[38]

Caiel's view reflected the usual position of the leading male voices in the international peace movement[39] as well as the position of the indisputable woman leader of the international peace movement, Bertha von Suttner. In no uncertain terms, von Suttner warned in 1897, "friends of peace should not take up the armaments question; [arms reduction] can only follow from a preceding understanding and creation of a legal order."[40]

Evidently Wiesniewska recognized the danger of emphasizing disarmament apart from any other recommendation for defence or security. She assured her own compatriots

> Frenchwomen, we are chauvinists--at least [we must] remain armed . . . to defend the country against an invader as long as our neighbours do not disarm.[41]

By 1899, the word "disarmament" was dropped from the title of the society and the newly named *Alliance des Femmes pour la Paix* emerged. At the Paris Exposition of 1900, the *Alliance* held its own separate peace congress, not participating in the Universal Peace Congress. There, Wiesniewska clarified her intentions:

> We ask for international disarmament in the name of humanity to end the sufferings of war victims, the tears of their mothers and widows . . . .
> The aim of our society is certainly not the disarmament of *la patrie*; it only takes aim at the armed peace which will ruin

and depopulate Europe before a war even breaks out--to the political and industrial benefit of America and the Asiatics.

Our league respects the sacred cause of the defence of the motherland and the integrity of all its colonial possessions which every patriot must defend, until war shall disappear before the jurisdiction of arbitral courts, which, while guaranteeing the independence of each nation, will eliminate the causes of collision; national independence will thus be assured in justice and the reciprocal equity of peoples.[42]

Thus, the programme of the women's league for disarmament changed to reflect the centrist position of the international peace movement. However, before her death, Wiesniewska abandoned her strategy of elitism. She came to conclude that the objectives of the peace movement would never be achieved until women got the vote. In 1903 she urged Mme. Edmond Spalikowska, who was to represent the Alliance at an international peace congress, to press the importance of suffrage at that congress.[43] It is fascinating to note that this relatively conservative woman reached the same position as the radical Eugénie Potonié-Pierre, who also argued that women would never vote for militarist candidates.

The third women's peace society established in Paris was founded by Sylvie Flammarion and called *l'Association "La paix et le désarmement par les femmes."*[44] Flammarion, a vice-president of Wiesniewska's group, struck out on her own in 1899 to create the Association, perhaps because the *Alliance* had strayed from its attack on the arms race. Flammarion, married to a well known astronomer, Camille, had developed her own reputation in that field and as a writer. In forming *l'Association,* she announced several differences from Wiesniewska's *Alliance.* The group would be run entirely by women and only feature women speakers. It would emphasize the dangers of the arms race. Finally, it would go out among ordinary women and working people to prosyletize. Normally a reserved and quiet woman, Flammarion climbed on boxes and carts in public squares and markets, proclaiming the dangers of armaments, the importance of peace to working people and working-class women, the need for common folk to press governments on behalf of arbitration, and the connection between arms expenses and poverty. Ignoring hecklers who attacked her for abandoning Alsace-Lorraine, she denounced war as "useless carnage, imbecile massacre [and] the total observance of masculine law."[45] The word "disarmament" was never eliminated from the title of her organization and women continued to manage its affairs in every area.[46] Of all the French middle-class women's peace societies that survived until the war, Flammarion's association remained the most determinedly sex-separate. One of her most important contributions to the peace movement was the recruitment of the journalist Séverine (Carolyn Rémy) to the cause. Of all the leading pre-war peace activists, Séverine remained the most resistant, in 1914-15, to the brandishments of patriotism and was a very early protester in France of the war's legitimacy.[47]

The creation of women's peace societies occurred about a decade later in Italy.[48] Italian feminists were prominent in Italian peace societies as individual members, first in 1878-9 and then after 1889, when peace societies began to multiply in the peninsula. In 1908, however, a new direction began as a result of the appearance of a whirlwind feminist crusader, Teresita Pasini dei Bonfatti, who was known publicly by her pseudonym, Alma dolens.[49] A writer for and organizer of philanthropic causes, Alma dolens spent about six months touring central Italy with the purpose of establishing peace committees and societies, at least half a dozen of which were women's groups. At the fifth national congress of Italian peace societies in Rome in 1909 she was heartily welcomed for her labours and pleaded with the congress to take steps to attract more women to the cause. "Women," explained Alma dolens,

> have remained aloof from the peace movement mainly because of the false concept that has confused pacifism with anti-militarism and anti-patriotism as well as the mistaken idea that the problem of arbitration and gradual disarmament are arguments exclusively for masculine competence.[50]

The purpose of separate women's peace societies was to insure that women developed the confidence to discuss issues previously beyond their experience. In fact, she arrived at the right movement. A previous Italian peace congress had committed itself to support the movement for women's rights and "emancipation" on the grounds that the success of the peace movement depended on the development of "donne coscienti."[51] But there is no evidence that the peace groups had made the kind of effort which Alma dolens undertook to bring in women.

A second woman peace activist, Rosalia Gwis-Adami, who was an author and frequent contributor to La Vita Internazionale, the leading Italian pacifist journal, also took up the problem of attracting women to the cause in 1909. Gwis-Adami, aided by several Milanese women high school teachers, organized the Società delle giovinette italiane per la pace which managed to grow to several thousand members in one year. Women students and teachers came to lectures on international peace, arbitration and law; established model arbitration tribunals, organized debates and recruited other students. The clear purpose of this group was to educate young women to the dangers of the current international system (or anarchy) and demonstrate alternatives to it; it was to implant what Gwis-Adami considered a healthy patriotism--that love of country did not necessarily mean destruction of a neighbouring country. Furthermore, the society provided a new kind of education, one in which students were participants and not merely passive recipients. Gwis-Adami, for instance, frequently spoke to students on literary topics, including a critical evaluation of heroic poetry and fables. Her eventual dream was to extend the society on an international plane, creating a trans-national organization of high school youth educated in the teachings of the peace movement. Gwis-Adami was a gifted propagandist but not an original thinker. Her entire analysis was derived from her mentors, the president of the Milanese peace society and Italy's Nobel Peace prize winner, Ernesto T. Moneta, and the Roman professor of linguistics, Angelo De Gubernatis, both of whom she idolized.

Despite its promising beginnings in 1908-9, women's peace activism in Italy came to a bitter and abrupt end in 1911. In September of that year the Italian government declared war on Turkey and invaded Lybia-Cirenaica, basing its actions on typical imperialist arguments and the needs of the *Banca di Roma* at that time. Almost immediately after the declaration of war, Moneta's *Unione Lombarda* and de Gubernatis' peace society in Rome announced their support of the war.[52] The peace movement in Italy was sundered between those who supported the war and those who did not--and who attacked pacifists favouring the expansion of Italy. In Europe, there was universal agreement among pacifists that the Moneta faction had abandoned its twenty-year record. Gwis-Adami followed her male mentors; Alma dolens championed the anti-war forces and the open war of words between these two women leaders became bitter and personal. Alma dolens not only campaigned publicly against the war; privately she wrote to the Berne peace bureau, which had just obtained a large grant from the new Carnegie Foundation, to ask that funds be sent to support the beleaguered anti-war pacifists in Italy.[53] The executive secretary of the central office, Albert Gobat, quietly obliged, and Alma dolens, along with Edoardo Giretti and others, managed to re-organize the Italian peace movement and support publications that remained pacifist. On her own initiative, she organized a new workers' peace society in Milan, the *Società Operaia "Pro Arbitrato e Disarmo,"* with the aid of a metal workers' union official. Quite illegally, Alma dolens and members of the workers' peace society leafletted Milan, held marches and put up posters denouncing the war.[54]

For her part, Gwis-Adami took over Moneta's role because of his age and failing health. She became a prominent propagandist, arguing for "patriotic pacifism" and denouncing Alma dolens, Gobat and the entire international peace movement. It was her first step in a long journey that later included defending Italy's entrance into World War I, attacking Romain Rolland during the war for his pacifism and denouncing the Treaty of Versailles in 1919 for not giving Trieste to Italy.[55] Never did Gwis-Adami consider herself anything but a pacifist--one who believed, however, that a nation's self-interest came before anything else.

Neither gender nor class explains the different behavior of Italy's two women pacifist leaders. Both Alma dolens and Gwis-Adami had supportive husbands and came from well-to-do families of Risorgimento patriots who admired Mazzini and Garibaldi. What was essentially different was the inspiration that brought them into the peace movement. Alma dolens was moved by concern for women and the oppressed; Gwis-Adami followed the leadership of two eminent men, leaders in journalism, politics and academe. She had never been active in any women's movement and, although she vaguely believed in women's emancipation, she often expressed her dislike of non-feminine women leaders and English radical suffragists. The war in 1911 heralded the decline of the Italian peace movement and generated conditions resembling the impact that 1914 had on the entire international movement.

Gwis-Adami's effort to bring in young women as recruits for a next generation of pacifist leaders--before 1911--was one of several such efforts made by women's peace groups to have an impact on education. When she organized her group of high school teachers and students in 1909, she was evidently unaware of the fact that other efforts of this type had been made earlier in France and Belgium. In 1901, two members of the *Alliance des Femmes pour la Paix*, Madeleine Carlier and Marguerite Bodin, who lived in separate provinces in France, announced the creation of a new group, the *Société d'education pacifique*. It was not their objective to establish yet another pacifist society--France had many already--but to create a network of teachers who would engage in bringing peace education into the classroom. In addition, the *Société* planned to lobby national congresses of teachers' organizations (*amicales*) on curricular reform. Children should be taught that "there are not two moralities--one for nations and one for individuals."[56] Young children should learn respect for life, rights and dignity--not heroism. War should not be taught as an inevitable result of political struggle but as a phenomenon which can be controlled through arbitration. Games and classroom exercises should be introduced to teach children how to resolve differences through compromise, mediation and negotiation. Bodin presented the outlines of the society's program in 1901 at a teachers' congress in Bordeaux. There she also addressed history teaching, one of the most sensitive subjects anyone could raise in a country reeling from the Dreyfus case and the Fashoda crisis. Bodin urged high school teachers to teach history as the rise of civilization across national boundaries and not the chronicle of battles and victorious generals which it so frequently became. The common achievements of peoples in industry, science and the arts, and not the making of political boundaries, she argued, made up the real thread of the past. Younger children should sit in classrooms decorated with scenes of people working--not battlefield carnage. The congress was enthusiastic and, by 1910, the *Société d'education pacifique* included membership from approximately one-third of France's provinces.[57] In Belgium, a sister organization was created in 1906 by Marie Rosseels in Anvers which held annual teachers' conferences nearly every summer up to World War I.[58] A Swedish affiliate founded and run by Fanny Petterson specialized in international student exchange.[59]

Educating children and high school students in alternative thinking evidently became a major concern of the Peace and Arbitration Committee of the International Council on Women. It, too, worked to transform textbooks from nationalist heroics to studies in civilization, to revamp history teaching and focus on peaceful solutions that worked in the past. The Committee struggled to have May 18 celebrated as Peace Day in schools--May 18, 1899 was the opening day of the first Hague Conference. This effort was most successful in parts of the United States, Denmark, Switzerland, the Netherlands and England. For very young children, the Committee rewrote fairy tales and Mother Goose stories to eliminate murder, violence and bloodshed. Major scholars were approached to write new history emphasizing man and his march towards civilization and not his march over fellow man.[60] It was in the field of education--broadly construed--that women peace activists laboured most persistently. Considering the career options available to educated women, it is no surprise to find so many involved in peace education prior to World War I.

In France, Italy, Belgium and the Scandinavian nations, women were active as organizers of women's peace societies, both conservative and militant; in education and educational reform as well as in peace societies including both sexes. In Germany leading women pacifists came out of feminist circles and were the organizers of huge petition campaigns. The event which galvanized the first of these campaigns was the Rescript issued by Nicholas II in August, 1898, calling for an international conference to discuss the arms race, ways of cutting down armaments and the institution of arbitration. The Rescript led to the first Hague Peace Conference in May-June, 1899.

At a congress of the Federation of German Women's Associations in October, 1898, one delegate, Marguerite L. Selenka, convinced the audience that an enormous international demonstration of women supporting the objectives of the Rescript be organized. Selenka found herself in charge of all the organizing after the Federation approved her initiative. She laboured up to the eve of the official opening, contacting women all over the world--as far afield as Japan.[61] When the diplomats gathered, they were confronted with petitions bearing nearly one million signatures. In addition, demonstrations were organized at The Hague and in hundreds of cities by women to support the objectives of the Conference. None of the demonstrators knew, of course, that between August, 1898, and May, 1899, diplomats and ministers throughout Europe had negotiated the thrust of the Tsar's call into oblivion--particularly the sections on arms reduction. Nonetheless, the women's presence was felt. On the eve of the conference, a large public crowd in Copenhagen celebrated the conference, listening to a choir of 100 women dressed in white and to speakers led by Mathilde Bajér; in Milan and Turin, Paolina Schiff and Emilia Mariani organized and addressed about 20 different meetings of men and women on behalf of The Hague Conference; a 2000-person crowd listened to Marya Cheliga in Paris, representing the *Alliance des Femmes pour la Paix*; a last minute effort in Stockholm rounded up 200 women signatories to a telegram sent to The Hague; hundreds of new members joined the Dutch women's peace society and Wiesniewska's network came through with thousands of signatures--as did May W. Sewell.[62] Selenka evaluated the outpouring as the beginning of a new era for women and, thus, for history. Women were no longer vaguely and sentimentally opposing war. She saw their anger and opposition as arising from their new social and political voices and their more rational attitude towards patriotism.

> As it lies in the hands of women to foster the fond attachment to home, . . . it is she who can . . . best inculcate true love of country, . . . for native soil, for mother tongue

by opposing the chauvinist press and calls to "racial hatred."[63]

The impressive results of Selenka's campaign were not lost on male pacifists. The dean of European pacifists, Frédéric Passy, gratefully thanked her for adding women "to our male voices which for so long have been alone in protest."[64] Italian pacifists hailed her for her struggle to have May 18 recognized as Peace Day everywhere.[65] On the other hand, the German plenipotentiary to The Hague, Count Muenster--who detested the conference--viewed Selenka and the other pacifists somewhat differently:

> The Conference has attracted the worst political rabble of the entire world. The lowest journalists such as Stead, distasteful Jews like Bloch, peace widows like Frau von Suttner, who was feted yesterday by the Russian delegation, Frau Selenka, etc. This whole rabble (including Young Turks, Armenians . . . socialists) work openly under Russian protection.[66]

The pacifist presence at the first Hague Conference was the first large-scale lobbying effort of private peace activists at a diplomatic conference ever to occur. Earlier international conferences, such as the Brussels meeting of 1874, or the Geneva conference in 1862 which led to the Red Cross convention, had been visited by a handful of self-selected peace crusaders. But 1899 was the first major meeting where large numbers of peace activists congregated and in that group the women's presence was very clear. Besides Selenka, Wasklewicz-Van Schilfgaarde and, particularly, Bertha von Suttner spent six weeks button-holing diplomats each evening after official sessions closed.

No major women's petition and demonstration campaign preceded the second Hague Peace Conference in 1907, but in 1910 the German-American feminist and pacifist, Anna Eckstein organized another mass crusade for signatures. Eckstein's world-wide petition was aimed at encouraging the convocation of a third Hague Peace Congress, and she appeared at a meeting of the German national peace association in 1910 with hundreds of thousands of signatures.[67] She also brought the petition to the 1910 Universal Peace Congress in Stockholm. It demanded better results than the first two Hague Conferences had achieved on arms control and the extension of arbitration as an obligatory requirement among the major powers. The language of Eckstein's petition went considerably farther than the more guarded resolutions of the peace congresses, but in essence its demands were similar. Bluntly she claimed that "if women take up the cause of peace, they take up their own cause and at the same time, that of men." She was also applauded and supported. By 1910, all national and international peace congresses were becoming impatient, awaiting official government announcements for the third Hague Conference which, it was expected, would occur either in 1913, 1914 or 1915. Part of Eckstein's purpose was to push for the earliest date possible and for a firm commitment on the part of governments to find an arms reduction formula.

No examination of the role of women in the pre-1914 struggle to avoid war by the organization for peace is even half complete without some word about Bertha von Suttner. Born in 1843 into the Austrian nobility, descended from a family of military officers, von Suttner created a career as a journalist, writer and political commentator of some distinction by the 1880s. In 1889 she published her novel, *Die Waffen nieder! (Lay Down Your Arms)*, the story of the life and misfortunes of one fictional Martha Trilling whose marital happiness was destroyed by war and bloodshed. Graphic depictions of the horrors of battlefields and the 1871 siege of Paris--where Trilling's beloved husband died--turned the novel into one of the world's all-time best sellers. Its author became known as the Harriet Beecher Stowe of peace.[68] By 1914, the novel had been translated into sixteen languages and sold over a million copies. It was about to be released as a motion picture in Vienna in the summer of 1914. That showing never took place.

Shortly after the novel's appearance, von Suttner made contact with leaders of peace movements in western Europe. In Vienna, she founded the *Oesterreiche Friedensgesellschaft* (Austrian Peace Society) in 1891, then toured Germany creating peace societies in a number of cities. Thus was launched her 25-year career as a peace activist; some would say she was a one-woman peace movement. She joined the *Bureau international de la paix* as a permanent member of its directorate in 1892; shaped the agendas of international peace congresses; wrote and edited peace journals in German and was able to contribute to French, Italian and English journals easily, since she knew all the languages thoroughly. Her articles on contemporary affairs and the peace movement appeared in the liberal *Neue Freie Presse* in Vienna, and her friendship with Alfred Nobel probably contributed to his decision to draw up his amazing will.[69] (There is absolutely no evidence that she knew its contents before Nobel died.)

In the international peace movement, von Suttner occupied a position as mediator among conflicting positions. During the nineties when she saw the international movement as a "fragile plant" she struggled to keep divisive issues--particularly Alsace-Lorraine--off the agendas.[70] Given the ardent militarism of most of her compatriots, she argued that discussions of arms reduction would only drive away central European members from the movement. Von Suttner spent most of her hours as a propagandist trying to persuade eminent Austrian and German leaders of the value of international arbitration. Nothing separates her position from that of the centrist mainstream of international pacifism before 1914--indeed, she helped to fashion it. When invited to write an article on "peace from a woman's point of view," she candidly admitted that she would have preferred a different title--she saw no difference between men's and women's viewpoints on peace.[71] The methods and ideas in favour of peace, in von Suttner's estimation, had nothing to do with sex. Evidently the founders of the Women's International League for Peace and Freedom in 1919 saw nothing amiss in von Suttner's position either--they put her portrait in as the frontispiece of their published minutes. In her own day, organizers of women's peace societies, meetings and lectures vied to have her speak. She was asked to serve as honorary chair of several women's societies which she accepted. In 1907 at a special meeting of women on peace questions connected to the Munich Universal Peace Congress, von Suttner's speech evoked a ten minute standing ovation from over a thousand women.[72]

Apart from her organizational work, which was considerable, von Suttner's main contribution to the movement was as a popularizer. She "translated" the complex legal analyses of international theorists on topics such as arbitration, sanctions and methods of providing "good offices" into comprehensible lay language; she explained the differences between the types of arbitration treaties which nations had signed and laid forth the provisions of the Hague conventions to a wider public. Behind her technical writings lay a profound conviction that civilized nations had better find a way to avoid war if they wished to preserve civilization. Von Suttner understood that civilization was a very fragile result of centuries of human labour which would be eradicated by modern weapons. To her, this insight was sufficiently significant to overcome all hesitations and cavils--it meant that the peace question overrode all other issues. She truly believed that it transcended political and class differences and wanted desperately for her vision to be shared by the ruling circles of Europe. There is no exaggerating her rapture when she read the language of the Tsar's Rescript. Here, finally, was a monarch who wrote like a pacifist.

Von Suttner has been occasionally evaluated as a sentimentalist, a Pollyanna capable of producing reams of purple prose. Beneath her cheerful optimism and her constant reminders that change comes very slowly was a powerful recognition that the movement to which she gave her life could be exploded at any moment by an irrational act of those with power. Fortunately for her, she died a few days before Sarajevo.

Given the long record of women's peace activism, especially from 1899 up to the eve of the war, it is difficult to claim that women invented peace activism in 1915. What the congress in 1915 did was brave a torrent of hostility in order to meet--as well as brave some serious physical dangers. The most immediate demand that emerged from the women's meeting in 1915 was a very practical one conditioned by war itself--a hope that the great neutral power across the Atlantic would provide mediation and good offices to end the war as quickly as possible. The post-war agenda, however, was not particularly different from the pre-war agenda of the peace movement. This observation is not surprising and certainly not insulting, for, after all, how many ways were there for organizing peace in a world where no nation was willing to relinquish sovereignty *and* the nations were roughly equal in power. In the course of the discussions at The Hague, the participants often found themselves facing extremely difficult problems--as had earlier congresses of peace activists. Just how far, for instance, should the principle of national self-determination go? While most people were willing to admit the right of Poles to self-government, should national self-determination break up Belgium into component parts? or transfer Trieste to Italy? and what should be recommended about the Irish? Dr. Aletta Jacobs and Jane Addams, who managed the congress, found themselves in 1915 in approximately the same uncomfortable position as Bertha von Suttner had occupied when French pacifists wanted to discuss Alsace-Lorraine and Italians wanted to discuss Austrian treatment of Italians in the Tyrol. At a Universal Peace Congress in 1912, English pacifists had also squirmed as an erudite young Egyptian provided the international congress with a description of the British occupation of his ancient nation. The problem for peace congresses--be they pre-war or the 1915 Hague women's meeting--was that the international law formulations on which they all depended so completely were meaningless for peoples who had no nations. Yet, there was really no other set of ideas available for peace activists to defend.

Women's peace propaganda--in 1915 and earlier--was a brew mixing "sentimental" appeals to authority that war was particularly destructive to women and children with hard-headed, rational and "scientific" arguments on behalf of law and order. Women peace activists varied among themselves as greatly as did men. Some insisted, in the tradition of Marie Goegg, that international peace efforts required the support of educated and emancipated women; further, that women's absence from active political rights and life retarded the peace cause. In varying ways, this position was held by Eugénie Potonié-Pierre, Alma dolens, eventually the Princess Wiesniewska, Marguerite Selenka, Ellen Key (who came to her first international peace congress in 1910 in Stockholm), the women educators in the peace movement and, certainly, Séverine. Others, such as von Suttner and Gwis-Adami, understood the peace movement as something separate and even more important than other social and human rights endeavours, believing that without internationally organized institutions curbing violence, little else would develop. From neither group came any advocacy of unilateral disarmament. Indeed, almost all women's peace associations--with the possible exception of Flammarion's--emphasized the importance of extending the Hague conventions, of building the practice of arbitration among nations, of developing codes of international law before tackling arms reductions. In this sense, the 1915 Hague meeting differed slightly--they did not argue that arms reduction would be a long term result of legal internationalism; they wanted both, simultaneously, at the end of the war--which they wanted immediately.

The quarter century culminating in World War I, a period of unrelieved crises, rampant nationalism and a dizzying arms race, was an environment that forced rational men and women to examine alternatives to destruction and attempt to press the case for international similarities. The men and women of the organized, middle-class peace movement in Europe chose to argue for peaceful means of conflict resolution. They did not elect to follow Tolstoi's call for absolute pacifism and refusal to bear arms any more than they accepted Quaker arguments; they skirted the ticklish issue of conscientious objection on the continent where standing armies of conscripts had become standard practice; they did not advocate sabotage and subversion against the military training system, nor did they call for a general strike when war was declared. In fact, neither did most socialists who had discussed these options for twenty-five years. The peace movement, a combination of liberal internationalism and republican or radical internationalism, was a loose coalition or network. Considering the overwhelming odds that it confronted, the movement would have committed suicide had it excluded women or confined them to lesser roles. Those who complained in later years that the movement was timid, passive and negative were luxuriating in selective memory, if not historical amnesia.

Comments

Ursula Herrmann

Sandi Cooper has spoken about the *Ligue internationale de la paix et de la liberté* (International League of Peace and Liberty) in 1867 and has mentioned the position of Marx with regard to this organization. I would like to give you Marx's own words on this subject at the sitting of the General Council of the International Workingmen's Association on 20th August 1867. Marx said, and I quote from the minutes, "Citizen Marx called attention to the peace congress to be held in Geneva. He said it was desirable that as many delegates as could make it should attend the peace congress in their individual capacity, but that it would be an injustice to take part officially as representatives of the

International Workingmen's Association. The International Workingmen's Congress, meeting at the same time in Switzerland, was in itself a peace conference in the sense that the union of the working classes in the democratic countries must ultimately make international wars impossible."

Sandi Cooper

I would suggest you go from 1867 to 1868 when Marx discovered that the largest group from the International Workingmen's Association attending the Ligue internationale at its second meeting came from Bakunin's group. I've read the minutes of the First International, from '67-71 and some correspondence. To me, the outcome was a tragedy. Here was the first attempt on the part of socialists and radicals to work together and it was destroyed. I've no doubt about Marx's commitment to the issue. What happened, however, was that a great many people who came to the first meeting in Geneva came as independent individuals--such as Chemalé from Paris, and Cremer from England; and they came and remained independent. In the second year, 1868, and during the second Congress of the League, Bakunin attempted to take over the entire Association. A very nasty political struggle developed. The League voted on a principle it had tried to avoid--that principle being the belief in the necessity of private property as a requisite for freedom. Bakunin's group left. I think what was attempted in Europe in 1867-68 was the creation of a peace and social issues group which tried to be a coalition and a bridge between ideological positions. And the effort failed; the rigid ideologues' positions won. Marie Goegg herself wrote to Cesar Paepe in Belgium, asking to appear at the meeting of the International in 1868 which was being held in Brussels. She received no answer. She was, however, invited to appear at the *Ligue internationale de la paix*. To the Papacy, of course, there was no difference between the socialists and republicans. Rome denounced the peace activists in Geneva. Marx and other socialists also wanted the Peace Society to disband and join the socialists.

Shirley Faringer

We're currently engaged in an anti-war-toys campaign. Did the women who were worried about the education of children before World War I also look at the toys children were playing with?

Sandi Cooper

Yes, I should have mentioned that. They were concerned with toys, with music; in fact, there were some experiments with reconstructing the classroom so it would not be an authoritarian experience, using circles, encouraging creativity. Of course, the Italian woman, Montessori, the famous educator, comes out of this period.

Notes

[1]Congrès International des Femmes, 28 avril - 1 mai, 1915, The Hague, Report, Rapport, Bericht (Amsterdam, n.d., probably 1915), pp. 35-41.

[2]Ibid., Introduction, p. x.

[3]Gertrude Bussey and Margaret Tims, Pioneers for Peace, Women's International League for Peace and Freedom, 1915-1965 (London: Alden, 1980), p. 17.

[4]Lela B. Costin, "Feminism, Pacifism and Internationalism," in Judith H. Stiehm, ed., Women and Men's Wars, special issue of Women's Studies International Forum V, 3/4 (1982): 302.

[5]Quoted in Blanche W. Cook, Introduction to Marie Louise Degen, The History of the Woman's Peace Party (New York: Garland reprint, 1972), p. 7.

[6]See, for example, Congrès International des Femmes, op. cit., pp. 106-11; 310-13. A similar point is aptly made by Marijke Mossink, "Womanly pacifism, a parable," (unpublished research paper, University of Nijmegan), pp. 3-5.

[7]For a parallel argument about French feminism see Karen Offen, "Depopulation, Nationalism and Feminism in Fin de Siècle France," The American Historical Review 89, 3 (June 1984): 674-6.

[8]Histories of the peace movement for this period include Merle Curti, The American Peace Crusade, 1815-1860 (Duke, 1929); Christina Phelps, The Anglo-American Peace Movement in the Mid-Nineteenth Century (New York: Columbia, 1930); Gavin B. Henderson, "The Pacifists of the Fifties," Journal of Modern History (September 1937): 314-41; J. A. Hobson and Richard Cobden, The International Man (London, 1919; new edition with an introduction by Neville Masterman, 1968); J. ter Meulen, Die Gedanke der Internationalen Organisation, 2 vols. (The Hague, 1917-40); A. C. F. Beales, The History of Peace (orig. London, 1931; reprinted with a new introduction by Charles Chatfield, New York: Garland, 1971); Ettore Rota, "I movimenti pacifisti dell '800 e del '900 e le organizzazioni internazionali" in E. Rota, ed., Questioni di Storia Contemporanea (Milan: Marzoarti, 1952) II, 1963-2018 [should be used with care]; Théodore Ruyssen, Les Sources doctrinales de l'internationalisme (Paris: P.U.F., 1954-61) vol. II; Christian Lange and August Schou, Histoire de l'internationalisme, III, Du Congrès de Vienne jusqu'à la Première guerre mondiale (1964); F. H. Hinsley, Power and Pursuit of Peace (Cambridge, 1963): F.S.L. Lyons, Internationalism in Europe, 1815-1914 (Leyden, 1963); Peter Brock, Pacifism in the United States (Princeton, 1968) and Pacifism in Europe

to 1914 (Princeton, 1972); S. E. Cooper, ed., Internationalism in Nineteenth Century Europe: The Crisis of Ideas and Purpose (New York: Garland, 1976); Eric W. Sager, "The Social Origins of Victorian Pacifism" in Victorian Studies XXIII (Winter, 1980): 211-36; Georges P. Speeckaert, Le Premier Siècle de la Coopération internationale, 1815-1914 (Brussels: U.A.I., 1980).

[9]Alexander Tyrell, "Making the Millenium: The Mid-Nineteenth Century Peace Movement," The Historical Journal XX, 1 (1978): 75-95.

[10]Sandi E. Cooper, "The Impact of Nationalism on European Peace Movements and Liberal Internationalists, 1848-1914," Peace and Change VI, 1 & 2 (Winter, 1980): 26-7.

[11]A brief biography by Laura S. Strumingher is in Harold Josephson et al., eds., A Biographical Dictionary of Modern Peace Leaders, 1800-1975 (Westport: Greenwood, 1985), pp. 689-90.

[12]Alice F. Tyler, "The Crusade for Peace," Phases of American Social History to 1860 (Minneapolis, 1944).

[13]The standard study of the mid-century (after 1860) European peace movement is Irwin Abrams, "A History of European Peace Societies, 1867-1899" (unpublished dissertation, Harvard, 1938). See also Frédéric Passy, Pour la Paix: notes et documents (orig. Paris, 1909; reprinted with an introduction by Adolf Wild, New York: Garland, 1972), ch. 2.

[14]For the creation of the Ligue international de la paix et de la liberté, see Abrams, op. cit.; also Jules Barni, ed., Annales du Congrès de Génève, 9-12 séptembre, 1867 (Geneva: Vérésoff and Garrigues, 1868), pp. 9-12.

[15]"Proposition de créer une Association internationale des femmes en connexion avec la Ligue de la paix et de la liberté," Les Etats-Unis d'Europe I, 10 (March 8, 1868): 38. A brief biography of Goegg by S. E. Cooper is in Josephson, ed., op. cit., pp. 338-9.

[16]Speech reprinted in Les Etats-Unis d'Europe I, 26 (June 28, 1868): 102.

[17]Deux Discours (Geneva, 1878, reprint of 1868 speeches), 4-5.

[18]Barni, op. cit., p. 49. The poor relationship which developed after 1868 between the Genevan Ligue and the First International is also recorded in Jacques Freymond et al., La Première Internationale (Geneva: Droz, 1962). One of the founders of the International, the English trade union leader W. R. Cremer, was among the first to resign. Cremer was also a founder of the Genevan peace society. His initial commitment was to an organization of workers from Britain and the continent against war and he was completely uninterested in Marx's analysis. See Howard Evans, Sir Randal Cremer: His Life and Work (London, 1909; reprinted with an introduction by Naomi C. Miller, New York: Garland, 1971), chs. iii, iv, viii.

[19]Goegg, Deux Discours, introduction.

[20]Sandi E. Cooper, "Peace and Internationalism: European Ideological Movements Behind the Two Hague Conferences (1889-1907), " (unpublished dissertation, New York University, 1967),

ch. 1; Roger Chickering, Imperial Germany and a World Without War: The Peace Movement and German Society, 1892-1914 (Princeton, 1975), ch. 1; Jost Duelffer, Regeln gegen den Krieg? Die Haager Friedenskonferenzen, 1899 und 1907 in der internationalen Politik (Frankfurt/M.: Ullsten, 1981), pp. 7-17; Solomon Wank, ed., Introduction to Doves and Diplomats (Westport: Greenwood, 1978).

[21]The most remarkable work of prediction was the study by Jean Bloch, La Guerre (Paris 1896-8) which examined the nature of modern warfare and proposed most of the nightmarish conditions of trench warfare that would occur in a major war among the great powers. One volume of that six-volume study appeared in English as The Future of War (Boston, 1910). The six-volume French edition (it was also published in Russian, Polish and German) and the single English volume are available, with an introduction by S. E. Cooper in a Garland reprint, 1972-74. Bloch's impact on the Tsar is discussed in Peter van den Dungen, The Making of Peace: Jean de Bloch and the First Hague Peace Conference, Occasional Papers #12 (California State University at Los Angeles, Center for the Study of Armament and Disarmament, 1983, general editor: Udo Heyn), 57 pp.

[22]Bureau internationale de la Paix in "Appel aux Associations des Dames," Berne, 12 mai, 1892, in Bureau international de la Paix Archives (hereafter, BIP Archives) United Nations Library, Geneva, dossier V.A.4.

[23]Jules Bois, "Le Role Prépondérant de la Femmes pour l'éstablissement de la Paix," La Paix par le Droit VIII, 10 (Paris and Nîmes, December, 1898): 53.

[24]La Paix, organe des sections romandes de la Société romandes de la Société suisse de la paix (Lausanne, March, 1905): 6-8.

[25]In 1904, its president, the American May Wright Sewell affiliated the committee directly with the Berne Bureau. See BIP Archives, V.A.4, letter, January 15, 1904.

[26]See Liverpool and Birkenhead Women's Peace and Arbitration Society, Annual Report, List of Officers for 1894, 2 p. circular in BIP Archives, VII A.1 "History of Peace Societies."

[27]A brief biography by Thomas C. Kennedy is in Josephson, ed., op. cit. Peckover claimed several thousand members by 1894. See BIP Archives, VIII, A.1., letter to Elie Ducommun, 9 X 1894 and undated post card.

[28]BIP Archives, dossier "Femmes et paix," "Les Femmes d'Angleterre à leurs soeurs de France," April 28, 1895.

[29]Eugénie Pierre-Potonié, "Aux Femmes de tous les pays," Petits Plaidoyers contre la guerre XXX (1895) in BIP Archives, III, Q 2 Congrès de la Paix, Historique.

[30]BIP Archives, V. A. 4, 6 "Propagande par des sociétés des femmes." Undated ms, "Aux femmes françaises."

[31]BIP Archives, V.A.4, letter to Elie Ducommun, December 3, 1897.

[32]BIP V.A.4, letter to Elie Ducommun, April 8, 1896, requesting that the Bureau send delegates to a feminist congress.

[33]BIP Archives, V.A.4 "Propagande des femmes."

[34]A brief biography by H. Rombach is in Josephson, ed., op. cit., Waszklewicz-Van Schilfgaarde, a talented organizer and editor, was active in the national and international movement from 1898-1904 when she apparently lost interest in the movement. A brief biography of Wiesniewska by S. E. Cooper is also there.

[35]Letter to Austrian Women, copy in Bibliothèque Marguerite Durand (Paris), dossier "Paix."

[36]Letter to Norwegian Sisters, in Durand, loc. cit., also clipping from Echo de Paris, 15 October 1900 in loc. cit.

[37]Preface to Archer de Lima, Pour la Paix et pour l'Humanité (Lisbon, 1898).

[38]Caiel was quoting the words of Gaston Moch, a leading French pacifist in Caiel, La Femme et la Paix: Appel aux Mères Portugaises (Lisbon: Imp. Nacional, 1898), p. 53, brochure preserved in Bibliothèque de Documentation Contemporaine, Nanterre, Fonds Passy.

[39]The central position accorded to arbitration provided the international movement with its strongest unifying ideology. Many pacifists shared Gaston Moch's view that "the realization of a simultaneous agreement [on arms reduction] is materially impossible for the problem differs greatly from one nation to another--the configuration of the land, population density, wealth, importance of the colonial empire--produce very specific defensive conditions for each power, from which proceeds the impossibility of finding a common ground." Gaston Moch, "La Philosophie de la Paix: L'arbitrage universel" in Morale Générale II (Paris: Colin, 1903), p. 365. At an international peace congress, the same idea was passed as a resolution which asserted

> disarmament [would be] a result of the organization of peace rather than a means of arriving at peace. [The congress] is convinced that the application by the nations of a system of justice . . . will necessarily lead to a progressive and simultaneous reduction of armaments.

Congrès universel de la paix, Bulletin officiel, Monaco, 1902, p. 47.

[40]Bertha von Suttner, in Die Waffen nieder!, #20 (Vienna, 1897) quoted in Hans Wehburg, Die internationale Beschraenkung der Ruestungen (New York: Garland, 1973), reprinted with an introduction by S. Wank, p. 15.

Von Suttner (1843-1914) was the most eminent woman in the movement. A brief biography by Irwin Abrams is in Josephson, ed., op. cit. Longer studies include Beatrix Kampf, Bertha von Suttner: Das Leben einer grossen Frau, Schriftstellerin, Politikerin, Journalistin (Vienna: Oesterreicher Bundesverlag, 1964); Carolyn E. Playne, Bertha von Suttner and the Struggle to Avert World War I (London: Allen Unwin, 1936) and a fictionalized account, Hertha Pauli, Cry of the

Heart, The Story of Bertha von Suttner, tr. by R. and C. Winston (New York: Washburn, 1957).

[41]"Manifesto," Le Désarmement Géneral I, 2 (Paris, 1897): 5.

[42]Reprinted in Caiel, op. cit., p. 49.

[43]Letter to Mme. Edmond Spalikowska, 1 IX 1903, pp. 3-4 in Durand, loc. cit.

[44]A brief biography by S. E. Cooper is in Josephson, ed., op. cit.

[45]Séverine, "Mme. Camille Flammarion" in Le Congrès Spiritualiste (July, 1908) #7, clipping preserved in Durand, loc. cit.

[46]When Flammarion was unable to attend a meeting in Berne of the central committee of the peace bureau, she asked to be represented by "une déléguée"--a woman delegate--who would respect the women's approach to peace concerns. See BIP Archives, I. F., Commission du Bureau, 1892-95 (misfiled) letter to Albert Gobat, 28 IX 1911.

[47]A brief biography by Albert Hill is in Josephson, ed., op. cit.

[48]In reality, one society--the Comitato delle Signore per la Pace e l'Arbitrato internazionale had been founded in Palermo in 1891 and Signora Elvira Cimino remained its chair for over 20 years. This group appears to have confined itself to protests to the government during crises and occasional protests over military appropriations. Unfortunately, surviving information leaves no indication of its activities, its membership and its involvement in the national peace federation of Italy. The initial creation of this organization was the work of an English organizer, Hodgson Pratt, who headed the London based International Peace and Arbitration Association of which the Palermo group was an affiliate.

[49]A brief biography by S. E. Cooper is in Josephson, ed., op. cit.

[50]Speech to the fifth national congress of Italian peace societies, in La Vita Internazionale XIII, 1 (January 5, 1910): 6.

[51]Ibid. X, 19 (October 5, 1907): 435, report of the third national congress, Perugia.

[52]A brief biography of Gwis-Adami by S. E. Cooper is in Josephson, ed., op. cit. For a discussion of the Italian pacifist crisis in 1911 see Sandi E. Cooper, "The Impact of Nationalism on European Peace Movements and Liberal Internationalists," pp. 30-2.

[53]BIP Archives, Correspondence, letter to Albert Gobat, January 12, 1912.

[54]Ibid., letters to Albert Gobat, February 12, February 17, 1912.

[55]See, for example, Nella mischia. Riposta di una donna a Romain Rolland (Rome, 1918).

[56]BIP Archives "Paix et l'Education," Société d'Education Pacifique, Announce, 1902.

[57]Bureau International de la Paix, Annuaire du Mouvement pacifique pour l'année 1910 (Bienne, 1910), pp. 54-7.

[58]La Paix par le Droit XVI, 10 (October 1906): 397. (This journal of the French peace movement,published from 1891 to 1948, mainly in Paris, is available on microfiche from Clearwater Press, New York City).

[59]Bureau international de la paix, Annuaire. . .pour 1910, p. 80.

[60]May Wright Sewell, "Report on the Committee on Peace and Arbitration" in Countess Aberdeen, ed., International Council of Women, Report of the Quinquennial Meetings, Rome, 1914 (Karlsruhe, 1914), pp. 408-15.

[61]Maguerite L. Selenka, Die internationale Kundebung der Frauen zur Friedenskonferenz, 15 mai 1899 (Muenchen: Schupp, 1900), Introduction.

[62]Report in Correspondence Bi-mensuelle IV, 11 (Berne: Bureau international de la paix) June 10, 1899, pp. 75-7.

[63]Selenka, op. cit., p. x.

[64]Quoted in Vita Internazionale IV, 9 (May 5, 1901): 293.

[65]Ibid., p. 294. In addition to struggling for an international observance of Peace Day, Selenka and other German feminist pacifists worked unsuccessfully to eliminate the German national holiday, Sedan Day, celebrating the defeat of France in 1870. See "Contre la Fête de Sedan in La Paix par le Droit #8 (July, 1909): 334.

[66]Communique of Muenster to Foreign Minister, von Buelow, June 26, 1899, in Die Grosse Politik der Europaieschen Kabinette, XV, #4327, pp. 312-14.

[67]Der dritte deutschen Friedenskongress in Wiesbaden, 1910 (Verlag der Deutscher Friedensgesellschaft, n.d., probably 1911), pp. 20-1.

[68]An English translation, Lay Down Your Arms is available with an introduction by Irwin Abrams, (New York: Garland, 1972).

[69]Irwin Abrams, "Bertha von Suttner and the Nobel Peace Prize," Journal of Central European Affairs XXIII (1962): 286-301. I am grateful to Professor Abrams for a copy of his latest paper, "The Transformation of the Nobel Peace Prize" delivered at the International Studies Association, Spring, 1984 (Atlanta) which examines the differences between the prize in the years before 1914 and after 1919.

[70]Bertha von Suttner, Memoirs, 2 vols., reprinted with an introduction by Irwin Abrams (New York: Garland, 1972), I, p. 361.

[71]Bertha von Suttner, "Universal Peace from a Woman's Standpoint," North American Review CLXIX (July, 1899): 50.

[72]Congrès universel de la Paix, Bulletin officiel, Munich, 1907 (Berne: Buechler, 1908), Appendix. This special meeting was called to emphasize the importance of bringing women into the peace movement. Besides von Suttner, Lucia Mead, Sylvie Flammarion, and Priscilla H. Peckover spoke.

THE PARTICIPATION OF WOMEN IN THE BELGIAN PEACE MOVEMENT (1830-1914)

Nadine Lubelski-Bernard

This paper seeks to pinpoint the precise role played by Belgian women in the defence of peace prior to the First World War by attending to the particular ideologies they upheld as well as to the means they chose to attain their goal. Firstly, however, it is necessary to describe the particular status of women in Belgium. Secondly, the origins and development of the peace movement will be considered within its political context, both national and international, and thirdly a few details about the movement and its individual supporters will be given.

In the Middle Ages, women living in the area corresponding to modern Belgium enjoyed quite extensive rights. However, under the influence of Roman law, these rights were progressively eroded, resulting in a corresponding decline in the social status of women. From the 11th and 12th centuries onwards, the growth of the major cities in Flanders and the Brabant, as well as in the Liège region, was accompanied by a corresponding evolution of urban law. One of the most distinctive features of the latter was its tendency to favour the equality of the sexes, both within and outside marriage.[1] This egalitarian tendency increased up to the 16th century, but then lost ground in the two centuries that followed.[2]

Just before the onset of the French Revolution, Condorcet denounced the inferior status of women and demanded, on their behalf, the recognition of certain basic rights, including the right to vote, and the right of access to education and to certain jobs still barred to them. This was followed, in 1791, by the feminist "Déclaration des droits de la femme et de la citoyenne" (Declaration of the Rights of Woman and the Female Citizen) by Olympe de Gouges. However, scarcely two years later, a law was passed banning women from clubs, thus effectively prohibiting their participation in political life. The period of the Empire and the Napoleonic Code was, in fact, far from favourable for the emancipation of women. In our provinces, Napoleonic legislation led to "an appreciable worsening of the woman's subordination to her husband, which ran directly against the ideas that had prevailed and been freely aired in these parts up to that point."[3] Hopes raised at the outset of the French Revolution were thus quickly dashed and it was not until the Saint-Simonians and the idealistic socialists that one heard the slightest call for the political and legal equality of women, for an improvement in their economic prospects and even for sexual liberation. Shortly afterwards, such demands were brushed aside with the failure of the 1848 revolution, dashing hopes in this area once again. Moreover, Proudhon's theories on women[4] seriously restricted the women's socialist movement for several years to come.

Thus one finds women in the 19th century relegated to the legal status of 'minors,' or 'mental defectives'; moreover they were generally illiterate since there was no compulsory schooling. Those who did go to school received only a superficial education. In any case, pathetically few establishments of secondary education were open to girls. As far as the universities were concerned, these remained closed to women, in most disciplines, right up to the very end of the 19th century. What is more, women were kept out of public office since they possessed no political rights, the right to vote only being granted to them after the Second World War. Clearly, the status of women in Belgium was very different from that of their English-speaking counterparts who contributed far earlier to the movements for emancipation of all humankind. This does much to explain the tardy entry of Belgian women into the peace movements. In fact, they were very slow to realize the role they might play, both in society and the State, as a social group that was more or less equivalent to that of men. They were not to make any contribution to the peace movement until the final decade of the 19th century, and no sustained contribution until the beginning of the 20th.[5] However, there are numerous other reasons why their interest in matters of such crucial importance was so late in developing. These reasons are shared by both the men's and women's sectors of the peace movement. They arise from the international political context and internal political, economic and social conditions that, as elsewhere, influence the development of pacifist ideas.

The international political situation between 1830 and 1914 severely hampered the work of the pacifist movements. In 1830, Belgium obtained its independence from the Netherlands. Nine years of latent war followed this division. This external insecurity hardly encouraged Belgians to occupy themselves with the theoretical problems of peace maintenance. In addition, the international status enjoyed by Belgium--perpetual neutrality, guaranteed by the superpowers--tended to reduce immediate interest in peace, since many Belgians considered this neutral status adequate protection against international conflict.

The *Coup d'Etat* in France (1851), the Crimean War (1853-1856) and the Civil War in the United States (1860-1865) put a stop to the first demonstrations in favour of peace. It was not until the end of the 1860s that one sees a resurgence of peace movement initiatives, only to be halted again by the Franco-Prussian war (1870-1871). The ensuing peace, far from calming national rivalry, served only to step up the arms race. A raging military fever swept the European world, dividing it into two blocs. On the one side Germany tried to isolate France by making an alliance first with Austria-Hungary, and then, in 1882, with Italy; on the other side France, faced with this Triple Alliance, reacted by allying itself first with Russia, and then England, thus forming the Triple Entente. The development of the peace movement was, therefore, set within a context of armed peace, together with parallel currents of nationalism, protectionism, militarism, and an imperialism that was linked to the desire for both colonial and commercial expansion.

The internal political, economic and social situation was scarcely more favourable to peace initiatives. Lack of education constituted a major obstacle to the success of movements that presupposed a certain awareness of international affairs. If the population devoted little time and attention to the ways of avoiding war, even though these questions were of the utmost interest to them, this is mainly because they felt that they had no significant role to play in this area. Uninvolved in national politics, since the great majority had no voting rights, they did not try to influence the course of international events. The size of the country (Belgium being extremely small in surface area), its geographical position (encircled as it is by two powerful neighbours, France and Germany) as well as its newness (having been established only a short while before) were additional contributory factors that tended to push Belgians in the direction of moderation and caution insofar as foreign politics were concerned. Finally, the attitude adopted *vis-à-vis* war constituted another obstacle to the development of pacifist activities at that time. All those who had fought for peace before 1914 perceived the importance of developing attitudes on the subject. Indeed, the thinking of Joseph de Maître was shared by many traditional Catholics. For them war represented Divine punishment and it was not the place of mere mortals to rebel against the Will of God. Others, converted to Darwin's biological theories, felt that struggle, conflict and war itself should be accepted as elements that form part of existence as a whole. They affirmed that war was a natural phenomenon, both necessary and beneficial. Still others regarded it, like Malthus, as a means of resolving the problem of overpopulation.

In the 19th and early 20th centuries, Belgium was predominantly Catholic, especially Belgian women, and they were not interested in pacifist ideas. Their indifference may be explained in a number of ways. Most importantly, as suggested above, believers were influenced by the Church's attitude to war as being of Divine origin. In addition to this, becoming a pacifist meant renouncing war as a solution to any kind of problem; for many Catholics this also meant renouncing the reinstatement of the Pope on his temporal throne in the wars of Italian unification. As well as these religious and political reasons, one should not forget the economic considerations. In the middle of the 19th century, the pacifist movement adhered to the doctrine of Free Trade. The Catholic electorate, however, was mostly made up of landowners who had a vested interest in Protectionism and the maintenance of high prices for agricultural produce. Hence their lack of interest in pacifist enterprises. Moreover, even groups advocating peace through legal channels still faced obstacles of internal politics that prevented the collaboration of the Catholic majority. It was, indeed, unthinkable in a country where churchmen and non-churchmen were permanently at each other's throats, that a large number of Catholics should be able to take part in ventures involving liberals, sometimes protestants, Freemasons or socialists. Finally, in the peace field Belgium had nearly always relied on foreign initiatives, especially from France, but also from English-speaking countries. These same Belgian Catholics had no great liking for a Republican France that was both non-religious and responsible for anticlerical laws, preferring, instead, the ultra-Catholic Austria and the ultra-religious Germany. In both of the latter, however, the peace movement was still weak. If the great majority of the population remained indifferent to movements preoccupied with avoiding war, those in official circles chose to pretend to be unaware of their very existence. In order to justify their inactivity in this area, they took refuge behind a restrictive interpretation of Belgium's neutrality.

Bearing in mind the obstacles that slowed down the expansion of the peace movement, one can now move on to consider the political and social nature of its partisans. Pacifists belonged, broadly speaking, to two branches; one recruited from the middle classes, and the other from the working classes. In the former, members had generally had some form of higher education. They belonged to the professions and filled political posts or positions in industry and commerce. As to political, religious and philosophical affiliations, they were connected with all the progressive tendencies of both Liberal and Catholic parties, of the Catholic as well as the protestant church, as well as of Freemasonry. They believed that the burden of military expenditure could only be reduced in a climate of international détente, thus liberating the capital indispensable to the political, economic and social reform they wanted to achieve. Catholics who were interested in the search for peace represented a more conservative tendency. Religiously they sought the restoration of the notion of 'just war' and politically, an end to the rise of socialism and social unrest which they believed to be engendered by military expenditures. For all these reasons, the middle-class-supported peace societies campaigned for a policy of improving international relations through the extension of free trade, arms limitations, the development of international law, increased recourse to arbitration, the creation of an international court and the organization of the League of Nations. It was by embracing the doctrine of the Manchester School that they came to place great hope in the extension of free trade. Only rarely did they realize that in pleading this cause they were promoting the interests of the most financially, industrially and commercially advanced countries, to the disadvantage of less developed ones. They divided their support equally between efforts directed at education and propaganda in favour of peace. Their pacifist ideologies were thus of a religious, economic, juridical, military and political nature. Before 1914, there was no absolute, unconditional pacifism in Belgium. Everyone still agreed to rise to the defence of their country in case of invasion. War in self-defence was sacred; this was neither questioned nor discussed.

The second branch, working-class pacifists, consisted largely of socialists who campaigned from within the First and Second International. If socialist pacifists, like the pacifists with middle-class origins, shared the same aims with respect to peace, the similarity stops there. In fact, they disagreed considerably concerning both the nature of the peace envisioned, and the means to be used in achieving this aim. Rarely did the middle-class pacifists define the kind of peace to which they aspired. However, generally speaking, it represented for them a total absence of any kind of upheaval and the conservation of the established order or status quo, tempered by the desire for extensive political, economic and social reform. Convinced that the anarchy reigning in international relations was the principal source of conflicts, middle-class pacifists proposed the use of legal channels to alleviate this state of affairs. By contrast, the socialists saw the origins of war as rooted in capitalist society and in class conflict and poverty. For them, international peace was closely linked with social peace, and the latter could only be arrived at by bringing about the overthrow of the capitalist system and by achieving the international triumph of socialism. This was to be obtained either through revolution and the demolition of the military organization that was seen as the basis upon which the established order depended or, alternatively, through reform of the capitalist society. Depending on the times, the socialist movement was split between these revolutionary and reforming tendencies. The first advocated general military strikes and armed insurrection; the second favoured recourse to anti-military propaganda, parliamentary action, the intervention of the International Socialist Office, and the use of means such as those traditionally used by the middle-class pacifist movement. As 1914 drew closer, the Second International turned its back on general strike action and, instead, favoured the classic means of struggling against war. Revolution was abandoned in favour of reform.

Peace supporters, whatever branch of the movement they belonged to, were viewed by their contemporaries as pipe-dreamers, utopians, revolutionaries and even sometimes as dangerous criminals. The search for the best ways of fighting against war was indeed difficult at that time, given the contemporary climate of militarism and aggravated nationalism. One may well ask what motivated those involved in this arduous crusade, faced as they were by the total incomprehension of their countrymen and women. Underlying their commitment were the political, economic and religious motives referred to earlier, and also a genuinely humanitarian concern and an awareness of the hard realities of international life. In addition, external circumstances fostered the pacifist 'vocation.' These included contact with the London Peace Society and the English-speaking movement in general, membership in the Christian social movement, contact with

Paris-based groups sharing the same ideals and also with the many foreign exiles to be found in Belgium at that time. All these elements stirred up a desire for international brotherhood and social justice in certain democratic idealists. Adherence to the republican form of government led others to become interested in groups that saw a means of establishing peace in Europe through the spread of republicanism.[6] Free trade also stimulated a number of its supporters to become active within the peace leagues. Social reasons were widely influential in recruiting many pacifists, who sought to establish a new society guaranteeing the fullest opportunities for realising the potential of every individual. Alongside these reasons must be added the shock factor produced in those who experienced the real horror of war, which often led to a determination to do anything possible to prevent the renewal of such massacres.[7] Relationships with family and friends or encounters at congresses and trips abroad provided ample opportunity for fostering inclinations towards peace.

These peace supporters influenced their women colleagues when the latter started to become interested in the peace movement. But how, exactly, did the women benefit from experience in peace-campaigning? In 1848, Brussels provided the setting for the first European pacifist meeting. The British peace societies, which wanted to make their ideals known on the continent, were prevented from choosing Paris because of the revolutionary climate there and decided to organize their second congress in Brussels (the Second Congress of Friends of Universal Peace). English women Quakers took part in this meeting but did not take the floor.[8] The discussions that did take place revealed the means favoured by participants for the prevention of war. These were mostly directed at transforming individuals and national and international society in such a way as to attenuate their bellicose instincts.

The peace groups, created in Belgium before 1870, were few and far between and often short-lived. On the other hand, thanks to the unceasing devotion of its pioneers, Belgium did become a meeting place for European pacifists and a site for several conferences and international meetings in favour of peace. The Belgian capital was also chosen to be the headquarters for several international organizations whose aims included the search for the best ways of preventing international conflict. Certain Belgians managed to play leading roles in the foundation, direction, and presidency of various organizations aiming to prevent disharmony among nations, that developed in Europe after the Franco-Prussian war. In fact, after a period of disorganization caused by the 1870 war, pacifists, conscious of their weakness, tried to unite on an international level in order to carry more weight and to exercise more influence on public opinion and government.

Thus, in 1889, the Interparliamentary Union[9] and, two years later, the International Peace Bureau[10] were founded. The former, located in Brussels from 1909 to 1914, had as its first president the Belgian Catholic statesman, Auguste Beernaert[11]. In 1909, Beernaert was awarded the Nobel Peace prize, honouring his interparliamentary political work and his international contribution at the Hague. This honour had, in 1904, already been conferred on the Institute of International Law, founded in Ghent in 1893, for its contribution to the development of international arbitration. For a third time before the outbreak of the First World War, in 1913, this same prize was given to a Belgian, the Socialist Senator Henri La Fontaine,[12] who presided over the International Peace Bureau from 1907-1943, and was honoured for his unstinting devotion to peace and international harmony. The exceptional position of Belgian socialists within the Second International should also be noted. The Executive Committee of the International Socialist Bureau, one of whose principal missions was to watch over the maintenance of peace, had its headquarters in Brussels. Its members were Belgian, and its president was the Belgian Deputy, Emile Vandervelde[13] who, until 1914, performed an essential role for the international workers' entente against war. Before the First World War, therefore, the presidents of three major organizations devoted to the preservation of peace were Belgian. However, while the personal merits of our countrymen and their devotion to the pacifist ideal enabled them to play important roles on an international level, the fact that they belonged to a small neutral state which did not pose a threat to any major power probably facilitated their access to these privileged positions.

It is within this context that a few women, in the last decade of the nineteenth century, became interested in the peace movement. Who were they? As with their male counterparts, these women belonged to the two branches of the movement. The socialist one attracted only a few women. The other, by far the most important, was middle class, but a more conservative middle class than that from which the men's pacifist movement originated. This second branch grouped together Catholic or liberal women, most of whom had above-average education. The ideologies that they defended were identical to those of pacifist men. They followed obediently in the footsteps of the latter, adding no innovative or original contribution to the theory of pacifism. The means they favoured in their battle against war were non-violent and similar to those of their male counterparts. However, from the range of activities that were available to them, they chose education and peace propaganda, presumably because these were areas in which, given their isolation from political life, they could play a meaningful role.

With considerable conviction and perseverance, they managed to accomplish educational tasks within schools and in their contacts with other women. They were also involved in propagandist activities, such as the publishing of brochures, letters and petitions, the holding of meetings, and the organization of conferences. They maintained close contact with all European and British movements engaged in the campaign for peace. Their involvement in the peace cause was often due to the influence of family or friends, or was the expression of a need to devote themselves to a great humanitarian cause. Like pacifist men, they believed that they had a very real and particular role to play in this field. Pacifist men, for their part, saw in these women members their natural allies. They emphasized the crucial importance of the role women played within the family, as wives, mothers and sisters, as well as the vital place that they occupied in educating the younger generation. Moreover, they attributed to them a dominant influence on the orientation of values held by society as a whole. Lastly, they believed that women had an innate affinity[14] to peace and that, therefore, granting them equal political rights would change political behaviour in the direction of liberty, justice and peace. Experience in the twentieth century has proved the falsity of these assumptions and shown how much more complex human behaviour is[15] than was supposed in the preceding century. Today one is more aware of the extent to which women, and men, are the reflection of their background, their culture, and the socialization they receive[16] and how difficult it is to fight against such dominant forces as the respect for national and military values[17].

Although it was not until the end of the 19th century that Belgian women started to take part in the peace movement, as early as the 1860s various progressive peace groups were open to women.[18] However, not a single Belgian woman joined. One has to wait until 1889 and the creation of the Belgian section of the International Arbitration and Peace Association, in Brussels, under the influence of Hodgson Pratt, to see women among the members of a Belgian peace society. This association, averaging about 460 members, sixty of whom were female, recruited its supporters from middle-class liberals, non-churchgoers, and Freemasons. Women were openly welcomed as natural allies. Its activities were generally oriented towards pacifist propaganda. Mixed male and female sections soon appeared in various towns throughout the country to further this aim.[19]

A few years later, women created a Belgian Committee[20] of the *Union internationale des femmes pour la Paix* (International Union of Women for Peace), founded in Paris in 1895 by the feminist, socialist and pacifist, Eugénie Potonié-Pierre, with a view to organizing a vast women's movement in favour of general disarmament.[21] This committee was short-lived, but it opened the way for other initiatives that followed hard on its heels. In 1898, Sylvie Flammarion founded a group of women called *La Paix et le Désarmement par les femmes* (Peace and Disarmament by Women).[22] This, unlike the majority of other female organizations, placed a lot of importance on the education of working-class women and it led to the creation of sections elsewhere in the world. In Belgium, a section was created under the leadership of Hélène de Harven,[23] but it was not very active.

In Antwerp, in 1906, a large female pacifist society, the *Alliance belge des femmes pour la paix par l'Education* (the Belgian Alliance of Women for Peace through Education) was founded. This was a division[24] of the *Alliance Universelle des femmes pour la Paix par l'Education* (The Universal Women's Alliance for Peace by Education). Created in Paris in 1896 by Princess Wiesniewska,[25] this Alliance represented a current of women's pacifism that believed in the possibility of transforming individuals, of modifying attitudes and of obtaining peace through education. The Alliance recruited a thousand members from Belgium before 1914. Its activities were varied. Above all, it believed in transmitting ideas of peace, universal friendship and arbitration to people in all walks of life, but especially to school children. If education formed the basis of their work, pacifist propaganda was their means of action. For example, the Alliance supported the initiative of Miss Anna Eckstein, who tried to gather signatures throughout Europe for her "Pétition Universelle" in favour of peace. Several branches of the Alliance were created in various Belgian towns, and special attention was paid to a section for young people, entitled *La Jeune Belgique Pacifiste* (Belgian Pacifist Youth), which was founded in Antwerp in 1910 and designed to bring together all young people who were interested in the maintenance of peace. Between 1906 and 1914, the Alliance flourished as a dynamic and enterprising organization, whose membership increased steadily. The political neutrality of this women's association, bringing together liberals and Catholics alike, contributed to its appeal. It spread ideas promoting peace throughout Northern Belgium, thereby complementing the work of the *Société belge de l'Arbitrage et de la Paix.* Like the latter, its work was carried out mostly among the more comfortably-off middle classes who tended to regard it as a charitable activity. The war brought an end to both the Alliance's propaganda and educational activities which, until then, had been able to count on the support and collaboration of many women's groups, such as the *Conseil national des femmes belges* (National Council of Women of Belgium), in its attempt to gain the support of women and children for peace.

The third important Belgian peace association active up to the First World War was *la Ligue des catholiques belges pour la paix* (The League of Belgian Catholics for Peace). Founded in 1911, its aim was a return to the notion of a 'just war.' Women were invited to join the League, but, of its 1600 members, the number of women was negligible. Founded as it was just before the war, the League had no time to exert significant influence on Belgian Catholics, the majority of whom opposed pacifism.

In 1913, following the first National Peace Congress, the three peace associations in Belgium formed a permanent 'Delegation' of Belgian Peace Associations. Its purpose was to monitor the implementation of resolutions adopted by the Congress, to see to the preparation of future congresses, and also to coordinate, in an efficient manner, all pacifist activities throughout Belgium. War put a stop to what was a truly exceptional experiment in cooperation in a country where Catholic and liberal, cleric and anti-cleric knew no bounds in their opposition to each other.

The *Conseil national de femmes belges*, founded in Brussels, with

Marie Popelin as its President, included a section devoted to the problems of peace and arbitration. Its efforts were concentrated on the education of children, trying to inculcate in them the love of one's neighbour and human solidarity. It established May 18th as a Day of Peace to be regularly celebrated in schools, and it also influenced teaching in the direction of pacifism. To this end, books on the peace movement were distributed among school children and students and in universities and local libraries. Lectures were given throughout the various Belgian cities on arbitration and on other peaceful ways of settling conflicts.

Finally, it should be noted that a very small minority of the women who participated in these groups turned their attention to another struggle, that of the campaign for political rights for women. They thought, in fact, that priority should be given to this campaign, believing that once the vote had been won, it would give them ways of influencing political life both nationally and internationally in the direction of peace. As has already been stated, this hope was not to be fulfilled in the following century.

Alongside the middle-class women's movement there existed one for working-class women. Until the first World War, however, Belgian women socialists were not very active in the peace field. In this, they differed from their male counterparts, and even from working-class women elsewhere in Europe. At the Second International Congress in Stuttgart in 1907, socialist women decided to create an International Bureau of Socialist Women. Three years later they met in Copenhagen and added, in a resolution for the maintenance of peace, their support for resolutions taken on this subject by previous International Socialist Congresses. They asserted, like their male comrades, that the maintenance of peace would only be possible through determined and deliberate action by the proletariat and by the triumph of socialism. They advocated educating proletarian women on the causes of wars and on their origins within the capitalist order. But the Belgian Workers' Party sent no female representative to Copenhagen, because, as Camille Huysmans wrote, "their movement is practically nonexistent in our country."[26] However, there had been a League of Socialist Women in existence in Belgium since the beginning of the century.

While Belgian women did not enter into peace activities until the end of the nineteenth century, by the eve of the First World War they had become the main driving force of Belgium's pacifist movement. By the sheer number of their supporters, by the extent of their propaganda and educational activities, as well as by the multiplicity of their initiatives, women's societies for peace overtook those of men. If, in spite of everything, they were unable to prevent men from killing each other in the field of battle, one should not be too hasty in concluding that this amounted to the total failure of their efforts. Not having chosen direct action or revolution in opposition to war but instead the slower process of changing attitudes and opinions, women could hardly have hoped to modify the habits of centuries in the space of 25 years or so. It would have been impossible for a small group of women, with no means of effective pressure, to persuade governments to renounce war as a favoured means of resolving international conflict.

Notes

[1]See J. Gilissen, "Le statut de la femme dans l'ancien droit belge," in La Femme, The Jean Bodin Society Collection for the Comparative History of Institutions, XII, part II (Brussels: La Librairie Encyclopédique, 1962): 256-67.

[2]Ibid., p. 320.

[3]Report of the 'Commission de la Justice du Sénat belge' (Justice Commission of the Belgian Senate), 1957, the Bill relating to the rights and duties of married persons. Senate, 1956-1957, Parliamentary documents, No. 346, p. 1; quoted by Gilissen, op cit., pp. 320-1.

[4]D. De Weerdt, "De historische aanloop tot de Vrouwenemancipatie Bewegingen," in Bulletin de la Fédération belge des Femmes diplômées des Universités, April, 1976, pp. 20-6.

[5]At that time, the terms 'pacifique' (pacifistic /pacific/peace-loving) and 'pacifiste' (pacifist) were used interchangeably. In French, the term 'pacifiste' did not yet have the pejorative connotations that were added between the two world wars, nor did it then have the meaning of 'absolute' pacifist that it sometimes carries nowadays.

[6]S. E. Cooper, "The Work of Women in Nineteenth Century Continental European Peace Movements," Peace and Change IX, 4 (Winter 1984): 13.

[7]Examples abound of those who turned to pacifism after the painful spectacle of the wars.

[8]S. E. Cooper, op. cit., p. 14 and W. H. Posthumus-van der Goot, "Les efforts féminins pour l'organisation de la paix aux XIXe et XXe siècles," in La Paix, The Jean Bodin Society Collection for the Comparative History of Institutions, XV, part II (Brussels: La Librarie Encyclopédique, 1961): 592.

[9]Private Assembly of Members of Parliament who wanted to organize international society juridically, and whose work laid the foundations for the discussions at the Conferences at the Hague between 1899 and 1907.

[10]Founded in Berne in 1891, the B.I.P. grouped together all peace groups and associations then existing throughout the world.

[11]A. Beernaert (1829-1912), Catholic statesman, member of the two Hague conferences, first President of the InterCouncil (1909-1912), member of the Permanent Court of Arbitration (1900), Nobel Prizewinner for Peace (1907), President of the International League of Catholic Pacifists and of the League of Belgian Catholics for Peace.

[12]H. La Fontaine, (1858-1943), lawyer, Socialist politician, pacifist Secretary General of the Belgian Section of the International

Federation of Arbitration and Peace, President of the IPB (1907-1943), member of the Interparliamentary Union, Nobel Peace prize winner (1913), mainspring of the federation of the three Belgian Peace associations.

[13]E. Vandervelde (1866-1938), Socialist statesman, President of the Executive Committee of the International Socialist Office (1900-1914) member of the Interparliamentary Union and of the Belgian section of the International Federation for Arbitration and Peace.

[14]See H. Krogh, and U. C. Wasmuht, "Sexism and Bellicism or Women and Peace," International Peace Research Newsletter XXII, 3 (1984): 20.

[15]On this subject see E. Senghaas-Knobloch, "The Rising Consciousness of Women and Politics against Violence," in E. Jahn and Y. Sakamoto, eds., Elements of World Instability: Armaments, Communication, Food, International Division of Labour, Proceedings of the International Peace Research Association, Eighth General Conference (Frankfurt a.M.: Campus Verlag, 1981), pp. 365-73.

[16]N. Lubelski-Bernard, "La Paix par l'éducation," in Les mouvements et les idéologies pacifistes en Belgique 1830-1914 (Ph.D. thesis, Université Libre de Bruxelles, 1977), vol. 3, pp. 977-97.

[17]In countries at war, women and men alike often tend to side with the quarrels of their governments. They very often identify with the policies of their country.

[18]Examples include la ligue Universelle du Bien Public (1864) of Edmond Potonié and the Ligue internationale de la Paix et de la Liberté (1867) of Charles Lemonnier. See Potonié-Pierre, ed., Un peu plus tard, (Paris: Librarie Mondaine L. Breton, 1893), pp. 140-58 and 201-29; Historique du mouvement pacifique, (Berne: Impr. de Steiger, 1889), p. 177; Posthumus-Van der Goot, op. cit., p. 594; S. E. Cooper, op. cit., p. 13.

[19]In 1912, one branch was created in Forest (Brussels), and another in Liège. The latter was named Groupe Emile de Laveleye and soon had over a hundred members. Emile de Laveleye (1822-1892) was a liberal economist, protestant, and professor at the University of Liège. He maintained close connections with pacifist circles in England. From 1889 to 1892, he was President of the Belgian Section of the International Federation for Arbitration and Peace.

[20]This Belgian committee had Marie Popelin (1846-1913) among its members; she was the first woman to be made Doctor of Law at the Université Libre des Bruxelles (Free University of Brussels) and was refused admission to the bar because of being a woman. Her sister, Louise, a teacher, also sat on this committee. See S. E. Cooper, op. cit., note 40, pp. 26-7.

[21]Ibid., pp. 19-20.

[22]Ibid., pp. 20-1.

[23]Hélène de Harven (1864-1949), woman of letters, painter, pacifist, and friend of Sylvie Flammarion. She was to spend two years

(1890-1892) on the Canadian Prairie, amongst Indian tribes, before travelling to Japan and China.

[24]In 1909, another branch was created in Tirlemont.

[25]S. E. Cooper, op. cit., p. 20.

[26]Letter of C. Huysmans to Klara Zetkin, the President of the International Conference of Socialist Women, 6th August, 1910: "the P.O. in Belgium did not delegate women representatives to Copenhagen, because their movement is almost non-existent in our country. Women accompanying their husbands will attend, however. I shall be too busy on the 26th and 27th of August to be available to help you, but there will be someone, maybe a woman, to nominally represent poor old Belgium." D. Deweerdt, and W. Geldoff, Camille Huysmans, documenten, deel I, C. Huysmans in Brussels (Antwerpen: Standaard, Wetenshappelijke Uitgeverij), document·16, p. 58.

SOCIAL DEMOCRATIC WOMEN IN GERMANY AND THE STRUGGLE FOR PEACE BEFORE AND DURING THE FIRST WORLD WAR

Ursula Herrmann

Six months before the outbreak of the First World War, Rosa Luxemburg declared, while defending herself in court:

> If, however, a vast majority of the people come to realize . . . that wars are a barbaric, profoundly immoral and reactionary phenomenon inimical to the interests of the working people, wars will become impossible . . . The decision as to whether present-day militarism will continue to exist or not rests with the mass of working men and women, old and young.[1]

Rosa Luxemburg was on trial because she had addressed meetings, calling for actions against the mounting danger of an imperialist world war and urging the workers not to shoot at their class brothers in other countries. Today, her words are more relevant than ever. The issue now is the prevention of a nuclear holocaust. Whereas the First World War took a toll of nine million dead and twenty million wounded, the human race is now facing the threat of total annihilation. The requirements of the present day make it imperative for us to take careful account of the historical experience.

The peace movement today is far broader and more comprehensive than it was in those days. The women of the world represent a tremendous political force in the contemporary campaign for peace and social progress. This finds its expression in the "Declaration on the Participation of Women in Promoting International Peace and Cooperation" adopted by the 37th session of the UN General Assembly in New York.[2] All evidence, past and present, shows that the role of women in the struggle for peace and their political and social equality are inextricably bound up with each other. This is reflected in the motto "Equality, Development, Peace" chosen for the UN Women's Decade. It can also be seen from the experience of the struggle waged by Social Democratic women in Germany before and during the First World War.

Although in Germany it was not possible until 1908 for women to take part in political meetings and organizations, the German Social Democrats had drawn women into the political and trade union struggle right from the start.[3] Compared with other countries, women in the German Empire were organized in large numbers. However, only a small portion of the 10 million women in employment were aligned with the Social Democrats. As of 1910 the party had 82,642 female members, and the Social Democratic trade unions had 16,512.[4] Rosa Luxemburg was correct in pointing out that:

> the trade union and Social Democratic organizations have so far done more than anyone else for the spiritual and moral awakening and education of women . . . The Social Democrats and the trade unions have lifted them out of the stifling and oppressive atmosphere of their domestic concerns. The proletarian class struggle has widened their horizons, made their minds more flexible, trained their mental faculties and set them challenging goals.[5]

On the eve of the First World War, the struggle of the imperialist powers for a redivision of the world grew in intensity as the contradictions between the imperialist countries sharpened. Monopolies and governments were engaged in an arms race never before witnessed. Chauvinistic agitation reached fever pitch. Books were published that glamourized war and vilified the peace movement as an alleged threat to the people.

But in a parallel development, the Russian Revolution of 1905-07 had made broad masses of the population aware of the strength inherent in the working class once it acted in a revolutionary manner. The working class movement experienced an upswing in all countries. At powerful peace rallies, workers protested against imperialist adventures. Many women attended these rallies, which attracted hundreds of thousands.[6]

The conclusion drawn by socialist-organized women from the tense world situation was to draw closer together on an international scale. On 17 and 19 August 1907, fifty-eight delegates from twelve countries assembled for the First International Conference of Socialist Women in Stuttgart. They set up an international head office based in Stuttgart and chose the Social Democratic women's journal *Die Gleichheit* (Equality) to be their international mouthpiece. Clara Zetkin[7] was elected Secretary of the international Women's Secretariat, which relied on correspondents in various countries.[8] At the subsequent International Socialist Congress the women put forward their resolutions concerning the struggle for women's equality. They endorsed the resolution against militarism which called on the working class to oppose the danger of war through powerful actions and, in the eventuality of war, pledged the socialists in the various countries to make every effort to end the war and to accelerate the overthrow of capitalist rule.[9]

At the Second International Conference of Socialist Women, held in Copenhagen on 26 and 27 August 1910, more than 100 delegates from 17 nations adopted a resolution on the "Preservation of Peace." The Conference attributed "war to the social contradictions generated by the capitalist mode of production." Hence the struggle against war required informing women about the causes of war, "making the entire working class more conscious of its own power" and educating children in such a way that they joined the ranks of the "army of peace" and socialism.[10]

Another resolution provided that a "Social Democratic Women's Day," initially without a general binding date, should be observed internationally, and this was the starting point to the International Women's Day of Action for Peace and Social Progress as we know it today. The resolution was evidence of an endeavour to employ new and more powerful forms of struggle in the face of a growing arms build-up and mounting war hysteria. The idea behind making Women's Day international in character, with May Day serving as an example, was to enhance the strength of the socialist women's movement, to increase the number of women workers thinking and acting along political lines, and to bring home to them that vigorous mass campaigns are necessary in order to win rights for women.

Women's Day in 1911 was to become the most powerful demonstration for women's equality to be held thus far. The number of participants in Germany amounted to over one million, most of them women, but men took part as well. The number of women in the Social Democratic Party rose by 25,000.[11] Half of all female party members in 1914 had joined the party after 1910. But despite impressive mass rallies, especially in July 1914, it was impossible for the mass of the people to prevent the war.

The ruling classes played a demagogical role. They concealed their aims. The war of annexation was depicted as "Defence of the Fatherland."[12] In truth in 1914 the German imperialists were seeking the annexation of Belgium and Poland, of large parts of France and Russia, and of a colonial empire in Central Africa. They were out to gain supremacy in Europe and, if possible, in the whole world.[13] Although the First World War ended in defeat for German imperialism, the war was a most lucrative affair for the arms industry. The war profits of German monopoly capital are estimated at 50 thousand million Marks. For the four years of World War I the German monopoly company Krupp, well-known for its armaments production, amassed profits it would have taken a period of 20 years of thriving business in peacetime to make.[14]

The slogan "Defence of the Fatherland" confused the mass of the people. The middle-class German Women's Federation was put in consultation with the Minister of the Interior with a view to drumming up support for the imperialist war among the women's organizations. The Social Democratic Party and trade union leaders proclaimed a "truce" with the ruling classes and supported the war. They voluntarily renounced the right to strike. They left women at the mercy of the military machine and of ruthless exploiters.

The First World War had a profound impact on the lives of women and their families. The war deprived women of their husbands and sons, millions of whom were permanently maimed, exposed to gas warfare or doomed to die on the battlefields. Women were drawn into the arms industry to an increased extent. In late 1917 women accounted for 52 percent of all workers on compulsory health insurance, thereby outnumbering their male counterparts. Although women carried out the work of men called up for military service, they were, as a rule, paid only about one-half of their wages. An emergency decree revoked legislation on safety regulations at work that had been won through many years of struggle. A 12-hour day became the rule. Outright famine conditions prevailed in 1917-1918. Hunger, exhaustion and epidemics took a heavy toll among the civilian population.[15] The revolutionary working-class movement had advocated women's employment as the means of achieving social independence. But now employment was directed against women's vital interests. Their work was being used for the prolongation of wholesale slaughter and was taking place under conditions causing serious damage to the health of the women and girls involved.

The Government imposed a state of emergency on 31 July 1914, whereby executive power was transferred from the civilian authorities to the military commands. Public rallies and demonstrations were banned, with violations being punishable by imprisonment. The press was subjected to censorship. Virtually the entire Social Democratic press was in the hands of those who supported the war. Deprived of their instruments of struggle, misled by nationalism and social chauvinism, and exposed to conditions resembling those in a military prison, the working-class movement and the women's movement suffered a severe setback.

In this situation only one section of German Social Democracy was immediately determined to offer vigorous resistance to the imperialist mass slaughter: the German Left. Their revolutionary Marxism enabled them to recognize the entirely imperialist character of the war. This anti-war Left was headed by Rosa Luxemburg, Karl Liebknecht, and Clara Zetkin. Supporters were organized in the International Group, the Spartacus Group and other left-wing groups, some of which would come together in 1918 to found the Communist Party of Germany.

They deemed it their most urgent task to expose the true nature of the war and to steer working men and women away from the "truce" towards class struggle against imperialism in order to end the war through a revolution, overthrow the monarchy in Germany and wrest power from the forces responsible for war: the monopolists and the *Junkers* (landed gentry). This made it necessary to expose the policies of the mainstream Social Democrats and to cooperate with anti-war activists in other countries and with the middle-class pacifists in Germany.

The Left's anti-militarist struggle was waged under exceedingly difficult conditions. Persecuted by the military authorities, thrown into jail, called up for military service as far as the men were concerned, deprived of means of expression and harassed by the Social Democratic Party leadership, they were unable at first to launch any mass campaigns. Yet they managed all the same to create a clandestine network of connections in late 1914 and early 1915. By mid-1915 they had established firm links with 300 towns. Extensive studies into local history yield ever new examples of women and girls fearlessly joining the ranks of those fighting against the imperialist war, sending underground literature to frontline soldiers and organizing demonstrations and strikes in protest against hunger and war.[16]

Political education among women workers and other female employees was assuming great importance here. Clara Zetkin was editing *Die Gleichheit* in this spirit even though the language employed was that of slaves and the journal often contained vast blank spaces-- passages deleted by the censor. In early November 1914 she addressed an appeal "To the Socialist Women of All Lands" in which she came out against the imperialist war and called for broad campaigns in support of peace.[17]

On 17 November 1914, Kaete Duncker[18] submitted theses on "The Economic Causes of the World War" to some 200 organizers and tutors of women's reading circles in Berlin. She demonstrated that the war had its origin in "world capitalist profit needs and imperialist contradictions." "The rivalry over colonial possessions and 'spheres of interest' and the armaments policy tend to generate continuing tensions among the capitalist states which are apt to erupt into a warlike conflict." Displaying remarkable foresight, she concluded: "Even after the termination of the present war the continued existence of capitalism will . . . provoke new world wars over world markets and world supremacy." The "vital interests of the proletariat," therefore, required "the inevitable struggle against imperialism."[19]

An International Socialist Women's Conference was held in Bern from 26 to 28 March 1915 on the initiative of Clara Zetkin and representatives of the Social Democratic Workers' Party of Russia (Bolsheviks). It was attended by 25 delegates from Germany, Britain, France, Italy, the Netherlands, Poland, Russia and Switzerland. In a manifesto addressed to the "women of the working people" they demonstrated that the capitalists were the only ones to benefit from the war. "The workers stand to gain nothing from this war and to lose everything they hold dear." They called for effective political peace campaigns and concluded: "Down with capitalism, which sacrifices hecatombs of people to the wealth and power of the propertied classes! Down with war! Forward to socialism!"[20] The manifesto was illegally distributed in Germany as a pamphlet printed in 200,000 copies. Men and women alike were sent to jail if they were caught with it.[21]

The national conference of the Spartacus Group in January and March 1916 strengthened the Left in organizational terms. They stressed the need for street demonstrations and strikes against the war and laid down measures designed to draw more women and young people into these activities. The March 1916 conference emphasized: "The greatest emphasis will have to be laid on activities by women, who are called upon to play a highly important political role during the war."[22]

In 1915/16 some twenty major cities were the scene of hunger riots involving mostly women. The anti-war movement reached a high point on 1 May 1916. In Berlin, the Spartacus Group organized a demonstration attended by about 10,000 people, among them many women. Karl Liebknecht, who was leading the march, demanded: "Down with war! Down with the government!" Peace demonstrations were also held in other towns.[23]

Nevertheless, the social chauvinists wielded their influence. They controlled the Social Democratic party organization and nearly all publications, and they were not subjected to any persecution. In June 1917 Clara Zetkin was dismissed by the Party Executive as editor of the international women's journal *Die Gleichheit*.[24] At this time, when the imperialist war led to a dramatic worsening of women's living and working conditions, the Party Executive dissolved the Social Democratic Women's Bureau. It became more and more apparent that it would be impossible within that party to rally the force committed to end the war. So the Independent Social Democratic Party of Germany was founded in early April 1917. Despite the ambiguous nature of this Party, its foundation gave a boost to anti-war activities.

The February 1917 Revolution in Russia, which had overthrown the Tsar and established a bourgeois-democratic republic, put the German workers in a more militant mood. Under the influence of this uprising and in the face of renewed cuts in food rations, they embarked on the biggest and most comprehensive anti-war action so far on 16 April 1917. Hundreds of thousands of men and women, primarily in the arms industry, went on strike despite resistance from trade union and party leaders. In Berlin they numbered 300,000 and in Leipzig 30,000. Other towns followed suit. There are no exact data regarding the proportion of women involved, but all the evidence suggests that they were well represented. The strikes dealt a rude blow to the war industry. Despite having failed to prevent them, the social chauvinist party and trade union leaders managed to secure a swift end to the strikes after the employers had promised higher pay.[25]

The Independent Social Democratic Party established a National Women's Committee. At its first meeting, on 17 June 1917, the Women's Committee expressed its "resolve to bend all its energies to the task of achieving a peace based on international understanding, a peace without annexations and war reparations. But it also claims the right for women to help shape the peace conditions which will be of crucial importance for the cultural development and independence of the peoples concerned."[26] The conference thus emphasized that women were entitled to bring their influence to bear on fundamental decisions in world politics.

The gulf between the longing for peace felt by millions of working people and the imperialist war policy pursued by the monopolies, Junkers and military leaders continued to widen. Finding a way of ending the imperialist mass slaughter became the overriding issue. It was against this background that word came of the victorious social revolution in Russia. This set an example, providing inspiration and an orientation for the revolutionary workers' and women's movement. The decrees issued by the new Soviet government reflected not only the demands of the Russian working people, but also the interests of the German and international proletariat. The first decree was that on peace. On 26 October (8 November) the Second All-Russia Congress of Soviets declared war to be the worst crime against humanity. The Soviet government dissociated itself from all annexationist treaties, called for the abolition of secret diplomacy and invited all nations and governments to conclude a general and just peace forthwith,[27] thereby demonstrating its commitment to the unity between socialism and peace. In late 1917 the Soviet government matched its words with deeds, taking Russia out of the war.

The new Soviet government also set an example to the world with regard to the political and social equality of women.[28] The "Declaration of the Rights of the Working and Exploited People" provided for the full equality of men and women. Thus the October Revolution marked the dawn of a new era for women and their social status. After millenia of oppression in social systems based on private ownership of the means of production, women were promised full involvement in social development as equal members of the community. This provided "the firm and solid foundation for women's full equality within the family, society and the state," as Clara Zetkin pointed out, "enabling women to realize all their potentialities while performing socially useful work within and for the community."[29]

Clara Zetkin familiarized part of the German women's movement with the essence and the lessons of the October Revolution through the articles she wrote in 1917. She stressed that "the revolutionary proletariat of Russia faced the nations of the world as the foremost champion of peace."[30] Her article of November 1917 entitled "The Struggle for Power and Peace in Russia" paid tribute to the historic initiative taken for peace in the world by the Bolshevik government. "The most important prerequisite for implementing the revolutionary programme is peace," Clara Zetkin noted.[31] She told the German proletariat that it would have to alter the power structure in order to bring about peace. Referring to the peace policy ushered in by the October Revolution, she demonstrated the political strength inherent in revolutionary masses. In a pamphlet of December 1917 the Spartacus Group stated:

> Hunger and wholesale misery as we know it today will not cease as long as those interested in war, i.e., the government and the bourgeois classes, remain in the saddle. It is

imperative to overthrow the rule of the reactionaries and the imperialist classes in Germany if we want to put an end to the slaughter of whole peoples . . . Only mass struggle, mass rebellions and mass strikes bringing the wheels of industry and of the whole arms sector to a standstill, only revolution and the establishment of a people's republic in Germany by the working class will make it possible to end the butchery and bring about universal peace.[32]

The strike in the German arms industry from 28 January to 4 February 1918 was motivated by a firm resolve to win peace as the Russian workers had done. It evolved into the biggest action for peace in Germany with more women taking part than at any other time during the First World War. When it reached its high point, more than a million workers were on strike[33] The principal demands were an immediate peace without annexations and war reparations, and the participation of workers in the peace negotiations. A police report from Berlin noted that women played "a prominent part in the strike itself and in street demonstrations."[34] After a week the strikers suffered a defeat.

Despite numerous strikes, demonstrations and hunger riots, the women taking an active stand against the war remained in a minority. The demagogical peace rhetoric of the government and of reformist Social Democrats was a major factor here.

The ruling classes sought to prevent a revolution not only through sterner repressive measures, but also through promises of reform. One sign of this was the haggling over the women's franchise, which was a major topic of public debate in 1917/18. There was no lack of words, but what were the facts? When the Emperor promised a change in the electoral law in July 1917, he did not mention the female suffrage. When the ruling classes found themselves compelled, in October 1918, to appoint a coalition government, including Social Democratic ministers, the programme of the government did not even mention the granting of equal rights to women.[35]

On the strength of their own experience many working men and women began to realize that only a revolution would bring peace and fulfill women's political and social demands. This was confirmed by the outbreak of the November Revolution of 1918 in Germany.[36] The revolutionary mass actions of men and women during the November Revolution changed the status of women. The November Revolution put an end to the First World War and enforced universal and equal suffrage for women. Under the Constitution of the Weimar Republic of 1919 all citizens were theoretically equal before the law, entitled to an eight-hour day, and other social and democratic rights. But the November revolution in Germany did not give rise to any profound changes in the relations of ownership and power. The bourgeoisie, the Junkers and the militarists held sway in the Weimar Republic--to the detriment of the rights of women. They were still bound to respect the superior legal status of men as fixed in the Civil Code. Women were still being denied equal pay for equal work. Facilities designed to relieve them of their household chores were provided only in isolated instances. Clara Zetkin observed: "The German November Revolution was bound to disappoint women, because it disappointed the working classes." In Germany, "bourgeois property, capitalism has triumphed over women's rights."[37]

Lessons of the struggle against war during the period dealt with here are very relevant for the peace movement of our day: that peace and women's political and social status are inseparably bound up with each other; that peace can be safeguarded only through powerful mass action by the working people; and that it is in the best interests of women to join in the struggle for peace. Popular opposition alone--men and women together--can overcome those pressing for war and prevent a nuclear holocaust. Therefore, responsible personal commitment, political consciousness and the resolve of each individual are in greater demand than ever. "The strength of the weak"--to use the words of the writer Anna Seghers--must be brought together on an international scale.

Comments

Frances Early

I enjoyed your talk very much. I think that in terms of some of the themes that we have developed and are developing here, you are implicitly showing a relationship between capitalism and patriarchy which is one of the themes that Berenice Carroll mentioned. We have to look at the root causes of patriarchy and find out how it operates and where. My reading of history shows that patriarchy remains, however, even after capitalism is overturned, and I think a good example of this would be what is happening in Nicaragua today. There has recently been a film made by the National Film Board of Canada on Nicaraguan women which shows that patriarchy works at deeper levels than political systems.[38] What I would like to ask, even though it isn't part of your talk, is whether you could elaborate a bit on the theme of the relationship between women, or among women, across different political systems. It seems that in this period in Europe, before World War I and after World War I, it is striking how women from socialist countries, and of socialist persuasion, could work in an international peace organization, despite their differences. I wonder if you could comment on that further, because it seems to me that that would help bring out some of the points that Carroll said we need to look at more thoroughly.

Ursula Herrmann

I can only underline your main point because I too believe that it is necessary that the women's movements from all countries should work together for the goal of world peace.

Notes

[1]Rosa Luxemburg, Gesammelte Werke (Berlin, 1973), vol. 3, p. 400. See also Annelies Laschitza and Guenter Radczun, Rosa Luxemburg: Ihr Wirken in der deutschen Arbeiterbewegung (Berlin: Dietz Verlag, 1980).

[2]Article 1 of the Declaration states: "Women and men have an equal and vital interest in contributing to international peace and cooperation. To this end women must be enabled to exercise their right to participate in the economic, social, cultural, civil and political affairs of society on an equal footing with men." Quoted from Bulletin of the GDR Committee for Human Rights 2/83 (Berlin): 34.

[3]See Zur Rolle der Frau in der Geschichte des deutschen Volkes (1830 bis 1945): Eine Chronik (Leipzig, 1984); Dokumente der revolutionaeren deutschen Arbeiterbewegung zur Frauenfrage 1848-1874: Eine Auswahl (Leipzig, 1975); Die Frau und die Gesellschaft (Leipzig, 1974).

[4]See D. Fricke, Die deutsche Arbeiterbewegung 1869-1914: Ein Handbuch ueber die Organisation and Taetigkeit im Klassenkampf (Berlin, 1976), pp. 326, 327, 672, 724.

[5]Rosa Luxemburg, "Frauenwahlrecht and Klassenkampf" (written for the pamphlet Frauenwahlrecht to mark International Women's Day in 1912) in Gesammelte Werke, vol. 3, p. 164.

[6]See Die internationale Arbeiterbewegung: Fragen der Geschichte und der Theorie, 7 vols. (Moscow, 1982), vol. 3; Antivoennye traditaii mezhdunarodnovo rabochevo dvizheniya (Moscow, 1972), pp. 104ff., 117ff., 144ff.; Geschichte der deutschen Arbeiterbewegung, 8 vols. (Berlin, 1966), vol. 2, pp. 83ff.

[7]See Luise Dornemann, Clara Zetkin: Leben und Wirken, 5th enlarged and revised edition, (Berlin: Dietz Verlag, 1974.); Clara Zetkin, Ausgewaehlte Reden und Schriften, vols. 1-3 (Berlin, 1957, 1960).

[8]See Die Geschichte der II. Internationale (Moscow, 1983), vol. 2, pp. 403ff.; J. Kirchner, "Herausbildung und Geschichte der Sozialistischen Fraueninternationale und zu den Anfaengen des Internationalen Frauentages - ein Beitrag zur Geschichte der II. Internationale," (Ph.D. thesis, Dresden, 1983).

[9]See Die Geschichte der Zweiten Internationale, vol. 2, pp. 104ff.

[10]Die Gleichheit, Stuttgart, 10 October 1910.

[11]See 70 Jahre Internationaler Frauentag (Leipzig, 1980), pp. 21ff; Die Gleichheit, 27 March 1911; Protokoll ueber die Verhandlungen des Parteitages der Sozialdemokratischen Partei Deutschlands,

abgehalten in Jena vom 10. bis 16. September 1911 (Berlin, 1911), pp. 18, 21, 45.

[12]Comprehensive studies include Deutschland im ersten Weltkrieg, vols. I-III (Berlin, 1970, 1971), and Geschichte der deutschen Arbeiterbewegung, vol. 2, pp. 207ff.; Dokumente und Materialien zur Geschichte der Deutschen Arbeiterbewegung, Series II, vol. 1, July 1914 - October 1917 (Berlin, 1958) (hereafter referred to as DuM II/1), p. 17.

[13]See Weltherrschaft im Visier: Dokumente zu den Europa-und Weltherrschaftsplaenen des deutschen Imperialismus von der Jahrhundertwende bis Mai 1945, edited and with an introduction by W. Schumann and L. Nestler in collaboration with W. Gutsche and W. Ruge (Berlin, 1975).

[14]See Deutschland im ersten Weltkrieg, vol. III, pp. 569ff.; W. Richter, Gewerkschaften, Monopolkapital und Staat im ersten Weltkrieg und in der Novemberrevolution (1914-1919) (Berlin, 1959), pp. 96ff.; A. Schroeter, Krieg - Staat - Monopol, 1914 bis 1918: Die Zusammenhaenge von imperialistischer Kriegswirtschaft, Militarisierung der Volkswirtschaft und staatsmonopolistischem Kapitalismus in Deutschland waehrend des ersten Weltkrieges (Berlin, 1965).

[15]See R. Helbig, W. Langbein, L. Zymara, "Beitraege zur Lage des weiblichen Proletariats und dessen aktive Einbeziehung in den Kampf der deutschen Arbeiterklasse gegen den Imperialismus, Militarismus und Krieg in der dritten Hauptperiode der Geschichte der deutschen Arbeiterbewegung" (Ph.D. thesis, Leipziger, 1973), pp. 125ff.; Frauen-Beilage der Leipziger Volkszeitung, unter staendiger Mitarbeit von Frau Klara Zetkin (referred to as LVZ hereinafter), 25 January 1918.

[16]See Zur Rolle der Frau. . .Chronik, pp. 92ff; S. Scholze, "Zur proletarischen Frauenbewegung in den Weltkriegsjahren 1914 bis 1917," in Beitraege zur Geschichte der Arbeiterbewegung 6 (Berlin, 1973): 992.

[17]See C. Zetkin, Ausgewaehlte Reden und Schriften, vol. 1, pp. 635ff.

[18]See R. Kirsch, Kaete Duncker: Aus ihrem Leben (Berlin, 1982).

[19]Reprinted in H. Wohlgemuth, Deutschland und die deutsche Arbeiterbewegung von der Jahrhundertwende bis 1917, mit einem Dokumentenanhang (Berlin, 1963), pp. 282ff.

[20]DuM, II/1, pp. 126, 127.

[21]See DuM, II/1, pp. 198ff, 201ff.

[22]DuM, II/1, p. 319.

[23]See DuM, II/1, pp. 432ff.

[24]DuM, II/1, p. 647; see R. Helbig et al., pp. 403ff.

[25]See H. Scheel, "Der Aprilstreik 1917 in Berlin," in Revolutionaere Ereignisse und Probleme in Deutschland waehrend der Periode der Grossen Sozialistischen Oktoberrevolution 1917/1918 (Berlin, 1957), pp. 1ff. The Spartacus Group pamphlet on the "Lessons of

the Big Mass Strike" refers to "over 300,000 workers, men and women" (DuM, II/1, p. 621).

[26]Frauen-Beilage LVZ, 13 July 1917.

[27]V. Ulyanov-Lenin, Die ersten Dekrete der Sowjetmacht (Berlin, 1970), pp. 23ff.

[28]See Dekrety sovetskoi vlasti, vol. I (Moscow, 1957), e.g., pp. 237ff., 247ff., 314ff.; vol. II (Moscow, 1959), pp. 545ff.; V. Ulyanov-Lenin, pp. 70ff., 77ff, 87ff., 181ff.; Zhenshchiny strany sovetov (Moscow, 1977).

[29]C. Zetkin, Fuer die Sowjetmacht: Artikel, Reden und Briefe 1917-1933 (Berlin, 1977), pp. 181-2.

[30]Ibid., p. 37.

[31]Ibid., p. 46.

[32]Dokumente und Materialien zur Geschichte der deutschen Arbeiterbewegung, Series II, Vol. 2, November 1917- December 1918 (Berlin, 1957), p. 51.

[33]See P. Kuhlbrodt,"Die proletarische Frauenbewegung in Deutschland am Vorabend und waehrend der Novemberrevolution (Herbst 1917 bis Anfang Mai 1919)" (Ph.D. thesis, Leipzig, 1981), p. 415.

[34]See Central State Archives, Potsdam, Foreign Office, No. 35 992, p. 203.

[35]See P. Kuhlbrodt, pp. 121ff.

[36]Concerning the November Revolution, see Geschichte der deutschen Arbeiterbewegung, vol. 3 (Berlin, 1966), pp. 87ff.; Illustrierte Geschichte der deutschen Novemberrevolution 1918/1919 (Berlin, 1978).

[37]C. Zetkin, Fuer die Sowjetmacht, p. 200.

[38]Dream of a Free Country: A Message from Nicaraguan Women, directed by Kathleen Shannon and Ginny Stikeman (National Film Board of Canada, 1983).

FEMINISM AND PACIFISM: THE FRENCH CONNECTION

Judith Wishnia

In March 1918, as the mud and machine guns of the trenches continued the destruction of millions of young lives, an elementary school teacher from a working-class suburb of Paris was brought before the Council of War. Charged with aiding the enemy by disseminating what the government called "defeatist" propaganda, the defendant, Hélène Brion, had already spent four months in prison. While defending herself against the charge of defeatism, Brion never denied that she had distributed literature calling for an end to the terrible slaughter. Indeed, she had helped to distribute a pamphlet, *Les Instituteurs Syndicalistes et la Guerre (Syndicalist Teachers and the War)*, written by François and Marie Mayoux, an activist couple in the teachers' union. She had put up posters which read "Assez d'hommes tués: La Paix!" ("Enough dead men--Peace!") She was an active member of the socialist minority, the Zimmerwaldians, who called for a negotiated end to hostilities. The crime of Hélène Brion was not defeatist, but hatred of war--pacifism.

During the course of the trial, Brion, a life-long feminist and author of a 1917 pamphlet *La Voie Féministe (The Feminist Path)*, was accused of using feminism to cover up her activities against the war. In a written statement which she read to the court, Brion answered those charges. Beginning with a reference to the irony of her situation--she stood charged with a political crime while, as a woman, she was denied all political rights (French women did not get the right to vote until 1946)--she explained that her feminism was not a pretext for her pacifist activities. In fact, the opposite was true. She was an enemy of war *because* she was a feminist. Her work for peace was a continuation of her ongoing activities as a feminist. At the heart of all her political activity was her desire to have her sisters answer the call, "Femme, Ose Etre!" ("Women, dare to be!")[1]

The political activities of Hélène Brion were indeed numerous. In addition to being a full-time teacher, she was, at the time of her trial, the secretary (equivalent to director) of the *Fédération Nationale des Syndicats des Instituteurs et Institutrices* (National Teachers' Union), the secretary of the workers' orphanage, a member of the central committee of the major union federation, the *Confédération Générale du*

103

Travail (CGT), the archivist of the Socialist Party of her community and a member of the action council of the *Comité pour la Reprise des Relations Internationales* (Committee for the Re-establishment of International Relations), the major left-wing peace organization. And at the heart of her activities, there were the feminist organizations-- feminist teachers' groups and suffrage organizations, such as *L'Union Française pour la Suffrage des Femmes* and *La Ligue Française pour le Droit des Femmes*. In addition, Brion had, for a decade, written articles on women's rights for many of the socialist and union newspapers and periodicals. During her imprisonment and trial, she continued to compile a huge encyclopedia of famous women. Among the witnesses at the trial were the noted feminists Séverine and Marguerite Durand.

The trial of Brion was a major cause célèbre of the last days of the war and her name received much publicity, but Brion was certainly not the only female teacher to face dismissal, trial and prison for anti-war activity. Marie Mayoux was in prison, along with her husband, for having written the pamphlet that Brion was accused of distributing. Other teachers had been fired and threatened with prison. Brion's political activity and devotion to feminism was particularly intense, but other teachers, like Marie Guillot, Marie Guérin and Marthe Bigot, also worked throughout the war for the same organizations and causes. In fact, Hélène Brion was just one member of a remarkable group of women teachers who, in the critical first decades of the twentieth century, were not only feminists, but socialists, unionists and pacifists. This paper, concentrating primarily on women teachers in France but with examples of other women active in the anti-war movement, will indicate how, for all these women, there was no separation between the politics of feminism, the pacifist movement and the politics of the working class. Their feminism was an integral part of a revolutionary political consciousness.

It is not surprising that so many of these political activists were teachers. When the Third Republic of France attacked the educational power of the church in the 1880s by expanding secular public education, it recruited thousands of young men and women, particularly from small towns and isolated villages, to become part of the vast army of primary school teachers who would become a gigantic network of propagandists for secular education and republican ideology. This identification with anti-clericalism and pro-republicanism automatically placed the teachers on the left of the political spectrum. Although the pay was notoriously low, to be a teacher was, for many sons and daughters of peasants and village artisans, one step, albeit a small one, up the ladder from poverty and tightening rural conditions. For young women, the opportunity to teach was even more important. One of the few occupations open to women, the expanding teaching profession meant not only higher education and economic independence for female teachers, it also offered to these daughters of the people the opportunity to teach millions of French girls, to offer them, for the first time, a modern education.

But life was not easy for these pioneers of republican education. In many villages there was antagonism to secular schools. Teachers were harassed by parents, by local notables, by priests. For the young women teachers, the difficulties were compounded. Hired to replace nuns, many were expected to behave like secular nuns, to live celibate, devoted, and, of course, poverty-stricken lives. There were conflicts with the community, with authoritarian directors and with male teachers who feared the "feminization" of teaching. From the beginning, despite the higher proportion of women with advanced degrees, female teachers were paid less than male teachers and restricted either to girls' schools or to the lowest levels of co-educational schools. Isolated and harassed, but determined to persevere, the women teachers turned to each other for comfort and intellectual companionship. In 1903, Marie Guillot, a teacher from Lorraine, founded the first *Groupe Féministe Universitaire*, "to struggle against the laws, mores and poor education which have for centuries kept women in a state of dependence and inferiority."[2] She called on women teachers to place themselves in the vanguard of feminism. Although they were never more than four or five percent of the women teachers, these feminist groups spread throughout the country (at one point there were about fifty groups) and emerged as a formidable centre of political activity with influence far greater than their numbers might indicate.[3]

While the women's groups were forming, teachers of both sexes who wanted to improve their working conditions were establishing organizations which would enable them to fight for the economic and social justice they demanded from their employer, the French state. Forbidden by law to use the blue collar organizational form, the union (*syndicat*), the majority of teachers organized into benevolent societies (*amicales*). There were, however, a small group of teachers, many of whom were socialists, anarchists or revolutionary syndicalists, who, attempting to create an alliance with blue collar workers, dared to risk their jobs by forming real unions. Women from the *Fédération Féministe Universitaire* were active in both organizations, but it was in the more radical, illegal unions where they put their major energies. It was the women of the *Fédération Féministe Universitaire* who helped to organize in the provinces and who, as officers and council members, helped to keep the fledgling unions alive. While working for the demands of all teachers, the feminist teachers continued to bring before the teacher organizations, in meetings, in annual congresses, and in their periodicals, the special concerns of women and women teachers.

In October 1910, the National Teachers' Union issued the first of its weekly journal, *L'Ecole Emancipée* (The Emancipated School). Though filled with lesson plans and teaching information, its mission went far beyond pedagogy. *L'Ecole Emancipée*, revolutionary syndicalist in orientation, brought to its readers issues of concern to the union and to the working class in general, as well as discussions of wider political significance. From its inception, the journal encouraged women to air their views. A weekly column, *La Tribune Féministe*, written by Marie Guillot but often using other feminist writers, discussed votes for women, the problems of housework, economic independence for women (it was not until 1907 that married women could legally keep their salaries), reproductive freedom[4] and, of course, issues of concern to women teachers--co-education, equal pay and open employment in all schools. Often debates on women's issues spilled over from the column onto the general political pages. While most male teachers had gone beyond the Proudhonist ideology that women belonged in the home, this still hampered many blue collar workers. For many males and some females in the syndicalist movement who were committed to class struggle and the social revolution which would bring about the end of capitalism, the existence of a separate feminist syndicalist group, with connections to the bourgeois suffrage groups, was anathema. They feared bourgeois feminism as anti-male, anti-working class, anti-revolution.[5] If women wanted to be active, let them join the union. Marie Guillot used her column to answer this criticism by emphasizing that it was through political activity that women came to unionism and to syndicalism and that millions of women had to be brought into the political mainstream before they could be active in changing society. "You are paying now," she charged, "for the political ignorance of women."[6]

Underlying this discussion was the question of where activist working women should put their energies--in the union movement or in the feminist movement. For most of these feminist teachers, there was no choice. As Cécile Panis explained, the struggle for workers' rights and women's rights were inseparable. Marie Guillot further explained why women's rights had to be a special part of the working-class struggle. "We have as women a double battle to wage, the common struggle of all the proletariat against economic servitude and the special struggle for the conquest of our rights as human beings."[7] As long as women were treated differently in society, they must have separate organizations, she wrote. "We must be feminists and revolutionaries."[8]

Even as these debates were taking place, another issue was gradually becoming more important and potentially more ominous. The great European powers were rapidly moving along the path of militarism and toward a deadly war. In the nineteenth century, many republican teachers, like others on the left, nurtured on the glories of the People's Army of the Revolution and the idea of revenge for the German occupation of Alsace-Lorraine, were fiercely patriotic and nationalistic. The growth of the military, the use of this military in imperialist ventures and, finally, the national agony of the Dreyfus affair, helped to turn teachers and others on the left away from the nationalism which had now become the ideology of the reactionary right. Though still patriotically attached to the French nation, socialist and unionized teachers rejected aggressive nationalism. War could only mean the death of workers and peasants; it was to be opposed. As early as 1901, the feminist pacifist teacher Marguerite Bodin had asked the teachers' congress to vote a resolution against the teaching of chauvinism and the glorification of carnage. Just as the blue collar federation, the CGT, and the French Socialist Party had promised to stop any war with a massive general strike, so the teachers pledged to fight the move toward war with all its educational and political resources.

The war of course was not stopped. There was no general strike, the great anti-war socialist leader and hero to all teachers, Jean Jaurès, was assassinated, and socialists and syndicalists alike, filled with patriotic fervour, rallied to the call of the government for an alliance of all parties--the *Union Sacrée*, the Sacred Union. The teacher organizations were in disarray--the men off to the front, whole areas occupied by the Germans or under fire, the terrible casualties mounting daily. The activist women picked up the pieces, first on behalf of the union and then on behalf of peace. Hélène Brion became national secretary of the union; she and Frédéric Loriot kept the teachers' union going throughout the war. Marie Guillot, Marie Mayoux and others immediately established contact with the tiny socialist and syndicalist minority which rejected the *Union Sacrée*. Women socialists, the first to call an international socialist meeting on the question of ending the war, met secretly in Berne in March, 1915. Dissatisfied with the inactivity of the teachers on the peace question, Marie Mayoux took the initiative and called a national meeting of the union in June, 1915. On July 1, Mayoux edited and issued a manifesto which began with the words, "Assez de sang versé" ("enough spilled blood"). "It was time," the statement continued, "for the Allies to end the butchery, to initiate peace talks."[9] The manifesto galvanized the teachers into action. Meeting in Paris a few weeks later, the national leadership and delegates from provincial unions voted to support the campaign for peace. Hélène Brion, who had until then supported the war effort, now came over to the side of peace. In September, socialists and syndicalists met in Switzerland at Zimmerwald (note: six months after the socialist women met) to inaugurate the movement to establish a new socialist international, one which would try to end the war.

In the periodical, *L'Ecole Emancipée*, now heavily censored by the government and forced to change its format and its name to the less provocative *L'Ecole de la Fédération*, all talk of peace was forbidden. Issue after issue appeared with huge gaps; whole pages were often blank. But the *Tribune Féministe* continued. Marie Guillot and others pressed for feminist causes. They campaigned for the overworked and underpaid women who were employed in war factories, supporting the *Comité Inter-Syndical contre l'Exploitation de la Femme* (Inter-Syndical Committee Against the Exploitation of Women), demanding rest periods, child and health care facilities, as well as adequate pay. They defended women teachers who had taken over the classes of the departed men and were then accused of stealing men's jobs, of "feminizing" the primary school system. The writers of the *Tribune Féministe* urged women to be active in the union movement and in the peace movement. And always they spoke of the future. There would be no permanent and just peace, no true social change, if women were not granted their economic and political rights. In October 1916, Hélène Brion addressed the peace organization with a statement which began: "We who have been unable to do anything to stop the war because we have no civil rights are heart and soul with you in wanting to end it."[10] But this had to be done with women, and women's rights must be granted, she insisted. In 1917, Brion published *La Voie Féministe (The Feminist Path)*, subtitled "Les Partis d'Avant-Guerre et le Féminisme" ("The Pre-War Parties and Feminism").

Through a penetrating analysis of women's private and political spheres, of the false separation between family life and political life, Brion admonished syndicalists and socialists to integrate the struggle for women's rights into the struggle for workers' rights, to change not only the relationships of production, but to revolutionize all social relations.[11]

* * *

The activity of Hélène Brion and the feminists in the teachers' union has been emphasized in this paper, but it is just one example of the vital linkage between feminism, socialism and peace made by women in the anti-war movement. Even as the first troop mobilizations were taking place in late July 1914, a leading woman socialist, Louise Saumoneau, in yet another doomed attempt to prevent the war, authored a tract calling on women to stop the impending carnage, to form a "living barrier against murderous barbarism." A founder of the *Groupe des Femmes Socialistes* in 1913, Saumoneau, who had always believed that women's liberation would come through socialism rather than bourgeois feminism, merged the goals of women and international socialism in her anti-war activities. The only French representative to the March 1915 International Conference of Socialist Women, Saumoneau returned to France to spur the anti-war movement within the Socialist Party by circulating Clara Zetkin's appeal to socialist women to "make war on war." Arrested in September 1915, she spent seven weeks in prison before protests by socialists, syndicalists and feminists persuaded the government to release her rather than risk making her trial a rallying point for anti-war activists.

Throughout the war, Saumoneau continued to work with the other anti-war socialists, male and female, to turn the Socialist Party away from its support of the government's war efforts. She also continued her special appeal to women by organizing the *Comité d'Action Féminine Socialiste pour la Paix contre le Chauvinisme* (Socialist Women's Action Committee for Peace and Against Chauvinism) and through her writings. In a tract addressed to "Femmes du Prolétariat" ("Women of the Proletariat"), she asked working-class women to join the ranks of those against the war and against capitalism which exploits and kills.[12]

In 1915, yet another feminist group joined the movement against the war. Influenced by their meetings with Jane Addams of the United

States and Dr. Aletta Jacobs of the Netherlands, a small group of feminists organized the French section of the International Women's Committee for a Permanent Peace. Founded at a meeting in The Hague in April 1915, the Committee issued a programme which called for an international congress of women to be held at the same time as the peace conference at the end of the war to ensure a just peace. The Committee further pledged to work for two goals: the settlement of international disputes by peaceful means and suffrage for women. The leadership of this Committee had also come to their anti-war activities through socialism and feminism. One of the founders, Jeanne Halbwachs, was a socialist and the other, Mathilde Duchêne, as pre-war president of the labour section of the *Conseil National des Femmes Françaises* (National Council of French Women), had initiated that organization's investigations into the evils of home work and sweat shops.[13]

Within a month of its founding, the Committee issued a pamphlet, "Un Devoir Urgent Pour les Femmes." Describing the horrors of the war, so devastating to soldiers and civilians, the pamphlet asked for women to demand an end to this conflict in which there could be no victors. It further asked women to vow to work for a just peace which would conform to international law. This vow was to be the basis of Wilson's fourteen points. In early December, the police raided the Duchêne house and the Committee headquarters, confiscating the pamphlets as well as other printed material as "defeatist propaganda." The raids put an end to their publications but the Committee continued to hold meetings and to work in other organizations. By 1917, Madame Duchêne and other members of the Committee were part of the organization for a League of Nations, and Duchêne, continuing her efforts on behalf of working women, was part of the Committee Against the Exploitation of Women, yet another example of the continuing connections between pacifism, feminism and the concerns of the working class.[14]

The year 1917 brought an intensification of the women's struggle for peace and for their rights. The war had exacerbated the economic exploitation of women workers. With prices rising and working conditions deteriorating, women workers in textiles, food and other feminized industries were told by employers, who were making huge profits, that demands for higher wages and shorter hours would have to wait until the end of the war. Women working in munitions plants were told that they would be unpatriotic, that they would be hurting their sons and husbands if they dared to demand an improvement in their long hours and dangerous working conditions. Feminists and socialists like Saumoneau, Duchêne, Marthe Bigot and Marcelle Capy had continually publicized these wretched conditions in their publications and through organizations like the Committee Against the Exploitation of Women. Finally in the late spring and early summer of 1917, a wave of strikes erupted. The working-class movement and the entire country were stunned by the enormity and intensity of these totally female actions. Textile workers, dressmakers, trolley conductors, laundry workers, sugar refinery workers, and war workers demanded and won more pay and a shorter work week, colloquially called the "English week" (*la semaine anglaise*), Saturday afternoon off, fifty-four hours work for sixty hours pay.[15] On the back of the signs demanding the shorter work week, there appeared the words "Nous voulons nos poilus" ("We want our GIs"), "A bas la guerre" ("Down with War").

That same summer brought a wave of anti-war protest in the army. Soldiers returning from leave cried out against the war from the windows of trains carrying them back to the front. When the military police surged on to.the platforms and trains, in town after town, they found bits of tissue paper, some printed, some hand-written. "Enough killing, Peace." "Women want peace and their rights." "Soldiers on leave. Your wives and children cry out to you. Don't go back to the front where a stupid death awaits you." There were mutinies at the front. Feminist propaganda was blamed.[16]

The year 1917 brought as well an increase in the strength of the pro-peace socialist minority. Louise Saumoneau issued her appeal to working women, the Mayoux published their pamphlet, *Syndicalist Teachers and the War*. In November there was the Bolshevik Revolution. The government counter-attacked; activities on behalf of peace were "defeatist," "pro-German," "treasonous." The teacher activist Lucie Colliard was tried and threatened with internment, the Mayoux were convicted and sent to prison for two years,[17] and, finally, there was the trial of Hélène Brion who was also convicted but given a suspended sentence.

When the peace the women had worked so hard to achieve finally came, it ushered in a period of intense political activity. Although they were still denied access to the ballot box, the women activists, joined now by a new generation of feminists whose consciousness had been formed during four years of war, continued to work in the feminist organizations, in the unions, in the Socialist Party, in the newly formed Communist Party, and in the pacifist organizations.

The story outlined in this paper does not intend to imply that all feminists are automatically anti-war. Indeed, most of the major French middle-class feminist organizations, as did their sisters in Great Britain, the United States and Germany, supported their governments' war efforts, attempting to win approval with their hard work and patriotism. While Mathilde Duchêne, Jeanne Halbwachs, Hélène Brion and others were campaigning for a just peace, one that would ensure peaceful solutions to conflicts, and women's rights, Madame Schlumberger of the Women's Suffrage Association was asking French women to do their duty after the war, to "give to the nation the children who would replace those who died."[18] Nor does it imply that only women oppose war. The activists discussed in this paper worked closely with men in the socialist, syndicalist and anti-war movements. This story of the feminist teachers and other anti-war activists provides, rather, one historical example of how feminist consciousness grows not in isolation, but in the milieu of work and general political activity. Feminism, while an essential aspect of the political and personal lives of these French women, was also part of wider political consciousness and activity within the working-class movement. The example underscores the vital linkage between female liberation and human liberation.

Notes

[1]The trial record, newspaper accounts and articles and tracts defending Brion, i.e., Madeleine Vernet, Hélène Brion: Une Belle Conscience et une Sombre Affaire (1918), are in the Dossier Brion at the Bibliothèque Marguerite Durand, in the Brion archives at the Archives de l'Histoire Sociale (Fonds Brion 14 AS 183(4) c) and Archives Nationales (Série F7 13575).

[2]Max Ferré, Histoire du Mouvement Syndicaliste Révolutionnaire chez les Instituteurs (Paris, 1955), p. 194.

[3]The activities of female teachers are discussed in Danielle Delhome, Nicole Gault, Josiane Gonthier, Les Premières Institutrices Laiques (Paris, 1980); Max Ferré, Histoire du Mouvement Syndicaliste Révolutionnaire chez les Instituteurs (Paris, 1955); Jacques Ozouf, Nous les Maîtres de l'Ecole (Paris, 1967); François Bernard, Louis Bouët, Maurice Dommanguet, Gilbert Serret, Le Syndicalisme dans l'Enseignement (Grenoble, 1968); Marie-Hélène Zylberberg-Hocquard, Féminisme et Syndicalisme en France (Paris, 1978); Thierry Flammant, L'Ecole Emancipée (Les Monédières, Treignac, 1982); Anne-Marie Sohn, "Féminisme et Syndicalisme" (unpublished thèse en doctorat, Nanterre, 1973); Persis Charles Hunt, "Revolutionary Syndicalism and Feminism Among Teachers in France" (Ph.D. thesis, Tufts University, 1975); and parts of Judith Wishnia, "French Fonctionnaires: The Development of Class Consciousness and Unionization" (Ph.D. thesis, State University of New York at Stony Brook, 1978).

[4]In the pre-war period, while much more emphasis was placed on demands for social aid for working-class mothers and children, most of the feminist teachers supported the "neo-malthusians" and joined such feminist organizations as the Conseil National des Femmes Françaises in opposing laws against abortion, see *l'Ecole Emancipée*, June 17, 1911. The February 20, 1918 issue of *La Lutte Féministe*, edited by Hélène Brion, referring to the anti-abortion law being considered by the Senate, stated, "La femme, la femme *seule* doit être souveraine maîtresse de disposer de sa personne. . ." A number of feminist teachers, Brion, Henriette Izambard and Antoinette Bigot, chose to be mothers without getting married. After the war, another feminist teacher, Henriette Alquier, was tried in 1927 for publishing a book *La maternité--un Devoir Social* which advocated family allowances and birth control.

[5]The attitude of male workers toward female workers is described in Sylberberg-Hocquard, Féminisme et Syndicalisme, especially chapter III.

[6]*L'Ecole Emancipée*, September 2 and 9, 1911.

[7]*L'Ecole Emancipée*, July 6, 1913.

[8]*L'Ecole Emancipée*, July 27, 1912.

[9]The Manifesto is in the Archives Nationales, F7 13575. On teachers in the war, see F7 13568, 13574, 13575, 13576, 13743.

[10]Huguette Bouchardeau, ed., Hélène Brion: La Voie Féministe (Paris, 1978), p. 93.

[11]Bouchardeau, Hélène Brion: La Voie Féministe. I have summarized Brion's ideas.

[12]The wartime activities of Louise Saumoneau are in the Archives de la Préfecture de Police de Paris (BA 295 provisoire), Archives Nationales (F7 13374) and Charles Sowerwine, Les Femmes et le Socialisme (Paris, 1978), especially chapters 8 and 9.

[13]A report by Mathilde Duchêne, Le Travail à Domicile, was printed before the war. It discusses international conditions of sweated home labour as well as conditions in France where she estimated that nearly one million women worked at home manufacture. During the war, army clothing, for example, was made at home. Fonds Brion 14 AS 183(4) c.

[14]The Comité International des Femmes pour une Paix Pérmanente, Mathilde Duchêne and their publications are discussed in BA 295 provisoire in the Archives de la Préfecture de la Police de Paris and in F7 13375 in the Archives Nationales. The Comité Intersyndical contre l'Exploitation de la Femme is in Fonds Brion 14 AS 183(4) c.

[15]The strikes are recorded in Fonds Brion 14 AS 183(4) c and in James McMillan, "Housewife or Harlot: The Place of Women in French Society 1870-1940" (Ph.D. thesis, New York University, 1981), Chapter 7.

[16]Archives Nationales, F7 13370.

[17]Les Instituteurs Syndicalistes et la Guerre. Archives Nationales, F7 13376; a description of the trial, Marie et François Mayoux, Notre Affaire, is in the Fonds Monatte 14 AS 150.

[18]March 20, 1916. Archives de la Préfecture de Police de Paris (BA 1651).

FEMINIST CONSCIOUSNESS AND THE FIRST WORLD WAR

Jo Vellacott

This paper* will deal with the impact of the First World War on the thinking of some British women who were already feminists or at least suffragists.

The suffrage movement in Britain has been quite extensively written about, yet the story and analysis are both far from complete. A look at its historiography is enlightening, and also sobering. Not only has it been affected by the attention of sensation-seeking media at the time, and the neglect or bias of male historians, but it has also been markedly distorted by the partiality of the accounts left by women who themselves played various roles in the movement.[1] The most obvious distortions, only now in the earliest stages of correction,[2] are the excessive attention given to the so-called "militants," the suffragettes, at the expense of the work of the "constitutional suffragists," and the related neglect of the working-class component in favour of a view of the movement as having been entirely middle class, a characteristic for which it is then often belittled.

Less familiar is the disaster which has befallen the story of the 1915 controversy within the non-militant organization, the National Union of Women's Suffrage Societies (NUWSS), when new issues raised by the war split the executive down the middle and led to the resignation of all the officers except the President and the Honorary Treasurer, and of more than half the executive. Germane as are the fundamental causes of the controversy, the details are irrelevant here, and I mention it at this point only to explain why there may be a whole area of pre-war and wartime feminism that has been inadequately chronicled.

---

*I wish to acknowledge with appreciation the use of materials from the following collections and the assistance given me by the curators at every place: Catherine E. Marshall Papers, Cumbria Record Office; the Fawcett Collection, City of London Polytechnic; papers of the British WIL, British Library of Political and Economic Science; papers of the WILPF, International Section, University of Colorado; papers of the U.S. WILPF, Swarthmore College Peace Collection; Bertrand Russell Archives, McMaster University. This paper will also appear in History Workshop Journal 23 (Spring 1987).

Briefly, the National Union (NU) was divided on the response to the war, with the disagreement focussed on two specific issues: should it concern itself with education for peace? should it lend support to the women's peace conference to be held at the Hague in April, 1915? In addition, immense heat and personal pain surrounded the subsidiary issue of certain public statements made by Millicent Garrett Fawcett, the respected and deeply-loved doyenne of the NU, which were seen by the "pacifist" faction as being pro-war and in direct contravention of an understanding to abstain from such statements while the division within the executive was unresolved.[3]

What all this is leading up to is the fact that the accounts of the non-militant wing published by those who took part in the struggle were, with very few exceptions,[4] written by Fawcett herself or by her close friend and unfaltering supporter, Ray Strachey. In an otherwise generally fair account of the growth and triumph of the nineteenth-century women's movement and in particular of the suffrage campaign, Strachey not only condenses the controversy of 1915 to almost nothing[5] but also wipes the leaders of the dissidents out of the annals of *pre-war* suffrage history, omitting all mention of their names in connection with the striking new political policies which they had largely inspired and administered before the war, let alone the extraordinary and talented organizational spadework which they had carried out between them.[6] Fawcett's own writings do the same. It is probably not coincidental that very little correspondence with these leading members of the executive before or during the war survives in the Fawcett collection.[7]

Letters from Ray Strachey to her family at the time of the dispute characterized the opponents whom she planned to "beat . . . and drive . . . out"[8] as "the lunatic section;"[9] at other times she merely described them as "the socialists" and "pacifists" and once, interestingly, as "the wild women of theory."[10] The latter epithets reflect reality. My interest is in examining the thought of what was indeed a left-wing group of feminists moving towards a far more radical view than was officially represented by their organization, struggling towards an integration of feminism, socialism and pacifism, with some awareness of theoretical underpinnings, and with a great deal about it that is of interest to present-day feminists.

Every variety of response to the war can be found in different individual suffragists, although patterns of characteristic reaction emerge within each organization. We can safely presume that a relation could be found between the pre-war practice and theory of each group and its stance in wartime. Little attention has been or, alas, was paid to those suffrage organizations opposed to the war, such as Sylvia Pankhurst and her East London Federation,[11] or to those women's groups, such as the Women's Co-operative Guild, which had a long-term, albeit often low-key, commitment to working for peace.

Feminism is not the only route to pacifism; opinion is divided as to whether pacifism is a logically inevitable corollary of feminism. During the First World War, a number of more or less isolated individuals[12] found it to be so for them. My purpose here is to trace the thought of a group who have left sufficient record of their views to make it possible for me to suggest the logic of their development.

The group that I want to look at became the dissident wing of the NUWSS in 1914-15. I shall begin a few years earlier in order to show that their sophisticated feminist view of the war was the continuation of their theoretical and practical development in the forcing-house of a beleaguered suffrage campaign. My focus will be on the emergence of a new consciousness and a new theory rather than on the details of suffrage activity.

The story of the campaign of the non-militants from 1907 to 1914 has certainly not been over-extensively written up; what has been written--good recent works include those of Leslie Parker Hume, and of Jill Norris and Jill Liddington,[13]--concentrates on unravelling the complexity of events, adding to our knowledge of the people involved and evaluating strategy.[14] These facets are all directly relevant to my examination of the developing theory that was to link the suffrage cause in the minds of some women with a far wider feminist perspective.

Before it took a new lease on life, "the product of irritation and of hope,"[15] around 1907, the NUWSS, while far from moribund, had some earmarks of a somewhat staid bourgeois organization, which would move slowly and respectably (and I think inevitably) towards its goal. This was true, at least, of the London headquarters and of its most visible affiliate, the London Women's Suffrage Association.[16] Even then, it is anachronistic, and unjust, to forget that to support women's suffrage was still more than a little avant-garde and took courage, especially for any whose family and friends mocked the movement. Suffragists came from all parties, but except in the north where there was a strong movement among Labour women, the majority were Liberals.

Classical liberal theory is one of the strongest threads running through the arguments for women's suffrage. John Stuart Mill,[17] and doubtless Harriet Taylor Mill, had done the women's cause great service by setting out the argument for women's enfranchisement as a logical extension of liberal ideology. In that part of the suffrage movement which was mainly middle class, this remained an important, perhaps the most important, thread for many years. One of the reasons, of course, for the location of much suffrage activism in the drawing rooms of the upper-middle class, and again particularly in London, is that this class was politically aware and interested, and that awareness extended increasingly to the distaff side, especially as women's education improved. As W. S. Gilbert wrote:

> ... Nature always does contrive,
> That every boy and every gal,
>   That's born into the world alive,
> Is either a little Liberal,
>   Or else a little Conservative![18]

Catherine Marshall, for example, read John Stuart Mill at an early age. She read his *Liberalism, Representative Government* and *The Subjection of Women*, later commenting wryly that most boys "read the first two and leave out the third."[19] It was not women's suffrage that first became her religion as a result of this indoctrination and of the climate of her Liberal home, but liberalism. Suffrage initially was for her, as I believe it must have been for many young Liberal women, just a component of liberalism, though an exceptionally important component since they expected its enactment to affect their own lives directly. A major factor in the escalation of the suffrage campaign after 1906 was the recognition by many Liberal suffrage women that "their" party, now in power, was going to need much more prodding than they had thought. Apparently the boys indeed had not grown up reading *The Subjection of Women*. Many former members of Women's Liberal Associations (WLAs) began to work for the NU, not because they had given up on liberalism or the Liberal Party, but because they saw a need to apply more public pressure than the generally deferential WLAs would do.[20] This strong identification of the suffrage issue with liberal ideology tends to be masked by the determined non-party stance of the NU, but is revealed, for example, in several speeches given by Marshall to Liberal clubs and associations, men's and women's, and in some of her correspondence with Liberal ministers.[21]

But the arguments used by the suffragists varied. At this stage[22] all women suffragists wanted admission to the established political structure, as voters.[23] Beyond that, support for the claim might go in any, or several directions. The demand for the vote on the same basis "as it is or shall be"[24] held by men was ideologically Liberal, even if its political effect, if enacted, might have been to favour the Conservatives. All women suffragists felt they had a right to the vote. This far, they claimed equality with men; it is a mistake to suppose that by "equality" they necessarily meant "sameness."[25] The argument from Right was married to the argument from Need--that women's pressing concerns would not get attention until they had the power of the ballot-box; and from Duty--that woman had an important role to play in the affairs of the nation. This last came across as classical social feminism; the country had need of women's special skills, moral strengths, and insights, especially now that many of the issues dealt with by governments fell within women's traditional sphere. Much use was made of the analogy of motherhood; the nation needed a mother to do its housekeeping, as well as a father to deal with the public interface of economy and international relations.[26] Coherent theory is not a strong point of political activism and particularly of protest campaigns. Any one polemical speech or article may contain a fine hodge-podge of these and other arguments, the priority--if the speaker is a good one--varying with the audience addressed. We should beware of overstraining analysis in our attempts to sort them all out retrospectively.

H. H. Asquith's pre-war Liberal Government may have done a service to feminism by its intransigence on the subject of the franchise.

Had the vote been won easily, middle-class women suffragists would have needed neither a new strategy nor new allies.[27] This new blood flowed into the NUWSS from 1907 on; the constitution was revised and made more democratic in that year, regional structures were formalized in 1910, new branches were created at a great rate, and some difficult housecleaning was carried out at headquarters.[28] While in London the membership appears to have been predominantly middle class, even upper-middle class, more and more attention was paid to the strong suffrage movement among women workers in the north of England, which had long existed on its own merits, and also to the need and possibility of bringing working-class male voters round to a supportive position.[29] While some suffragist leaders may have seen this only as an obvious response to Asquith's misguided and unintentional challenge to them to prove they had an extensive following,[30] others were changed by the experience. Disappointment with the Liberal Party's dilatoriness turned, by late 1912, into disgust with what was seen as its bad faith. After the debacle of the Speaker's ruling on the Reform Bill, in January 1913,[31] some accepted the new election alliance with Labour in a punitive spirit, some justified it solely as a Machiavellian strategy, some never did condone it, and some of the more radical began to see it as a logical and appropriate step.

Meanwhile, from the time of its founding in 1909, we find the NU journal, the *Common Cause*, taking a broad view of the suffrage cause, or rather of suffrage as a part of feminism. Under the editorship of Helena Swanwick, the *Common Cause* did not restrict itself to strategy, exhortation or reportage; rather, it assumed that its readers would be interested in all matters affecting the condition of women and it published well-researched articles on a wide range of feminist issues, many of them still depressingly familiar. For Swanwick herself, the scope allowed her was still insufficient; her resignation as editor in 1912 was largely because of this. In her valedictory leader, she wrote:

> In a paper which is to be the organ of such work [women's enfranchisement by constitutional methods] there is practically nothing human which is irrelevant. Everything there is in modern society is an 'argument' for women's suffrage ... The bother with the mass of the Press ... is that it does not recognize that human questions like war, or the birth-rate, or tariffs, or a miners' eight-hour day, have quite as much to do with women as with men ...[32]

The other issue which led to her resignation was the Executive's refusal to allow her to express freely her opinion that the "militant suffragists . . . are doing considerable immediate and far more considerable ultimate harm."[33] This also, as it turned out, had some relevance to the coming struggle.

Swanwick gave up the editorship voluntarily and quietly; she had felt the hostility of certain members of the Executive for some time, but had no wish to damage the organization. With her "too advanced"[34] views, she found the position of editor a vulnerable one, although in fairness to the Executive, it should be said that the *Common Cause* continued to present a broad view of feminism even after Swanwick's resignation, though certain topics were shunned.

The other "radicals" on the Executive, and especially Catherine Marshall and Kathleen Courtney, were protected from some of the potential criticism of their work by several factors. They were much less isolated than the *Common Cause* editor and they were immensely successful in enlisting Labour and Trade Union support among both men and women. Their organizational skills had gone a long way towards setting the NU on its feet as a responsive, well funded, democratic organization and their political astuteness was known and respected by parliamentary suffragists of all parties. In short, they were indispensable.[35] Further, the euphoria produced by the continued sense of forward motion resulting from the new and challenging alliance with the Labour Party, coming as it did at the apparent nadir of the suffrage cause, led the more conservative members to suppress, even in themselves, doubts they would otherwise have felt. While Helena Swanwick could not get away with visibly broadening the feminist platform in black and white, the political leaders who were broadening it in solid fact and action (and, as it turned out, radically broadening its theoretical base as well) were seen only as developing and implementing a bold strategy that was no real departure from traditional policy. Hindsight gave a different view; in 1927,[36] while Ray Strachey was writing her history of the women's movement, *The Cause*, Millicent Garrett Fawcett wrote to her:

> I agree with you in believing that the fundamental cause of the split was the adoption by the NU of all kinds of objects which many of us believe to be either useless or mischievous or both.[37]

In 1913, however, Fawcett actively defended the new policy from those who saw it as unwise or a betrayal of old allies. The Election Fighting Fund (EFF), conceived in 1912[38] and implemented immediately after the fiasco of the Speaker's ruling on the Reform Bill in 1913, was the outcome of final acceptance of the uselessness of pursuing the vote either by means of a Private Member's Bill or by means of an amendment tagged on to the Reform Bill of a hostile government. Suffrage could not rely on the goodwill, even when backed by pledges, of individual MPs.[39] The cause had to have official party backing; and the only party which could be persuaded to take it up was the Labour Party. While the Labour Party was in no position to implement the policy, EFF support given to Labour candidates at elections could help bring the vote nearer in three ways. The Liberal majority might be reduced, if only by stealing votes from the Liberals and letting Tories in. Liberal candidates who were not "tried and true friends of suffrage" might be given such a rough ride that the Party would hesitate to run them.[40]   Thirdly, the increased threat from Labour might well induce Liberal and Conservative candidates and MPs to press their leaders to adopt the suffrage cause.[41]

Although strategy was the sole publicized rationale for supporting Labour, the move brought the frontline leaders, generally the less traditional women, into much closer contact with the Left at exactly the time that the Liberal Party was discredited. The northern suffragists, who included large numbers of working women, many of them long active in trade unions, labour organizations and the Women's Co-operative Guild, found themselves in the mainstream as they had never been,[42] and some middle-class leaders, formerly strongly Liberal--notably Marshall--began to find much that was congenial and interesting in the Labour position. A sympathetic view of the industrial unrest of 1911 and 1912 readily suggested comparisons between the oppression of sex and the oppression of class. When a further mental link was made with the situation of the colonized peoples of India and Ireland, feminist consciousness was ready to move beyond a mere middle-class resentment at exclusion from the privileged structure on the one hand, and beyond the workers' defence of social and economic interests on the other. In December 1913, Marshall talked to Sir Edward Grey about the connections she saw. She spoke of the coming struggle between capital and labour, of the women's movement at home and abroad, and of a sense of "kinship with subject races." She applied her arguments concretely to the current British situation, and went on to claim:

> It matters enormously to [the] whole of civilization whether these 3 great movements run on sound and healthy lines, or are driven into revolution. *The women will have great effect on both.*[43]

By this time Marshall clearly believed that radical change was essential and was coming; whether it would be by peaceful or violent means would depend largely on how the Liberal Government chose to handle the women's cause. Although she did not spell it out, what is implicit here is anticipation of a real change in the nature of government, not a mere increase in the number of voters. In Sandra Holton's words, true for at least this group, "suffragists did not seek an entry to a male-defined society but the opportunity to re-define that society."[44]

An important element in what these women believed they could bring to polity was the substitution of non-violent principles in decision-making and conflict resolution for the doctrine "might is right." Before the 1914 war, this thinking was developed mainly, on the one hand, in response to to the anti-suffragists' claim that since force was the ultimate basis of government and women could not fight, they therefore could not vote; and, on the other hand, in response to the escalating violence of the Pankhursts' Women's Social and Political Union.[45] Among non-militant suffrage leaders there were some who already had a defined pacifist position,[46] but the war provided a catalyst welding together feminism, anti-militarism, and, perhaps more tenuously, socialism, in a far more closely-knit and coherent theory.

The difficulty which arose among suffragists over response to the war has been mentioned above and described elsewhere.[47] What is relevant here is that those whose suffrage claims still rested mainly on a demand to be admitted to the existing male political system, unchanged, generally supported uncritically the British Government's war effort. If this is not understood at a theoretical level, the immediate conversion of Emmeline and Christabel Pankhurst and their closest followers to a fervent jingoism may be startling; but there was no inconsistency because they had already recognized and adopted the role of force towards gaining the franchise.[48] In their pre-war campaign, their methods reflect an overall acceptance of a primary masculine value. Within the National Union, the division is more subtle because of the NU's commitment to legal methods, but it is illuminated by later correspondence, in which Ray Strachey, researching and writing the history of the suffrage movement, admitted to being "a good deal impressed by the militant side of it."[49]

The great qualities of Fawcett's leadership had been moderation combined with determination, and an ability to inspire affection and respect in her followers. The manifest acceptability, socially and politically, of Fawcett and the middle-class suffragists had enabled them to establish and maintain a bridgehead in political circles through a long period when more radical views and methods would simply have set the suffrage cause back.[50] Fawcett's theoretical basis was in classical liberalism; an important part of her creed was the rejection of all state interference such as free education, widows' pensions and mothers' allowances.[51] At the same time she subscribed to a view of women as essentially different from men, but, for her, this appears to have led to a traditional view of the appropriate role of women in wartime. In the absence of a radical view of societal change, this was reinforced by the realization that women's "good behaviour" during the war might further their admittance to the political system--on men's terms.[52]

On August 4, 1914, the day that Britain entered the First World War, an evening meeting of women was held in the Kingsway Hall in London. Sponsored by the National Union of Women's Suffrage Societies, it had been called at short notice before the actual declaration of war, when many still believed that Britain would remain neutral. Fawcett, as President of the National Union, chaired the meeting, despite her own "very grave doubts."[53] There was a large attendance, mainly of working women from the Women's Co-operative Guild, which has a fascinating history of opposition to war,[54] and women's labour organizations. Added interest and significance derived from the presence of members of the Executive of the International Women's

Suffrage Alliance currently meeting in London, several of whom spoke. Instead of coming obediently into line now that Britain was at war, the general mood was of disbelief and protest, almost the last flutter of the abortive movement for British neutrality which had begun to develop in the last few desperate days before the war.[55]

The aberrant behaviour of the women at the Kingsway Hall meeting and its possible consequences were brought home sharply to Fawcett the next day when she received a letter from Lord Robert Cecil, a leading Conservative Unionist suffragist, which I give in full because it epitomizes so neatly the generally unspoken conditions to be attached to women's admission to the public sphere:

> Permit me to express my great regret that you should have thought it right not only to take part in the "peace" meeting last night but also to have allowed the organisation of the National Union to be used for its promotion. Action of that kind will undoubtedly make it very difficult for the friends of Women's Suffrage in both the Unionist and Ministerial parties. Even to me the action seems so unreasonable under the circumstances as to shake my belief in the fitness of women to deal with great Imperial questions and I can only console myself by the belief that in this matter the National Union do not represent the opinions of their fellow country women.[56]

Ironically, of course, Fawcett was in accord with Cecil. The incident may have hardened her determination not to be trapped again into apparent acquiesence with a more radical view.[57]

The opportunities provided by the First World War for women to move into non-traditional jobs have obscured the fact that war, as ever, reinforced women's traditional role of supportive subservience. Women were to bear children, give their sons and lovers, provide nurturance for the warriors and the wounded, and undertake, temporarily, tasks which the men were too busy to perform.[58] Under the daily onslaught of appalling casualty lists, the sacrifices were made bearable only by acceptance of an unquestioning patriotism which made it all seem noble and worthwhile and which could make any hint of pacifism seem like disloyalty to the dead.[59] They were many; for example, before the war was over no fewer than twenty-nine of Millicent Fawcett's young male relatives had been killed.[60]

For those who wanted acceptance into the male political system on the men's own terms, there was logic in seeking to gain admission through excellent performance of the traditional roles. Those whose thinking had moved beyond this reacted differently. The war, and the apparent carelessness with which almost all Europe had slipped into it, sharply reinforced their view that radical restructuring of the political system was necessary. While they shared the perception of women's nature as different from that of men, they drew diametrically opposite conclusions. Women should not be wasting their lives and loves bearing and nurturing cannon-fodder; they should be turning their special skills towards developing peaceful alternative means of conflict resolution. For these feminists[61] there was an intimate connection between the women's suffrage issue and opposition to militarism; in a militaristic society women would never have an equal place; conversely, in a society where women were fully heard, militarism would not prevail. Swanwick wrote:

> ... to work for a right foundation of government; to endeavour to establish public right in control of physical force . . . is to work for the very foundation of a free and secure existence for women. Every suffrage society ought to be a pacifist society and realize that pacifist propaganda is an integral part of suffrage propaganda.[62]

Marshall was equally uncompromising. Writing an article on "The Future of Women in Politics," published in the 1916 *Labour Year Book*,[63] she began by declaring:

> The future of women in politics depends . . . on whether the war results in the discrediting of militarism, or whether it leaves all the nations more militarist than they were before.
>
> Conversely it is true that whether the civilised world does or does not surrender its soul to militarism will depend in no small measure on what place women are going to take in politics.
>
> The Militarist is one who believes in the supremacy of force . . . The mark of your militarist is that he would rather get what he wants by fighting than by any other way. He wants to force his enemy to yield, so that he may have him at his mercy and be able to impose what terms he chooses. I have heard Trade Unionists talk like this of Trade Union fights. I have heard socialists, who were ardent pacifists on international questions, talk like this of class warfare. I have heard suffragists talk like this of the struggle for sex-equality. *They were all talking pure militarism*--they were all moved by the desire to dominate rather than to co-operate, to vanquish and humiliate the enemy rather than to convert him into a friend.

Later in the same article, she described

> . . . another way in which women's experience fits them peculiarly to help men in the reorganization of international relations. . .Men's efforts to "preserve peace" (as if you could preserve that which is not there!) have been directed mainly to

preserving the status quo, to repressing any force that threatened to disturb the existing order. Now that is all very well for those who have all they want under the existing order--for the British Empire, for the capitalist, for the party in power. But what about those who are not satisfied with things as they are? Surely the business of those who desire a real living peace is to find some means other than war by which the existing order can be changed to meet legitimate needs and changing conditions?

Despite the stress often laid by these feminists on women's nurturant qualities, they held that this alone was not sufficient; women must study the hard questions of economics, foreign policy, international relations and defence. Swanwick was one of the founding members of the Union of Democratic Control in which she at once set to work to scotch plans for sidelining the women into a special women's branch.[64] While some of the pacifist feminists, including Swanwick, could then, and their modern counterparts can now, be accused of romanticizing women's virtues,[65] they had a practical approach to the task confronting them; but, sadly, even their most sober assessment can be seen now as having been over-optimistic.

The connection between pacifist feminism and socialism provides one clue to this over-optimism. There is, and was by 1918, a school of revolutionary marxist socialism, in which there were socialist feminists. This however prevailed mainly in Germany and Eastern Europe.[66] The kind of feminist socialism attractive to the renegade members of the NUWSS was the legitimate descendant of utopian socialism, and owed more to Guild Socialism than to Marx.[67] Proponents of peace sought each other out in the face of overwhelming press support for the prosecution of the war. The fact that the anti-war elements met together as such, at peace meetings, in anti-conscription groups, in the Union of Democratic Control, narrowed the spectrum of socialists whom the feminist pacifists regularly encountered.

The only party, and it was little more than an alienated subdivision of the Labour Party, to declare itself against the war was the Independent Labour Party (ILP), whose weekly paper, the *Labour Leader*, continued to publish anti-war, pro-negotiation, and anti-conscription articles,[68] and whose parliamentary Members, notably Philip Snowden, did a stalwart job of attempting to stand against the tide.

The small band of ILP leaders who opposed the war, and the Liberals (by then largely ex-Liberals) who joined them, mostly favoured Guild Socialism. When Bertrand Russell expounded his version of Guild Socialism in early 1916,[69] he did not see industrial rule by the workers as replacing political democracy, but as creating a parallel structure alongside the traditional democratic structure. One stream of traditional anti-war sentiment among socialists had been that workers should refuse to fight a capitalist war, rather than that they should abjure war altogether; but there were many socialists, especially in the No-Conscription Fellowship, for whom this political tenet was underpinned by a profound belief in the brotherhood of man.[70] Hence, although they worked for a change radical enough to have warranted the name revolution, they continued to have faith that it could take place with minimal violence. No wonder they saw in the first stage of the Russian Revolution, in March 1917, the miraculous upsurge of the people that they had been waiting for; no wonder they hoped that it would sweep across all Europe including Britain, ending the war and bringing a saner world. For the feminist pacifists there was even the essential component they were watching for; the first statement of principles issued by the new Provisional Government in Russia had declared for the adoption of universal suffrage.[71] When no such world-wide movement occurred, the euphoria passed and the war dragged on to its bitter end.

Once the war was over, pacifist socialists, and especially pacifist socialist feminists, were a small group in the larger body of labour and of international socialism. Not only that, but socialism in practice had moved conclusively towards centralized state socialism, turning its back on utopian guild socialism, with its emphasis on the greatest possible decentralization of power and decision-making.

Their realistic assessment of the magnitude of social and political change needed did not prevent the feminist pacifists from rejoicing that the vote was won,[72] but few there were indeed in this or perhaps in any other group who any longer saw it as the earthshaking event they had expected. The gilt was off all three "isms," feminism, pacifism and socialism. Utopian goals, far from being nearer, had receded immeasurably; the pacifists had indeed been proven right in their claim that a militaristic world was death to women's vision. But for the strongest of these women, the distant goals were still important to work towards. In 1920, we find Catherine Marshall, for example, seriously burnt out by her efforts on behalf of the No-Conscription Fellowship, and recovering from a long illness, but willing to work in support of the Labour Party,[73] not as if it were the one stepping-stone to the millennium, but as if it were the beginning of a long and uncertain road that seemed at least to lead in the general direction of equal opportunities for women, and social justice for workers.[74] We also find her, along with like-minded socialists, strenuously making out a case against "arming the proletariat" and resorting to class warfare. While admitting to being "deeply stirred by the great inspiration that has come from Russia," Marshall and indeed many British Labourites insisted on retaining "freedom to develop our own methods," believing and hoping that "it may be possible to achieve our revolution without resort to armed force."[75]

The most concrete achievement of the feminist pacifists, however, was the Women's International League for Peace and Freedom.[76] This was the creation of women from a number of different countries, nearly all of whom had been active in the suffrage movement before the war and most of whom had steadfastly resisted war fever. The founding conference at The Hague in April 1915 was a remarkable occasion, the first and the last such meeting during wartime. In 1919, when the war was finally over, the pacifist survivors were able again to meet, this time in Zurich.[77] The extent to which they had moved in their thinking and feeling beyond the confines of the male-dominated political system is striking. At this meeting were women whose countries had just concluded a bitter four-year war, a fight to the finish, in which virtually all of them must have lost close relatives. Here were women whose fellow countrymen, and -women, were screaming to have Germany and her allies squeezed "until the pips squeak" confronting women who had seen babies die because of the Allied blockade, and who in some instances were themselves emaciated from hunger.[78] There was an absence of recrimination on both sides, just a determination to do whatever women could do to bring about better conditions and to work for a lasting peace.

The international feminist pacifists at this Congress and in their ongoing organization at Geneva mustered an extraordinary array of intelligence, knowledge and creativity. Although their work between the two wars has been described in outline,[79] much still remains to be discovered about their thinking. My own impression is that they embodied much that was strongest in the school of thought I have been describing. They had a reasonably coherent theoretical feminist pacifist basis; they knew what changes had to be made. They believed women had special qualities, by nature or by nurture, to bring to the solution of national and international problems. They had the patience and ability to study economic, social and political questions, and they had the creativity to suggest non-linear solutions. They had political skills acquired in the suffrage struggle. They knew that the fate of women was inextricably tied to the decisions made by the male statesmen. Most of them now had the vote in their own countries and so could claim more confidently than ever before that they belonged in the public sphere.[80] They had some successes in publicizing and improving social conditions. Their achievements in the way of research and practical proposals were remarkable; they spoke out repeatedly about major international issues, from the need for Treaty revision on.[81] Their fault was not in what they said or did, and I refuse to lay the blame on the speaker for not being listened to.[82]

Yet we have to address the question of why they failed so totally to influence the course of events, to interrupt the march towards Hitler and 1939 which they had seen so clearly from that day in 1919 when they read with shock and horror the terms of the imposed Treaty of Versailles.[83] Was the vote a Pyrrhic victory in that, ironically, women had indeed been accepted into the political system on existing male terms--in practice, on condition of conformity? So that these women, arguably the most able and internationally well-versed of their time, who understood the system so well, but who could not accept its values, were everlastingly ignored no matter how important their message?[84]

Would it have been different had the feminist pacifists been able to carry the majority within the NU with them during the war?

This may be the central matter on which we should focus, on the tension that exists between the development of a holistic feminist theory, understood among women, and accepted by some men, and the absolute necessity, before it is too late, for productive interaction, involving discussion or pressure, with the men who rule the world.

Comments

Deborah Gorham

I think you make a very interesting parallel between militancy before the war and jingoistic support for the war during the war, but I think there are problems with it. What are you going to do about Mrs. Pethick-Lawrence and even Sylvia Pankhurst, both of whom to a certain extent supported a militant campaign and both of whom really did oppose the war? My problem with it is that I don't really think that Catherine Marshall was entirely right. I don't think that militancy really was militaristic. I think it was a curious kind of Victorian feminine strategy, to provoke men to violent attack against women in order to expose the true lack of respect underlying the pedestalization of women. I think it was non-violent except for its very last stages, for surely the arson campaign could have killed a lot of people if they hadn't been so lucky, but I think that equating the actions of the militants during the militant suffrage campaign with militarism has problems. And, specifically, I think one would have problems putting all the sheep on one side and all the goats on the other.

Jo Vellacott

I think it is certainly true that you can't divide them quite like that. I think it is an interesting thought that Emmeline Pethick-Lawrence, in fact, supported the militant campaign as long as it was not threatening to lives. She was out by the time it was turning to violence towards people. Sylvia Pankhurst is an exception to almost everything and a very nice exception I think. You could fit her in by saying that she was a genuine Marxist socialist pacifist, not prepared to get involved in capitalist wars. I think she was also a humane person so that she really was disgusted by the gross inhumanity during the war towards the poorer people in the country. I am quite sure you can't put suffragists all neatly in categories but I think it would be quite fun actually to go through the different suffrage groups and analyze their responses to the war in relation to the position they had taken on militancy before the war. The other thing about the Women's Social and Political Union (WSPU) is that, unlike the National Union, it was not a democratic organization and, therefore, it's extremely difficult, by 1912 or 1913, to know how many people really devotedly supported the escalation of militancy.

Naomi Black

The last point that you made is very close to one that I wanted to make. The suffragists never got that violent, and, although I think that they served their cause by being martyrs, that wasn't their intention. What is important is not the violence but the inner structure of the segments of the movement. The National Union was pretty democratic in practice and very much committed to it in principle. The WSPU was very hierarchical (I don't know whether that is the right word), but it was run in a very patriarchal fashion: orders from the top, quasi-military organization, even if they didn't actually do military things. And that seems to me to be very much related. This is the argument that many people make: it's structural violence, rather than actual violence. I think this is a very interesting and useful distinction because that's why the Pethick-Lawrences left, or were thrown out, over that issue, not just the violence but the anti-democratic organization. The other point I'd like to make is that perhaps you're being a little hard on the more conventional political activists. I'm not at all sure that the sort of things that Mrs. Fawcett and the others did means that they were expecting to come into the political system on men's terms. It strikes me more, and here one projects one's own experience, of course, as a calculation about how to get in. But the major point that I would make here is that most of them expected a very big change when they got in. I'll give one example, that of Lucy Stone, because it's one I feel strongly about.[85] She is often described, even in the excellent article in Dale Spender's book, as being conservative in her later days. Yet it is quite clear that she kept all her radical views about marriage; she just became convinced that one wouldn't get anywhere if one stood up in public and talked radical.

Jo Vellacott

You raised a lot of points here, with most of which I'm fully in agreement. I may sound hard on Millicent Fawcett's reaction to the war; however, I think it was the inbred reaction of someone who was herself brought up as a British imperialist. I think it is understandable, but I still think that it was a genuine sort of jingoism. I do think there is an element there of a much more limited vision than the group that I'm talking about. Fawcett and her group did not expect to change the structures and the system by getting inside; they expected a lot of social change. They expected to change attitudes but they thought it was a terrific system and once they were in, that would make it possible to change everything; but I really do think that to some extent it was a matter of getting in on the men's terms. I think the letter from Cecil-- admittedly he was Conservative and all the rest of it--really spelled it out from the point of view of the boys inside, the terms on which women would be allowed in and what was expected of them when they got in.

Jane Lewis

I was just trying to put this paper alongside other accounts of women's peace movements and feminists involved in peace, and I was having some difficulty, from a point of view mainly of definition. I am struck by the distinction drawn in Veronica Strong-Boag's paper between peace and internationalism.[86] In fact, that wasn't so much the message I got from your paper. Certainly the women we heard about in foregoing papers, the leaders anyway, seem to be involved very much in institutional lobbying, a sort of alternative female diplomacy, if you like. Very far removed from the peace marches and peace camps that we are familiar with today. I just wondered if you think it's a misperception to see all these early century efforts as internationalism rather than peace.

Jo Vellacott

I think when you get on to the inter-war years, it's perfectly true that the kind of internationalism they were dealing with had peace very much as a goal. Therefore, they became involved very quickly in questions such as treaty revisions and the economic conditions of Europe. I don't really see such an enormous difference between peace and internationalism in that context. There was always an attempt between the wars or before the wars, whenever you'd like to take it, to marginalize women to some extent (and I think we see it again very much now) by diverting them to social questions. We do now see more connections between the social questions and the major structural, systemic questions, I think. But the kind of thing that it was believed women ought to be working on in the League of Nations was the white slave trade. That's important, but the women like Helena Swanwick and Catherine Marshall were not going to stop at that. They were going to learn what was necessary to deal with the major questions, such as treaty revision and so on. They did their homework very well, but as I said at the end, they didn't get heard.

Notes

[1]The Pankhursts were the chief chroniclers of their own Women's Social and Political Union (WSPU). The super-abundance of materials on the small group of extreme militants led to its continuing to be the focus when interest in the suffrage movement revived. See, e.g., Roger Fulford, Votes for Women (London: Faber and Faber, 1957), and Andrew Rosen, Rise Up, Women! (London: Routledge and Kegan Paul, 1974).

[2]Jill Liddington and Jill Norris, One Hand Tied Behind Us: The Rise of the Women's Suffrage Movement (London: Virago, 1978); Doris Nield Chew, ed., Ada Nield Chew: The Life and Writings of a Working Woman (London: Virago, 1982); Hannah Mitchell, The Hard Way Up, edited by Geoffrey Mitchell (London: Virago, 1968 and 1977). My discussion of suffrage historiography arises in part from a conversation with Jill Liddington, June 1984. Sandra Holton, "Feminism and Democracy: The National Union of Women's Suffrage Societies, 1897-1918," (Ph.D. thesis, University of Stirling, 1980), also makes an important contribution in this area. Holton's book, now at the press, is eagerly awaited.

[3]Correspondence between George Armstrong and Fawcett, Fawcett Collection (Box 89); Ray Strachey, Millicent Garrett Fawcett (London: Murray, 1981), pp. 288-9. Emily Leaf wrote to Fawcett on November 2, 1916, asking her if she would agree to see Kathleen Courtney; Fawcett replied the next day that she thought it better not. Fawcett Collection (Box 89). In October 1917, Pippa Strachey said that "The O.G. [Old Girl=Fawcett]" was still "fearsome about the pacifists and their works," though she was prepared to work with the Women's International League for Peace and Freedom (WILPF) (presumably in relation to the proposed new Reform Bill). Seen by courtesy of Mrs. Barbara Halpern (hereafter, Halpern Collection).

[4]E.g., H. M. Swanwick, I Have Been Young (London: Victor Gollancz, 1935).

[5]Ray Strachey, The Cause: A Short History of the Women's Movement in Great Britain (London: Bell and Sons, 1928), p. 351. For a fuller and somewhat juster account of the 1915 controversy, see Strachey, Millicent Garrett Fawcett, pp. 282-95.

[6]The five women left out of the record were Margaret Ashton, Kathleen Courtney, Catherine Marshall, Maude Royden, and Helena Swanwick. See also Caroline Marshall (Catherine's mother), draft letter, not sent, to Eleanor Rathbone, n.d., and letter to Rathbone October 3, 1923; these are protests about the omission of the five from

books by Fawcett. On May 1, 1914, Fawcett had written to Mrs. Marshall, of Catherine, "I am more and more impressed by her great capacity for political work, combined with absolute openness and candour," and on August 13, 1914, had described her as "almost indispensable . . . our work now depends so much on her perception and judgment that we should feel very lost without her." Correspondence seen by courtesy of Frank Marshall. A striking example of how this kind of injustice is perpetuated occurs in Mary D. Stocks, Eleanor Rathbone (London: Gollancz, 1949), p. 115, where she refers to "the value of the Parliamentary goodwill evolved by Ray Strachey before 1919." Although Strachey was very active for a few weeks or months when the Speaker's Conference report was under discussion (1917), all the "goodwill" had been built up by Marshall before 1915. When Strachey took on the job of Parliamentary Secretary to the NU in June 1915, she admitted, "I am just filling a breach and keeping out some poisonous pacifists." Halpern Collection.

[7]NU correspondence has been "weeded" from time to time; the destruction of what must have been a considerable body of correspondence with, for instance, Marshall, may have been due to an unconscious bias rather than deliberate malevolence. Some papers were also destroyed in air raids during World War II.

[8]R. Strachey to Mary Berenson (her mother), May 20, 1915. Halpern Collection.

[9]R. Strachey to an aunt, April 29, 1915. Halpern Collection.

[10]Ray Strachey to "Aunty Loo" (Alys Russell), March 5, 1915. Halpern Collection.

[11]See also Andro Linklater, An Unhusbanded Life--Charlotte Despard: Suffragette, Socialist and Sinn Feiner (London: Hutchinson, 1980), pp. 176-7, for the reaction of Charlotte Despard and the Women's Freedom League.

[12]Sybil Oldfield, Spinsters of this Parish (London: Virago, 1984), p. 307, n. 1, has a useful list of some noted British women pacifists and/or pacificists in 1914, many of whom were well-known suffrage activists. The distinction between pacifists and pacificists is Martin Ceadel's; see his Pacifism in Britain, 1914-1945 (Oxford: Clarendon Press, 1980).

[13]Leslie Parker Hume, The National Union of Women's Suffrage Societies, 1897-1914 (New York and London: Garland Publishing, 1982); Liddington and Norris, op. cit.; Jill Liddington, The Life and Times of a Respectable Rebel: Selina Cooper, 1864-1946 (London: Virago, 1984). See also Sandra Holton, "Feminism and Democracy." Martin Pugh, Women's Suffrage in Britain: 1867-1928 (London: Historical Association, 1978) is useful.

[14]There are also a number of recent works which concern themselves strictly with the traditional political aspect, for example, Brian Harrison, "Women's Suffrage at Westminster, 1866-1928" in Michael Bentley and John Stevenson, eds., High and Low Politics in Modern Britain (Oxford: Oxford University Press, 1983).

[15]A. J. Grant on revolution, in A History of Europe: 1494-1610 (London: Methuen and Co., 1948).

[16]There is still much research needed on local suffrage organizations, militant and non-militant.

[17]J. S. Mill, The Subjection of Women (London: 1869).

[18]W. S. Gilbert, Iolanthe.

[19]MS. notes for speech to the Keswick Liberal Club, November 18, 1909.

[20]See Jo Vellacott, "Catherine E. Marshall: from liberalism to feminism, pacifism and socialism. A British case study: 1908-1918," unpublished paper, 1984. Extensive material in Catherine E. Marshall Papers (hereafter CEMP) relates. See also Constance Rover, Women's Suffrage and Party Politics in Britain: 1866-1914 (London: Routledge and Kegan Paul, 1967), pp. 140-3.

[21]MS. notes for Keswick, November 18, 1909; "Notes for Appleby, January 10, 1912;" Marshall to Sir John Simon, copy, August 10,1913; various notes for and of interviews with Sir E. Grey and F. D. Acland, December 1913; correspondence with Sir E. Grey, October-December 1913; etc. CEMP.

[22]This applies to the Western democracies. Where there was a less democratic structure and a revolutionary movement, feminism could be sharply divided between an ineffective bourgeois suffragism and a feminist support (also often bourgeois-led) for revolutionary activity, putting its trust in equality in a new order to come.

[23]The question of whether women should sit in Parliament, as well as vote, was always played down. Marshall's early speeches (various notes, 1908, 1909 in CEMP) begin with a specific disclaimer of this demand.

[24]This formula was adopted by nearly all suffrage groups, for strategic as well as ideological reasons. Harrison's belief (op. cit.) that the women clung to it solely because it made an ideological point ignores the extreme difficulty of coming up with any criterion that would command a broad spectrum of support.

[25]I see no reason why "equality" should be taken to mean "sameness;" the origins of the difficulty over this appear to me to lie in the earnest need for 19th-century women to demonstrate that they could accomplish what men accomplished. Cf., e.g., Emily Davies' insistence that Girton students must not accept any mitigation of the intellectual rigours of Cambridge.

[26]Marshall made frequent use in speeches and writings of the analogy of motherhood in the wider sphere, and also refers (which is not exactly the same thing) to the usefulness of women's nurturing and housekeeping skills in national and international affairs. See, inter alia, MS. "Women and War," March 22, 1915, CEMP, forthcoming in Margaret Kamester and Jo Vellacott, eds., Militarism versus Feminism: Women and Peace, 1915 (London: Virago, 1986). The complexity of the relationship between social feminism and equal rights feminism has been the subject of much recent debate. See Ellen

DuBois, "The Radicalism of the Woman Suffrage Movement: Notes Toward the Reconstruction of Nineteenth-Century Feminism," Feminist Studies 3, 1/2 (Fall 1975): 63-71; Ellen DuBois, et al., "Politics and Culture in Women's History: A Symposium," Feminist Studies 1 (Spring 1980): 26-64; Sandra Holton, "Women's Worlds, Women's Consciousness and Feminism," unpublished, given at the Sixth Berkshire Conference on the History of Women, Smith College, June, 1984.

[27]Cf., e.g., Canada. Carol Lee Bacchi, Liberation Deferred?: The Ideas of the English-Canadian Suffragists, 1877-1918 (Toronto: University of Toronto Press, 1983).

[28]No open controversy took place at NU headquarters, but there are hints in correspondence that there may have been some deliberate pruning of deadwood.

[29]Material in CEMP about various speakers' tours implies a largely male working-class audience at many meetings. See also a typescript of unpublished letters from Ray Strachey, giving an account of the Newnham College Suffrage Caravan's trip, July 1908, Halpern Collection.

[30]Hume, op. cit., p. 44.

[31]Ibid., pp. 186-7.

[32]Common Cause, quoted in Swanwick, I Have Been Young, p. 230.

[33]Ibid., p. 231.

[34]Swanwick to her husband, ibid., p. 227.

[35]Margaret Kamester, "The Secondary Feminist Interests of the WSPU and the NUWSS, as found in their journals for the period January 1, 1914 to August 4, 1914," unpublished paper.

[36]Fawcett to Caroline Marshall, August 13, 1912, and see note 6 above.

[37]April 9, 1927, Halpern Collection.

[38]The EFF was largely the brainchild of H. N. Brailsford, and set in operation by K. D. Courtney and Marshall. Extensive material, minutes of NU executive and of EFF, Fawcett collection; extensive material and correspondence in CEMP. See also Hume, ch. V.

[39]After the defeat of the Conciliation Bill in March, 1912, the NU analyzed the Division minutely in light of Members' pledges; besides the "pros," "antis" and "wobblies," they now had a list of "rats."

[40]Given favourable circumstances, the NU had already proved that it could cause problems for a candidate. In December 1910, Hilaire Belloc withdrew his Liberal candidacy in S. Salford after NU intervention. Vellacott, "Pressure and Persuasion," unpublished; Marshall, "a brief summary of events from one on the spot," CEMP; Common Cause, November 24, 1910; Hume, p. 93, n. 120.

[41]Hume, ch. V.; Vellacott, "Pressure."

[42]Liddington and Norris, op. cit., and Jill Liddington, Selina Cooper.

[43]MS. notes of interview with Sir E. Grey, December 15, 1913;

Marshall "The 'Entente Cordiale' between the Labour Party and the Women's Suffrage Movement" (ca. January 1914?), CEMP. See also P. W. Wilson, "Women's Suffrage and Party Policies," The Englishwoman, April 1914.

[44]Sandra Holton, "Women's Worlds." A weakness of this useful and stimulating paper is its failure to distinguish between the theoretical bases of the different suffrage groups.

[45]See Jo Vellacott Newberry, "Antiwar Suffragists," History 62, 206 (October 1977): 411-25.

[46]For example, Helena Swanwick, and Isabella Ford, a Leeds Quaker and Labour organizer.

[47]Vellacott, "Antiwar Suffragists." For useful discussion of the international suffrage response to war see Anne Wiltsher, Most Dangerous Women: Feminist Peace Campaigners of the Great War (London: Pandora, 1985). I appreciated the opportunity to read this in draft.

[48]Linklater, pp. 176-7, makes the connection between the Pankhursts' militancy and their militarism much as I have long done, and in addition illuminates the connection between both and the "purity campaign."

[49]Strachey to Carey Thomas, 1928. Other correspondence also refers. Halpern Collection.

[50]See note 6 above.

[51]Mary Berenson, unpublished biography of Ray Strachey, Halpern Collection; Stock, pp. 117-19.

[52]R. Strachey, Millicent Garrett Fawcett, pp. 300-1, claims that Fawcett "hardly gave a thought to questions of tactics and expediency" in her response to the war. I believe this to be true; Fawcett was sincere, but her vision of women's political role was narrow.

[53]Swanwick, I Have Been Young, p. 240.

[54]See Liddington and Norris. Also Naomi Black, "The Mothers' International: the Women's Cooperative Guild and Feminist Pacifism," Women's Studies International Forum 7, 6 (1984).

[55]Oldfield, pp. 177-79. See also Jo Vellacott: Bertrand Russell and the Pacifists in the First World War (Brighton: Harvester, 1980); Vellacott, "Anti-war Suffragists;" Irene Cooper Willis, England's Holy War, intro. by Jo Vellacott Newberry (New York: Garland, 1972, 1st pub. 1928).

[56]Fawcett collection.

[57]Cecil's letter, read together with Strachey's (M. G. Fawcett, pp. 288-290) account of the Kingsway Hall meeting in February 1915 at which Fawcett's public anti-pacifist stand so angered some of her colleagues, may help explain her action on that occasion.

[58]The special issue on "Women and Men's Wars" of Women's Studies International Forum 5 (1982) contains several articles of great interest on women's role in wartime, especially Jean Bethke Elshtain, "On Beautiful Souls, Just Warriors and Feminist Consciousness"; Nancy Huston, "Tales of War and Tears of Women"; Judith Hicks Stiehm, "The Protected, the Protector, the Defender."

[59]For an example of the tragic tension between loss and loyalty, see Bertrand Russell's wartime correspondence with Evelyn and Alfred North Whitehead. Bertrand Russell Archives. Also Vellacott, Bertrand Russell, pp. 57-8.

[60]Strachey, M. G. Fawcett, p. 282.

[61]See Oldfield's list (note 12, above). Many other nameless women were also pacifists, of course.

[62]Helena Swanwick, Women and War, with an Introduction by Blanche Wiesen Cook (New York: Garland, 1971, reprint of London, 1915, ed.), p. 11.

[63]Also MS. CEMP. Reprint forthcoming in Kamester and Vellacott, eds., Militarism versus Feminism. For the kind of detailed study of international issues which Marshall now saw as necessary, see notes "For Mr. Acland" (ca. December 3, 1914).

[64]Helena Swanwick, Builders of Peace: Ten Years of the Union of Democratic Control (New York: Garland, 1972, 1st pub., 1924). Correspondence, E. D. Morel papers, British Library of Political and Economic Science.

[65]Blanche Wiesen Cook, introduction to Garland reprint of Helena Swanwick, The War in its Effect upon Women and Women and War (New York, 1971), pp. 8-9.

[66]As in so many things, Sylvia Pankhurst was an exception.

[67]Simply put, Guild Socialism was a milder version of the Syndicalism which had been seen as such a threat to industrial relations in 1911-12. See Olive Banks, Faces of Feminism (Oxford: Martin Robertson, 1981), for the utopian socialist influence on feminism. A more complex and convincing account is given in Jane Rendall, The Origins of Modern Feminism: Women In Britain, France and the United States, 1780-1860. (London: Macmillan; New York: Schocken, 1984). See also Barbara Taylor, Eve and the New Jerusalem: Socialism and Feminism in the Nineteenth Century (London: Virago; New York: Pantheon, 1983).

[68]I. C. Willis, op. cit.

[69]Principles of Social Reconstruction (London, 1916); also published in the U.S.A. as Why Men Fight, reprinted New York, 1972.

[70]For the No-Conscription Fellowship, see Thomas C. Kennedy, The Hound of Conscience (Fayetteville: University of Arkansas Press, 1981); Vellacott, Bertrand Russell; Martin Ceadel, Pacifism in Britain, 1914-1945; J. W. Graham, Conscription and Conscience: A History, 1916-1919, with a Preface by Clifford Allen and an Introduction by John W. Chambers (London: 1922; reprint ed., New York: Garland, 1972); Arthur Marwick and Clifford Allen, The Open Conspirator (Edinburgh and London: Oliver and Boyd, 1964).

[71]See Vellacott, Bertrand Russell, ch. 11, "Pacifism and Revolution."

[72]See, for example, many letters to Fawcett in Fawcett Library Autograph Collection.

[73]Marshall to J. S. M[iddleton], MS. draft letter, May 6, 1920. Middleton was Secretary to the Labour Party. CEMP.

[74]Material in CEMP, especially relating to organization of Cumberland Labour Party, 1920.

[75]"I.L.P. Questions for Lenin," MS. rough notes in Marshall's writing (1920?). The occasion is not known but they probably related to the British delegation which visited the USSR in early 1920, and included, among others, Clifford Allen, Ethel Snowden and Russell.

[76]Gertrude Bussey and Margaret Tims, Women's International League for Peace and Freedom (London: Allen and Unwin, 1965); Vellacott, "Anti-war Suffragists"; Jane Addams, Emily Balch and Alice Hamilton, Women at The Hague (New York: Macmillan, 1915); Mercedes Randall, Improper Bostonian: Emily Green Balch (New York: Twayne Publishers, 1964); Lela B. Costin, "Feminism, Pacifism, Internationalism and the 1915 International Congress of Women," Women's Studies International Forum 5 (1982); Anne Wiltsher, op. cit.

[77]Ibid. Mary Sheepshanks had edited Ius Suffragii throughout the war, doing a remarkable job of maintaining pre-war bridges. Oldfield, ch. 9, sheds much light on British and international women's pacifism during the war. See also Wiltsher.

[78]Oldfield, pp. 216-17.

[79]See note 76 above.

[80]Ellen DuBois's distinction between the public and private spheres as opposed to feminine and masculine roles remains useful. "The Radicalism of the Woman Suffrage Movement."

[81]WILPF International archives, University of Colorado; WILPF, U.S. archives, Swarthmore College Peace Collection; WIL, British archives, British Library of Political and Economic Science.

[82]Certainly, in common with the whole peace movement, WILPF was effectively debilitated in the 1930s by the tension between collective security, absolute pacifism, sanctions and appeasement; but these difficulties arose from a kind of statemanship against which they had warned.

[83]Oldfield, pp. 217-18; Bussey and Tims.

[84]There was also the fact that admission to a political voice, marginally permissible in domestic affairs, was, and has remained, totally unacceptable in the bastions of male prerogative, foreign affairs and defence--neither of which, indeed, is ever fully open to scrutiny by elected representatives; this, of course, was the main target of the UDC's policy.

For an important analysis of feminism, women's role in the current peace movement, and the tension between the need to be heard *now* and the need to challenge the whole gender power system, see Jill Lewis, "Militarism and Gender: Danger--Men at War," in END Journal 5 (August-September 1983).

[85]Leslie Wheeler, "Lucy Stone: Radical Beginnings," in Dale Spender, ed., Feminist Theorists (London: The Women's Press, 1983), pp. 124-36.

[86]See Veronica Strong-Boag, "Peace-Making Women: Canada 1919-1939," in this volume, pp. 170-91.

VERA BRITTAIN, FLORA MACDONALD DENISON AND THE GREAT WAR: THE FAILURE OF NON-VIOLENCE

Deborah Gorham

Throughout the twentieth century there has been an active and sustained opposition to war. Moreover, as Sandi Cooper's work shows,[1] women of several countries were involved in anti-war organizations even in the decades before the outbreak of the Great War. But in spite of the existence of world-wide anti-war activism, in any country engaged in conflict in the twentieth century, only a small minority of individuals has been able to sustain a position of absolute non-violence during wartime. During actual conflict, men and women alike tend to support war, even if they have, beforehand, expressed anti-war sentiments.

Understanding why this is so should be of major importance to those interested in non-violence as a political principle and in the history of non-violence as a political program. This paper seeks to contribute to our understanding of the difficulties involved in arriving at and sustaining non-violent conviction in time of war through an examination of the experiences and responses of two individuals--both women--during the First World War.

The first of the two, the Canadian Flora MacDonald Denison (1867-1921), had been prominent for almost a decade as an activist for women's suffrage when the war broke out. Denison's views on the woman question and on other social issues were more radical than those of the majority of Canadian women activists, but in spite of this radicalism, her talents and energy had made her a leader in her home city of Toronto and nationally.[2] Denison, however, had been forced from her leadership position early in 1914 by a new wave of conservatism among Toronto suffrage women and in August, 1914, her influence within the Canadian suffrage movement was less than it had been for many years.

But she was still influential, as is apparent from the fact that the Canadian Suffrage Association published her essay *War and Women* as a pamphlet in 1914. It is evident from this pamphlet that Denison was aware of pre-war work for peace and arbitration and specifically of women's contributions, for the chief message of *War and Women* is that militarism results from the dominance of men in public life. "The male through centuries upon centuries has been combative and war has resulted," she says, whereas "woman's thought and action have always been constructive. . .The women of England have no quarrel with the women of Germany. Both were . . . asking . . . that international arbitration keep peace between nations and that women be given the power of the ballot. . ."[3]

An anti-war stance, derived from a belief that prevention of war is part of woman's special mission, was, of course, common among early twentieth-century women activists. Some of these women intensified their opposition to war as the Great War continued: in Canada, for example, the Winnipeg feminist journalist Francis Marion Beynon took a strong pacifist stand, which cost her her job with the *Grain Grower's Guide*.[4]

Denison, in contrast, did not sustain an uncompromising opposition to the war, and in this she was more typical of the majority of Canadian women's movement figures than was Beynon. While she never adopted the jingoistic, racist tone used by some suffragists during the war, by 1917 she was no longer stating, as she had in 1914, that the conflict was caused primarily by the male spirit of violence and by the world-wide disenfranchisement of women. In 1917 Denison worked in upstate New York as a paid speaker for the New York State Suffrage Party. In a United States newly at war, she addressed crowds from flag-draped platforms. In urging passage of suffrage legislation in the State, she said that women's claim was strengthened by their war work. She still insisted that the war was caused by masculine militarism, but by 1917 she had come to believe that Germany, because it was more militaristic, less democratic, and more male-dominated than its enemies, was the guilty party, and that its defeat was necessary and justified.[5]

What caused Denison's transformation from uncompromising opposition to reluctant acceptance of the war? The examination of an individual response has, I think, a wider significance. Denison was an influential public figure, but in her thinking she was a follower, not a leader. An examination of her changing responses provides some insight into the difficulties that an uncompromising non-violent stance encountered in gaining and holding adherents during the Great War.

Denison's life went through three phases during the Great War years. First, from late 1914 until late 1915, financial difficulties and personal pressures caused her to drop out of public life. Perhaps it was because she was living not in Toronto, but in the small town of Napanee, that she was unaware of the formation, in the United States, of the Woman's Peace Party in January, 1915, or of the International Conference of Women at The Hague in April, to which two Canadian women went as unofficial delegates.[6] Denison might well have been sympathetic to these developments had she known about them at this time, but her isolation, on the one hand, and the weakness of the anti-war movement, especially in Canada, on the other, meant that organized anti-war activism did not present itself to her as a possibility.

By the end of 1915, Denison's personal difficulties had eased enough to enable her to become involved once again in public life. But the activity in which she was engaged, in 1916, was not directly related either to the suffrage movement or to the war. Denison had long been interested in spiritualism, a religious alternative whose unorthodoxy made it more congenial to her than Christianity, and for many years this interest had been closely connected with her love of Walt Whitman's poetry. In the early twentieth century, Whitman had become a cult figure, a prophet of democracy. Whitmanism in the United States served as a focus for a blend of spiritualism and political radicalism. In the years 1916-1919, Denison was a leader among those attempting to institutionalize Whitmanism in Canada.

In order to promote the Walt Whitman Fellowship in Canada, Denison started publishing a journal, the *Sunset of Bon Echo*, from her remote country property Bon Echo, to which she had retreated in 1916. The four 1916 issues of the *Sunset* are revealing, as much for what is left out, as for what is included. While Denison did not entirely ignore the war in the *Sunset*, most of the material either extolls the beauties of nature or discusses the problems of the world on a spiritual plane. Denison did truly believe in democracy, peace and human fellowship, but the luxury of distance made it possible for her, in the year of the Battle of the Somme and of Passchendaele, to retreat into vague pronouncements about "the dear love of comrades" as a solution to world violence.

She could do this because of the nature of Canada's involvement in the war. In contrast to the United States, which remained neutral until the spring of 1917, Canada was at war when Britain went to war not merely because of the legal ties involved in the imperial union, but because the Canadian government vigorously supported the imperial effort. But although Canadian casualties were extensive and the war had a major impact on Canada, it was still possible, as it would not have been in Europe, to retreat, as Denison did in 1916, to a situation that was, both mentally and physically, the antithesis of trench warfare.

In the last months of 1916, personal circumstances brought the war closer to Denison. The most important person in Denison's life was her son Merrill, with whom she had an unusually intimate and egalitarian relationship. Born in the United States in 1893, Merrill had been raised in Canada. In 1915, he was studying in Pennsylvania. His mother wrote to him from Napanee almost daily, and he replied almost as frequently. What this voluminous correspondence reveals were the pressures to participate in the war faced by a young man who described himself in March, 1915, as "absolutely a pacifist." In May, when several of his Canadian friends had joined up, he wrote: "I might as well admit it--my viewpoint has changed since the war began and if it were not for you, I should go." In October 1916, in spite of his mother's continued opposition, Merrill went to France.[7]

After he left, Flora Denison's detachment was destroyed. Bon Echo might be a long way from the Western Front, but with Merrill there, she suffered from continual anxiety. Merrill's participation, I think, was responsible for the erosion of the anti-war position she had espoused in 1914. Because Merrill had decided that the Germans were truly the enemies of democracy, Flora Denison's own view shifted, and 1917 found her, as we saw earlier, using patriotic rhetoric from New York State suffrage platforms.

Denison's lapse into the rhetoric of patriotism during the war reveals the weaknesses of her political analysis. Her expressions of social concern had always been vague and sentimental: during the war, as we have seen, they became safely spiritual in nature and, therefore, completely ineffective. Moreover, the fact that she drifted away from the anti-war position she espoused in her 1914 pamphlet can be attributed to the inherent weakness of what could be called the feminine--not feminist--pacifism that was its mainspring. This feminine pacifism is easily eroded because it arises from a false view of masculinity and femininity, the Victorian ideology of separate spheres. To assert that women are intrinsically opposed to war is to condone war for men and to make opposition to war part of woman's separate sphere of activity. Like female philanthropy in a capitalist economy, this feminine pacifism can easily define itself as powerless and, when it does so, its opposition to war becomes simply a new form of what Nancy Huston[8] has called the symbolic women's tears that have long been a part of the martial tradition. By 1917 Denison's anti-war sentiments had come to fit this pattern.

I turn now to the second subject of this paper, the English woman Vera Brittain (1893-1970), who figures also in another contribution to this volume, that of Yvonne Bennett.[9] Brittain is best known for her autobiographical memoir of the Great War, *Testament of Youth*, published in 1933. That book is both a vivid presentation of the war from a woman's point of view and a passionate feminist statement. As Bennett's work demonstrates, Brittain did become a staunch advocate of non-violence in the 1930s. In the First World War, however, her youth, her social class and the milieu from which she came made it almost inevitable that, when war broke out, she would be caught up in active support for it.

Vera Brittain, who came from a conventional upper middle-class family, had been, since 1912, engaged in her own personal struggle to go to university, an ambition that was still unusual for a girl from her social milieu. In August, 1914, after two years of hard work, she was about to experience the realization of her ambition: she was to enter Somerville College, Oxford. She was also falling in love with Roland Leighton, a friend of her younger brother Edward. Both Edward and Roland had left their public school, Uppingham, in the spring and were also about to enter Oxford. So, as she says in *Testament of Youth*: "When the Great War broke out, it came to me not as a superlative tragedy, but as an interruption of the most exasperating kind to my personal plans."[10]

Brittain did go up to Somerville in the autumn of 1914, but not for long. Neither Edward nor Roland ever began their studies. Both volunteered for Army service, and Vera herself left Somerville after she completed her first year, to return only after the war. In June, 1915, she began service as a Voluntary Aid Detachment nurse. In the course of the war, not only were Roland and Edward both killed, but so also were two other close male friends. Vera herself served as a VAD, first in England, then in Malta and finally in France.

Those of you who know *Testament of Youth* might say that the task I address here--namely that of analyzing Brittain's responses to the Great War--has already been admirably performed by Brittain herself in that book. But *Testament of Youth* represents her interpretation of that experience when she was a mature woman with developed social and political convictions. What I wish to do is provide some direct understanding of the Vera Brittain who was a young woman in her early twenties during the Great War, without the mediation of the mature author of *Testament of Youth*; to ask what an historian might say using only those sources, namely her diaries and correspondence, dating from the war years themselves.[11]

These sources reveal a progression of reactions to the war. There was the first period when, after the initial shock of disbelief, she saw the war as an heroic adventure. By the end of 1915, when Roland Leighton was killed, she exhibited a growing sense of bitterness about the way in which the war was using up her generation. By the time she was nursing in France in 1917, where she cared for German prisoners as well as British wounded, the seeds of her future pacifism had been sown. She had begun to believe that government propaganda masked a callous indifference to the slaughter of innocent, victimized youth on both sides.

Why did Vera Brittain see the war, at first, as an heroic adventure? Why was she a willing participant, encouraging the young men to whom she was most attached to volunteer? Why did she herself choose to serve as a nurse? And why did she believe, even at the end of the war--and indeed for many years thereafter--that it had truly been the duty of the young to participate?

In August, 1914, twenty-year-old Vera was in many ways a conventional upper-middle-class young woman. She had done little thinking about politics, and even her feminism was relatively undeveloped. Therefore, it is not surprising that at the outbreak of the war she responded with conventional upper-middle-class patriotism. The evidence suggests that these values had been transmitted primarily through vicarious participation in the school experiences of her brother and his friends. As public school boys they had been exposed to a set of values about patriotism, bravery and duty which would have made it almost impossible for them to have resisted the call for volunteers that immediately followed the outbreak of war. Officers' Training Corps at Uppingham had taught them not only that they owed their country their services, but that, as members of the governing classes, they had duties as leaders.

Young Vera Brittain not only accepted, but admired, these

values. As she wrote in her diary while visiting Uppingham for Speech Day in July, 1914, where she was stirred by the sight of the boys in their OTC uniforms: "I can understand why Edward regrets leaving it so much. For girls--as yet--there is nothing equivalent to public school for boys--these fine traditions and unwritten laws that turn out so many splendid characters have been withheld from them--to their detriment."

When war was declared, it was Vera who urged Edward, then eighteen, to volunteer, and her diary gives her version of the family row that ensued: "Edward said that Daddy, not being a public school man or having had any training, could not possibly understand the impossibility of his remaining in inglorious safety while others scarcely older than he were offering their all."

In addition to conventional patriotism, there were other less obvious reasons, rooted in her emotional life, that made the war at its outset attractive to Vera. In her inner life, Vera longed to live at an intense level. It was this desire for intensity that attracted her to Roland Leighton when she met him in April, 1914. It was Roland who gave her, that same month, Olive Schreiner's *Story of an African Farm*, and from that time, until his death, references to it were woven into their courtship. As Alan Bishop has pointed out,[12] that novel, even more than Schreiner's *Woman and Labour*, influenced the young Vera. Why did this book appeal so strongly to these young people? The atmosphere of Schreiner's novel is one of overheated romanticism. Its themes include suffering, loneliness, and unfair persecution of the young by the old. It extolls high feeling, self-sacrifice and the beauty of death. In atmosphere and plot it offered a sharp contrast to Vera's own life up until 1914. For the evidence reveals that Vera's family life was unusually supportive: even with respect to her intellectual ambitions, while it is true that her parents did not understand them, they did give her ample encouragement and financial assistance in her goal to get to Oxford. What they could not nourish was her romantic spirit, and, when the war came, its power to do so was one of its undeniable attractions.

The war made soldiers of her male contemporaries. What circumstances caused her to become a VAD? Partly, the same motives that had originally led her to Oxford: she did not wish to be excluded because she was female. As she wrote to Roland in October, 1914: "Whether the war is noble or barbarous, I am quite sure that had I been a boy I should have gone off to take part in it long ago; indeed I have wasted many moments regretting that I am a girl. Women get all the dreariness of war and none of its exhilaration." But even more important than this girlish sense of adventure, this wish not to be left behind, was the same naive patriotism and romantic belief in self-sacrifice that led young men to volunteer for the army. This need to sacrifice, to prove that she too could work and suffer, became especially strong after Roland went to the Front in April, 1915. And by June, she had begun nursing.

By early 1915, when the atmosphere of unreality that had

prevailed in the early months had dissipated, and Brittain had begun to understand on a deeper level the destructiveness of the war, the shallow patriotic tone disappears from her diaries and letters. And, as the war continued, she grew increasingly skeptical of claims about its righteousness. But during the war itself the possibility of resistance to the war did not fully penetrate her consciousness: she still believed, even then, that the young who served the war effort were doing a necessary duty, and that the best young people had sacrificed themselves, leaving only the second-rate behind. Why? Because of the depth to which she had imbibed Victorian notions of duty and self-sacrifice, notions that remained central to her throughout her life. Duty meant to her, then, participation in the war, even when one had begun to question its justice. Later on, in the twenties and thirties, she came to believe that duty and self-sacrifice demanded conscientious objection to violence.

In *Testament of Youth*, Brittain wrote: "It is this glamour, this magic, this incomparable keying up of the spirit in a time of mortal conflict, which constitute the pacifist's real problem. We will never rescue civilization until we can somehow impart to the rational processes of constructive thought that element of sanctified loveliness which from time to time glorifies war."[13]

I agree with the mature Vera Brittain's own interpretation of the lesson to be learned from an analysis of the young Vera's war experiences. As the Jungian psychologist James Hillman[14] has said, it is not difficult to provide rational explanations for why people hate war--what needs explaining is why they sometimes love it. The major lesson to be drawn from an understanding of the young Vera's experiences is that this glamour had as much of a fatal attraction for her as it did for her male associates.

And the experiences of Brittain and her close male friends suggest that the young were exploited in the Great War not only through their naive idealism, but also through the emotional weaknesses that are almost inevitable in youth. The war offered some dangerously attractive shortcuts to these late adolescents. It provided, first of all, a shortcut to adulthood: it thrust boys like Roland and Edward into positions of authority, as officers. Vera said, in December, 1914, that both Edward and Roland seemed so much older than she was, all of a sudden. Edward, she said, "seemed to have grown up absolutely and suddenly." When one is nineteen, the possibility of growing up "absolutely and suddenly" has a seductive attractiveness.

The war also imparted a spurious simplicity to emotional life. Nancy Huston has written of the important role that war narrative plays in the perpetuation of war: "men's wars," she says, "are made of stories."[15] And war stories simplify moral and emotional realities. The traditional war hero is faultless. Brittain began making a war story out of the war as it was happening, and I believe that she was never aware of the extent to which, in all the versions of the story she produced over her lifetime, the war caused her to oversimplify. One example must suffice here: the Edward Brittain of *Testament of Youth* is a hero because he died on the Asiago Plateau; the brother-sister relationship Brittain creates in the book is virtually free of conflict. But in fact, Vera had the ambivalent feelings toward her younger brother that one would expect a real person, and not a war heroine, to have. The death of that brother made it impossible to express these feelings or to write frankly about the real Edward, whose story was far more complex than any of the published sources reveal. Depriving the young of their full possibilities for emotional development is less detrimental than depriving them of their lives; this examination of Brittain's experience does suggest, however, that it is one overlooked dimension of the way in which the Great War damaged a generation of young people.

Finally, how does Brittain's individual experience correspond with what contemporaries and historians have said about the Great War and women? Vera Brittain herself believed that the war did, indeed, bring about a decisive end to many of the Victorian restrictions that had hampered women of her social class, and no doubt this was true. But the war also thrust Vera back into adopting many of the stereotyped ideas and roles that she was, before the war, so determined to escape. When the war broke out, this Somerville Exhibitioner began knitting socks: "the only work it seems possible as yet for women to do."[16] And nursing, the real work to which she devoted herself, reflected feminine stereotypes much more closely than did the role of woman student. The critic Sandra Gilbert[17] overstates her case when she claims that the war "liberated" women. Vera Brittain did not need the war to release her "passionate energies," or to bring about a "revolution in her economic expectations," as Gilbert suggests; she had already paved the way for such goals by gaining admission to Oxford. The war interrupted the process for her.

In conclusion, Vera Brittain and Flora MacDonald Denison are contrasting figures, both in age and in nationality. But they shared certain characteristics: both were intelligent and genuinely humanitarian, and both were feminists. But neither was among the small minority offering sustained and unqualified opposition to the Great War, although both had qualities and beliefs that might have led them to such opposition. This paper has suggested why neither woman was pacifist in that war. In Denison's case, I have suggested that her anti-war sentiments were easily eroded because they were rooted in sentimentality. Brittain's case illustrates the extent to which young women as well as young men could get caught up in an acceptance of war as, in part at least, heroic and glamourous.

In both cases, the influence that ties to men who participated in the war could have on women is illustrated. And above all, we must remember how little opportunity they or anyone had to hear clearly stated non-violent beliefs during the war itself. As Vera Brittain herself was later to explain so eloquently in *Humiliation with Honour* (1943), in wartime, even in liberal democracies, the pacifist is usually regarded as a traitor and a coward. As Brittain rightly states, a clear perception of truth, and the right of minority expression are among the first casualties of war.

Comments

Ruth Roach Pierson

One of the things that I think you are doing that is very important is exploring the dual consciousness of women. We need to look at women opposed to war and what happens to them when the war actually breaks out. I liked the distinction that you were drawing between feminine pacifism and feminist pacifism and I think that very much underscores one of the arguments that Berenice Carroll is trying to develop in her paper. And another thing that I think is very good in your paper, but which drops out of your concluding analysis of Flora MacDonald Denison, is the importance of a woman having a son who is of the age for military service when a war breaks out and what effect that can have on the consciousness of the woman. One simply can't ignore that experience and its impact. Those of you who have read Hannah Mitchell's autobiography know that Hannah Mitchell was in the fortunate position of having actually convinced her son that absolute pacifism was the right stance. During the First World War he became one of the conscientious objectors and so she was spared the agony that she could foresee, that of sending off her son to kill the sons of other mothers. But many other women were not spared that agonizing experience and I think that that must have had a tremendous impact on the consciousness of those women and on how they stood with respect to their country's involvement in that war. I think it's interesting that Virginia Woolf says that what the pacifist feminist should do is withdraw her support from brothers who are strutting about in military clothes, but she doesn't talk about sons.

Deborah Gorham

Constraints of time didn't allow me to go into it in detail in the conclusion, but when I said male relatives that's what I meant. But I think in the case of both Flora MacDonald Denison and Vera Brittain you see in different ways this link to males in terms of the physical and emotional ties. With respect to what I think of feminist pacifism in relationship to Carroll's paper, it seems to me that what a feminist pacifist would do is start from an understanding that femininity and masculinity are cultural and not biological, and say that those characteristics that we have associated with femininity, not the passive ones but the genuinely pacific ones, should be globalized. That would be a beginning, and Carroll, of course, mentions this and it seems to me that that kind of sophisticated use of the differences between femininity and masculinity could lead you to a pacifism that did say something about gender differences but that was not rooted in a sentimental view of biology.

Ursula Franklin

I would like to extend your analysis, because it doesn't need a war. A War Measures Act or a cold war will do quite well. I think we should be quite clear that our male relatives are just as much accosted by the threat system at school and at work, and, therefore, pacifism doesn't begin at the outbreak of war. So I think that the process that you show is a process that every one of us has to face and face, I'm afraid, now. As a more and more militaristic public attitude moves people to the right, so I think we have to take our position and then see how we can convince our sons, our husbands and each other that pacifism is needed now and that the problem is with us here and now. I'm afraid it is going to be worse rather than better.

Notes

[1]Sandi E. Cooper, "Women and the European Peace Movements: The Effort to Prevent World War I," in this volume, pp. 51-75.

[2]See my essay on Denison: "Flora MacDonald Denison: Canadian Feminist" in Linda Kealey, ed., A Not Unreasonable Claim: Women and Reform in Canada (Toronto: The Women's Press, 1979), pp. 47-70.

[3]The pamphlet has been reprinted in Ramsay Cook and Wendy Mitchinson, eds., The Proper Sphere (Toronto: Oxford University Press, 1976), pp. 249-52.

[4]On Beynon see Ramsay Cook, "Francis Marion Beynon and the Crisis of Christian Reformism" in Carl Berger and Ramsay Cook, eds., The West and the Nation: Essays in Honour of W. L. Morton (Toronto: McClelland and Stewart, 1976), and Barbara Roberts, "'Here I have often felt alone': Feminist-pacifist responses in Canada to the Great War, 1914-1918," paper delivered at the Canadian Historical Association meetings, Montreal, May, 1985. On pacifism in Canada during the Great War see Thomas P. Socknat, "Canada's Liberal Pacifists and the Great War," Journal of Canadian Studies 18, 4 (Winter, 1983-84): 30-44.

[5]For Denison's speeches in New York State in 1917 see the Newspaper Clipping File in the Flora MacDonald Denison papers, University of Toronto. Some of the clippings are undated, but some are dated, and clippings and correspondence with representatives of the New York State Suffrage Party reveal that Denison was working as a speaker in upstate New York in the spring, summer and fall of 1917. As an example of her anti-German rhetoric see the clipping labelled N.Y. 1917 "Scores Faint Hearts in Fight for Votes": "'Although the status of the German women was much lower than that of women in other civilized countries,' said Mrs. Denison, 'they seemed contented with their lot, and were willing to be nothing but "hausfraus" and subservient to the men. . . .The German women are to me symbolic of just what is happening in the world today. Had they been as free as the women of the United States, this cruel, unjust war could not have been launched on the world. In Germany the women are classed as animals and man is the driver,' Mrs. Denison declared."

[6]See Marie Louise Degen, The History of the Woman's Peace Party, reprinted with a new introduction for the Garland Edition by Blanche Wiesen Cook (New York: Garland Publishing, 1972), pp. 77-8. And see Socknat, "Canada's Liberal Pacifists. . .," p. 35.

[7]Most of the correspondence between Flora Denison and her son Merrill is in the Merrill Denison papers, at Queen's University. For correspondence referred to, see box 9.

[8]Nancy Huston, "Tales of War and Tears of Women," Women's Studies International Forum 5, 3/4 (1982): 271-82.

[9]Yvonne Aleksandra Bennett, "Vera Brittain and the Peace Pledge Union: Women and Peace," in this volume, pp. 192-213.

[10]Vera Brittain, Testament of Youth (New York: The Macmillan Co., 1933), p. 17.

[11]The letters and diaries are to be found in the Vera Brittain Archive, housed at McMaster University. An edited edition of the war diary, with an excellent introduction and useful explanatory notes, has been published: Chronicle of Youth: Vera Brittain's War Diary: 1913-1917, edited by Alan Bishop with Terry Smart (London: Victor Gollancz, 1981). I have dealt with Brittain's responses to the First World War at greater length than I do in this paper in "Vera Brittain and the Great War," a paper presented at the Canadian Historical Association meetings, Montreal, May, 1985.

[12]See Alan Bishop, "'With suffering and through time': Olive Schreiner, Vera Brittain and the Great War," in Malvern van Wyk Smith and Don Maclennan, eds., Olive Schreiner and After: Essays on Southern African Literature in Honour of Guy Butler (Cape Town: David Philip, 1983), pp. 881-92.

[13]Testament of Youth, pp. 291-2.

[14]James Hillman made this comment in a lecture delivered at Carleton University: "Mars and War: the Martial Imagination and the Love of War," the 1984 McMartin Memorial Lecture, September 17, 1984.

[15]Huston, "Tales of War...," p. 271.

[16]See the diary entry for August 6th, 1914.

[17]Sandra M. Gilbert, "Soldier's Heart: Literary Men, Literary Women, and the Great War," Signs: Journal of Women in Culture and Society 8, 3 (Spring, 1983): 422-50.

THE PERILS OF 'UNBRIDLED MASCULINITY': PACIFIST ELEMENTS IN THE FEMINIST AND SOCIALIST THOUGHT OF CHARLOTTE PERKINS GILMAN**

Margaret Hobbs

In 1915, as war and hatred swept across Europe, prominent American feminist Charlotte Perkins Gilman shared with readers of her magazine, *The Forerunner*, an alternative vision of society. In the world she imagined, there was no warfare, no violence, no hatred. Nor was there hierarchy, poverty, greed and jealousy. All of the nastiness apparent in patriarchal capitalist societies during war and peace was absent. There were no horrible activities. There were not even any horrible ideas! Instead, patience, beauty, health, intellect and strength were cultivated and citizens were bound to one another by an uncompromising spirit of love and cooperation. This was more than the absence of war; this was a world enjoying absolute peace and harmony.[1]

Not coincidentally, "Herland" was also a world without men. For Gilman, masculinity, warfare and domination were inextricably connected, rooted firmly in men's sex traits and fostered by a male-dominated, or in her words "androcentric," culture. It was certainly not women who declared war and sought adventure through fighting, killing and conquering, she repeatedly pointed out. Men did these things. Women were predisposed by nature to be peaceful, nurturant and constructive. It followed logically that given the chance, women would create a society free from the aggressive, competitive qualities displayed in the world men had made.

Most turn-of-the century feminists and pacifists shared Gilman's conviction that sex differences prescribed separate male and female responses to war and peace. Indeed, the glorification of women as caring and nurturing mothers provided a powerful rationale for widening the female sphere from the private to the public arena, where women's 'natural' skills as peacemakers and peacekeepers could benefit the world at large. Unfortunately, however, the "ideology of nurturant

** I would like to thank Ruth Frager, Franca Iacovetta, Janice Newton, Ruth Pierson and Joan Sangster for their comments on an early draft of this paper.

motherhood" could serve contradictory ends. Feminists and anti-feminists, pacifists and those believing in either the necessity or inevitability of war, often huddled awkwardly beneath the same ideological umbrella. A recent analysis, for example, of two politically antagonistic groups during World War I--the Woman's Peace Party and the Woman's Section of the Navy League--has demonstrated how the premise and much of the imagery associated with the motherhood ideology were adopted by women who were in complete disagreement about its implications for women's role in the war.[2]

In spite of such inconsistencies and ambiguities, the stereotypes of men as inherently aggressive and women as innately peaceful have proven stubbornly appealing to several generations of peace advocates. Granted there have always been critics, such as Rebecca West, who in 1917 dismissed this line of argument as a useless form of "woman worship," and Mary Beard, who in 1946 called it naive and historically inaccurate.[3] But the fact remains that the idealization of motherhood, combined with assumptions of biological sexual differences, provided the emotional and theoretical core underlying most women's mobilization for peace in North America and Europe during the nineteenth and early twentieth centuries. And if feminist pacifists today are more wary of arguments steeped in biological determinism,[4] we are nonetheless still influenced by these early attempts to mobilize women and explain their unique potential as advocates of peace.

This essay explores the development of Charlotte Perkins Gilman's understanding of the relation of sex and gender to war and peace, and goes on to consider her response to the grim reality of World War I. Gilman is usually remembered not as a pacifist, but as one of America's most influential and witty feminist and socialist thinkers. Unlike her friend Jane Addams and many other female reformers, she was never a key activist in the various peace 'movements' of her day. Nor did any of her books focus exclusively, or even primarily, on war and peace. Nevertheless, Gilman's writings reflect a serious attempt to come to terms with the nature and origins of militarism and the meaning of peace. As a writer and lecturer of immense popularity from the late 1890s to the end of the war, her ideas helped mold the thought of a great many early social activitists.

Gilman's views on war and peace found a natural home in her assessment of male/female differences and her critique of patriarchy. More so than most reform-minded Americans, she characteristically emphasized the interconnectedness of issues. Indeed, her broad, web-like approach partly explains her reluctance to become too closely involved with any of the organizations whose cause she endorsed--the notable exception being her commitment, from 1890-1892, to the Bellamy-inspired nationalist socialist clubs in California. Despite this active work for Nationalism, Gilman was always more of a theorist than a political activist. It is therefore within the context of her development as a feminist and socialist theorist that her construction of a pacifist philosophy must be located and her reaction to World War I examined.

(i)

Born in 1860 into a long line of reformers and rebels, including Harriet Beecher Stowe, Catherine Beecher and Isabella Beecher Hooker, Gilman grew up amidst some powerful and unconventional female role models. Early on, as she struggled to reconcile her own varied, often contradictory needs, desires and ambitions with society's expectations of her, it became evident that her privately brewing turmoil would eventually spill over into the public arena. Like most feminists before and after her time, Gilman's emerging intellectual critique was informed at every stage by her personal experiences. But also like most feminists, she was not always consistent. Perhaps nowhere were the contradictions more apparent than when she tackled the question of sex and gender. Notions of male/female differences would always be problematic for Gilman--either personally, theoretically, or strategically--yet they formed the essential underpinnings of her particular brand of feminism, pacifism and socialism.

As a girl, Gilman generally accepted the prevailing Victorian polarization of male and female natures and roles; the problem was, her nature seemed neither exclusively feminine nor entirely masculine. Elements of both, she complained, waged a constant battle for supremacy, causing her endless anxiety. The young Gilman assumed that ultimately she would have to choose either to marry and live a domestic life or to pursue a career and involvement in the affairs of the world.[5] Of the two options, the latter seemed eminently more appealing. Marriage she viewed with a suspicion sometimes verging on horror, a reaction stemming in part from her more intimate bonding experiences with the female than the male sex,[6] but also from her observation that women gained little and lost much in marriage. Her own mother's experience was far from the romantic ideal. Having given up a promising talent in music to marry, Mary Perkins was abandoned by the husband she adored when Charlotte was still a child. She therefore raised her two children without the mythical male protector and provider, and without the comforts of a middle-class family home. Gilman's father, Frederick Perkins, a librarian and writer, sent the family money in dribs and drabs, if at all, and mounting debts forced his family into nineteen moves in eighteen years. Gilman later described her mother's life as "one of the most painfully thwarted I have ever known."[7] In contrast, her father enjoyed an emotional and intellectual freedom that Gilman found compelling. While resentful of his obviously greater commitment to books than to family, she grew to admire him. Impatient with the strictures of traditional womanhood, she sometimes exhibited an almost scornful attitude toward her own sex, despite her loving attachment to a young woman, Martha Luther. Before her twenty-first birthday she renounced her 'femininity' which, according to her biographer Mary Hill, "suggested her mother's dependence and vulnerability. Masculinity--meaning creativity, strength, her father's more worldly style of life--was the model she had chosen for herself."[8]

The problem, however, was not so simply resolved. Throughout her life Gilman would struggle with the tensions between 'masculinity' and 'femininity,' emotional need and independence, rebelliousness and convention, loving women and loving men. Shortly after losing Martha to a male suitor, a dejected Gilman swallowed her worst apprehensions and consented to marry Walter Stetson, a painter. The marriage turned out disastrously. She bore one child, attempted to content herself with motherhood and domesticity, but instead collapsed with a nervous breakdown. Gilman reclaimed her sanity by resisting Dr. S. Weir Mitchell's prescribed treatment for female "hysteria,"[9] leaving her husband and daughter, and plunging headlong into a writing and lecturing career. At age 40, she would again marry, this time with better results, but beforehand there was another love relationship with a woman.[10]

Painful though much of Gilman's past had been, her experiences acted as an important catalyst for her emotional and intellectual growth. After leaving Stetson and their daughter, Gilman increasingly began to identify her own difficulties with those of other women. Alongside a developing understanding of women's oppression emerged a more generous attitude towards women and a new faith in the potential of the female sex.[11] Her contact over the years with the California woman's movement and nationalist clubs, with British and American fabian socialists, and with the writings of several reform Darwinists-- most notably Lester Frank Ward, Patrick Geddes and J. Arthur Thomson--powerfully shaped her thought.

With the 1898 publication of her most famous book, *Women and Economics*, Gilman's matured ideas about sex and gender were widely read, exciting feminists and many socialists as well. Gilman would certainly never lose sight of the importance of sex differences, but she also wanted to emphasize the similarities between human males and females. "In our steady insistence on proclaiming sex-distinction," she argued, "we have grown to consider most human attributes as masculine attributes, for the simple reason that they were allowed to men and forbidden to women."[12] Gilman would continue to hammer home this crucial point in her later books, articles and lectures. Woman has always held "the place of a preposition in relation to man," she asserted:

> She has been considered above him or below him, before him, behind him, beside him, a wholly relative existence--"Sidney's sister," "Pembroke's mother"--but never by any chance Sydney or Pembroke herself.

Acting on this assumption, all human standards have been
based on male characteristics, and when we wish to praise the
work of a woman, we say she has "a masculine mind."[13]

Angered that women's lives had been so narrowly prescribed by
faulty reasoning, Gilman advanced an alternative interpretation of sex
differences and similarities which assured women of their right, indeed
their duty, to full participation in the world beyond the home. As she
explained in a 1914 *Forerunner* article, the human and animal kingdom
displayed what she identified as "race," "physiological" and "sex"
qualities. These she sometimes encouraged people to visualize as
segments of a circle. By far the largest portion of the circle was occupied
by race qualities that differed only between species. A very small
section represented physiological qualities, such as circulation,
respiration and digestion, "common to both sexes and to most species."
Another tiny slice represented sex qualities. These were either male or
female and were constant instincts apparent in *all* species in all
historical time periods.[14]

Gilman always found it easy to isolate the male sex qualities. The
strongest was desire; next was combat, which, through continual
exercise, males had incorrectly assumed to be "the major process in life";
finally, there was self-expression.[15] Gilman bolstered her case for the
masculine instincts of combat and self-expression with unmistakable
borrowing from Geddes and Thomson's ideas as expressed in *The
Evolution of Sex*, published in the US in 1890. In particular, Gilman
reasoned that self-expression, visible in the "proud bellowings of the
conquering stag as he trampled on his prostrate rival," was "inherently
and ineradicably masculine."

It rests on that most basic of distinctions between the sexes,
the centripetal and centrifugal forces of the universe. In the
very nature of the sperm-cell and the germ-cell we find this
difference: the one attracts, gathers, draws in; the other
repels, scatters, pushes out. The projective impulse is seen in
the male nature everywhere, the constant urge toward
expression, to all boasting and display.[16]

It proved more difficult for Gilman to identify the female sex
instincts. Usually she claimed that the female in all species shared
maternal qualities, such as "love, care, service, an active altruism."[17] In
Herland--the work in which Gilman dreamed most freely of the world
women might create were it not for masculine interference--these
motherhood qualities provided the foundation upon which all social
relations and all progress were built. Here was mothering at its
creative best.

There were problems, though, with Gilman's equation of
'femininity' with maternal impulses. First of all, she was often vague
about which of the qualities that society associated with motherhood

153

were sex instincts and which were culturally developed characteristics. More importantly, her sex instincts theory was fundamentally at odds with her frequently stinging critique of contemporary motherhood practices. Sometimes Gilman suggested that human females possessed only "rudimentary" maternal instincts, inherited from their most primitive ancestors. These instincts, she argued, had not kept up with social progress[18] (a fact which presumably explained why American motherhood bore so little resemblance to its counterpart in *Herland*). At other times, however, Gilman denied altogether the existence of maternal instincts in human females: the only real instincts for humans are "social instincts--and maternity is not a social process." All this talk of mother "instincts" was no more than sentimental idealism, she maintained in *The Home*, published in 1903. After all, she jibed:

> *Who*, in the name of all common sense, raises our huge and growing crop of idiots, imbeciles, cripples, defectives, and degenerates, the vicious and the criminal; as well as all the vast mass of slow-minded, prejudiced, ordinary people who clog the wheels of progress.[19]

These were strong words, especially coming from one whose case for world improvement hinged so crucially on the mothering potential of women.

Gilman's cleverest maneuvering could not possibly reconcile the basic inconsistencies in her handling of female sex traits. Aware of this problem, she admitted at least once to avoiding the specifics of the issue.[20] Although certainly unwilling to abandon the motherhood theory and imagery, she was uneasy about stressing women's special mothering instincts. Contradictions aside, she was likely also concerned because a maternal argument could inadvertently strengthen the case for the domestic imprisonment of women. By saying that female instincts (whatever their precise nature) could not alone ensure the proper care of children, Gilman found one way around the implication that women's lives should necessarily be devoted to privatized child care. The tasks of child rearing and education, she reasoned, were of such importance to the progress of society that they should actually be the exclusive responsibility of highly qualified specialists. Gilman always insisted that for humans, biological, professional and social motherhood should be independent functions. While she assumed all women wanted to and should give birth (unless they were physically, mentally, or morally "unfit"), only properly trained women were to attend to "the specific tasks of child rearing."[21] The category of social motherhood, however, pertained to all women in the form of an obligation to extend maternal care to the larger society.

Gilman firmly believed that the true purpose of "sex distinction" lay in its facilitation of sexual attraction and hence reproduction. It followed that sex instincts should be only barely visible, if at all, before adolescence. Boys would always "be more given to fighting and destroying" and girls "to caring for and constructing things," but childhood was properly a stage in which gentleness and calm, as well as "vigor and courage," were shared characteristics. Children, however, were rigidly socialized from birth according to sex. Boys learned to over-exercise their sex traits, but they were also encouraged to develop their "human" traits. Girls, on the other hand, were only permitted to cultivate their femininity. At bottom the problem was an economic one. "Because of the economic dependence of the human female on her mate," she argued, young women had a vested interest in developing and displaying their sexual distinctiveness, or femininity, to help attract a man and thereby earn a living. Forced to package and sell their bodies in order to eat, it was no wonder they were "over-sexed."[22]

Gilman's impatience with the "over-sexed" condition of women and with the "stunted" development of their "human" qualities was reminiscent of her girlhood disdain for femininity. But in fact she had acquired much greater respect for 'femininity' than 'masculinity.' "As a matter of sex," she wrote, "the female is the more important. Her share of the process which sex distinction serves is by far greater. To be feminine--if one were nothing else, is a far more extensive and dignified office than to be masculine--and nothing else." Perhaps anxious about appearing 'anti-male,' she often assured readers that she did not think maleness was all bad and femaleness all good. Rather, all sex instincts were right in their "proper place." But how could one wax enthusiastic for the masculine instincts of desire, combat and self-expression? Surely female maternalism, no matter how primitive and inadequate an instinct, was "more nearly in line with human progress" than were masculine sex instincts. Besides, male instincts were only "of a preliminary nature, leading merely to the union preceding parentage." Female instincts were broader in scope, more lasting and constructive in effect.[23]

In Gilman's assertions of female superiority and in much of her analysis of sex differences, the voice of her mentor Lester Ward was clearly echoed. Ward's gynaecocentric theory proved popular among feminists, not least of all because, as one historian observes, it offered scientific 'proof' of "how transient men really were, how dispensable, how second-rate."[24] Nature, Ward claimed, had designated the female sex as primary and the male as secondary. As Gilman put it in the sequel to *Herland*: "No one can study biology and sociology much and not see that on the first physiological lines the female is the whole show, so to speak, or at least most of it."[25] True, the male had managed to appropriate the superior, dominant position, but this was only a temporary reversal of the natural order. The female sex was destined to regain her rightful place in the world. Gilman was determined to help fulfill this prophecy, through writing, lecturing and thereby changing people's minds, especially the minds of women.

(ii)

Gilman's understanding of the nature of male-female distinctions made her fearful of the effects of male dominance on the world at large. Men had undoubtedly done much to advance civilization, she conceded; indeed, what progress had occurred was largely their achievement. Locked within their isolated dwellings and 'over indulging' their feminine qualities, women played little part in social development. But without the balancing influence of women to carry out "world work," industrial capitalist society was suffering deep, festering wounds that were the direct result of excessive masculinity:

> Being men, and men alone, they cannot restrain their masculinity. Unbridled masculinity means the kind of civilization we have so far produced; great and noble as it is, it is weakened by gross over-indulgence in food, in drink, in drugs; by vices that make crimes; by a rapacious and competitive business system that maintains poverty and injurious over-localized wealth; and by this fury of combat that vents itself in youth-destroying games; that crackles continuously in quarrels, prize-fights and murders; that bursts forth, over and over, in riot of open war.
> It is not humanity which does this; it is masculinity.[26]

War was nothing less than this "unbridled masculinity" at its "absurdest extremes." "Maleness means war," Gilman asserted in no uncertain terms.[27] Long before males fought for the possession of property, she explained, they fought for the possession of females. At this early evolutionary stage combat served a positive purpose, for in weeding out the physically weak it ensured the survival of the fittest and hence the improvement of the species. No such logic could legitimate warfare today, but because "men have carried over the combative instinct of a pre-social, polygamous period into a social and monogamous period, they continually kill one another."[28] Reflecting the prevailing turn-of-the-century concern with eugenics, Gilman pointed to the tragic irony that, instead of eliminating the unfit, modern warfare only "eliminates the fit, and leaves the unfit to perpetuate the race!" Armies, after all, were composed of the healthiest, most vigorous young men. While they were sent off to be slaughtered, who was left behind to father the next generation and determine the future quality of the race? Only the old, the very young, the sick, the cripples and "defectives."[29] Where was the sense in this, she wondered? Not only did combat weaken and kill soldiers and ultimately lower the racial standards of nations, it also decreased the birth rate and destroyed "the fruits of industry and progress." Furthermore, the culture of war fostered the growth of many negative mental attitudes, such as "Deceit, trickery, lying, every kind of skulking underhand effort to get information," competition, destruction, cruelty, and blind obedience to authority.[30]

Gilman knew how easily these harsh realities could be obscured in a male-dominated, or "androcentric," culture. History, literature and even religion were all saturated with the romantic glorification of military ideals in general and of the soldier in particular.[31] Interestingly enough, however, she did not always see through the facade as clearly as she claimed. Sometimes she too seemed to glorify militarism, or at least certain aspects of it. It seemed to her that the army was a cohesive unit that successfully inspired in its membership a spirit of cooperation, selflessness, group loyalty and total devotion. These qualities were central to Gilman's socialist ideals. A vehement anti-Marxist, her socialism most closely resembled that of the nationalist clubs that had mushroomed in the wake of the 1888 publication of Edward Bellamy's classic utopian novel, *Looking Backward*. "My Socialism was of the early humanitarian kind," she explained in her autobiography, "based on the first exponents, French and English, with the American enthusiasm of Bellamy. The narrow and rigid 'economic determinism' of Marx, with its 'class consciousness' and 'class struggle' I never accepted, nor the political methods pursued by Marxians."[32] The very language of class warfare was repugnant, smacking as it did of "masculinism." As far as this self-identified socialist was concerned, Marx had given socialism a bad name. For Gilman the major social and economic divisions in society were based on sex, not class. It was not the working class but women who she insisted were overdue for rebellion. And the nature of that rebellion would be peaceful and democratic.

In Bellamy's utopia the army was upheld as a working socialist model, promising economic independence for women together with the socialization of both domestic and industrial production. Gilman would never promote a rigid, militarist ideal to the extent that Bellamy did, but she was captivated by the new world he imagined could flourish within this structure. Even though Gilman was committed to a democratic revolution (she actually preferred the term evolution) she sometimes sanctioned the existence of a political body with coercive powers, to be aimed at individuals who would not, or could not, be made to conform to the expectations of the new social order. It is in "Moving the Mountain," Gilman's first utopian novel, that her authoritarian tendencies and eugenicist convictions make their most glaring appearance. Written in 1911, the story is set in America in 1940, twenty years after the citizens have opted for a socialist and "humanist" political, economic and social system. The otherwise impressive new society contains several shocking features: all new immigrants are put through a "Compulsory Socialization" process; biological parentage is denied to those deemed physically, mentally, or morally unsuitable, and before a woman is allowed to care for her children she must obtain the approval of the "Department of Child Culture." Criminals, "perverts," the insane, "hopeless degenerates" and prostitutes are almost always "cured" and then forgiven; but in the most stubborn cases, we are told that officials have been forced to "amputate." As one citizen explains with remarkable glibness: "If you're sick, you're sick--we'll cure it if possible. If not, you'll die--never mind, we all die--that's nothing."[33]

Though critical of the blind obedience with which soldiers submitted to military authority, Gilman's ideal citizens of the future displayed a similar willingness to subordinate their individual interests to those of the community. "The army," she observed, "very highly developed in a very low scheme of action, knows that neither self nor family must stand for a moment against the public service."[34] To Gilman there was great nobility in this sentiment, even though soldiers were hardly performing a useful public service by killing people. American society, bent on the individualistic, competitive ethos of industrial capitalism, could learn something from the military. In one of her short stories, called "An Unnatural Mother," she transferred the selfless group identity she associated with the soldier to a mother who risked her child's life and lost her own while attempting to save the whole community from a disastrous flood. Here was Gilman's conception of social motherhood in action. This mother would have sacrificed her one child to save all the others. Surely this was the correct moral choice; yet this brave woman was denounced by her neighbours as a heartless, "unnatural" mother.[35] Gilman believed that all citizens should emulate this unconditional devotion to community before family or self. She dreamed, however, that, unlike soldiers, who were manipulated into believing in destruction, the men and women of the future would act in accordance with a wise, agreed upon understanding of the nature of human progress.

The tragic irony of modern warfare was that it fostered honourable, even revolutionary, ideals of brotherhood in men who only wasted them on a process of mass destruction. The explanation was always apparent: male sex instincts. For Gilman herself, life was growth; for men, however, she believed that life--at least the main event of it--was combat. Thus for all her tendencies to glorify soldiers, at heart she felt they were "only men, a lot of men all being foolish together; wasting every good thing with both hands."[36]

(iii)

The outbreak of war in the late summer of 1914 found almost all American feminists pacifist in theory. Indeed, in the pre-war decade not just peace movement activists, but women in a wide array of reform organizations--like the National Council of Women, the Federation of Women's Clubs and the Women's Christian Temperance Union-- endorsed the cause of world peace.[37] The vast majority of these women premised their pacifism on the belief that women, being "free from aggressive instincts," could guarantee an end to military conflict if granted a larger public role at the national and international levels.[38] In this period, when the imminent threat of world war was anticipated by few, if any, North Americans, "peace was one of the most conventional of values."[39] So universally accepted was this ideal that it facilitated loose alliances between certain liberal feminists and Marxist socialist-feminists espousing pacifism. More than two years after Europe went to war, it seems that most Americans were relieved by President Wilson's policy of neutrality.[40]

The climate of opinion, however, would quickly change after Wilson announced America's entry into the conflict in April 1917. Almost overnight, nationalist sentiment rose to near hysterical heights and pacifism became a treasonous concept. The war rapidly became a convenient excuse for right-wing and racist assaults on pacifists, socialists, labour activists and immigrants.[41] Amidst such high-pitched emotion, the chorus of varied female voices so recently raised in unison against militarism was hushed. Among the female reform groups, all but the most radical branch of the Woman's Peace Party (led by Crystal Eastman in New York) supported the war effort to some extent.[42] Even the pioneer peace activist, Jane Addams, violated her principles by working for Herbert Hoover's Food Administration and also by allowing her settlement house to be used as a war registration centre.[43] Socialists too were divided by the war issue. While some leading party members were swept up in wartime patriotism, the American Socialist Party itself remained actively opposed to the war as a capitalist venture benefitting the captains of industry at the expense of the working class.[44]

Gilman's stand on the war was much closer to that of many feminist reformers than it was to the Socialist Party position. This was hardly surprising, given her scorn for the party's Marxist ideology. The October revolution in Russia, so inspiring to many socialists, only fueled her indignation and she attacked it in an outburst of anti-Semitism as "the Jewish-Russian nightmare."[45] As the war in Europe dragged on, Gilman attempted to forge her own identity as a pacifist. While she continued to articulate her theoretical understanding of war and peace as related to sex instincts and an androcentric culture, she had to clarify her ideas about pacifism and choose a political position on the war issue. It was 1916 before Gilman formally declared herself a pacifist and defined her meaning in *The Forerunner*:

> I am a pacifist, of settled conviction, meaning by that first the recognition that a condition of peace is a primary essential to all human growth, and that war is an absolute injury to that growth; further, in holding that this war should be stopped now--should have been stopped as soon as it began--yes, and before it began; still further, and most strongly, in seeing the immediate practical necessity for the beginnings of world-federation.[46]

Well aware of the ambiguity of the label 'pacifist,' Gilman drew attention to the disagreements among pacifists on a variety of fundamental questions. She made it clear that her pacifism did not entail a commitment to passive non-violence. "One may be an extremely peaceful citizen, quite gunless and knifeless, yet fight valiantly if it becomes necessary." She stressed that there "ought to be an extremely clear distinction made between Pacifism and Non-Resistance."[47] Even before the war, she had attacked non-resistance as "a sentimental negation" and a "pathetically useless attitude." Many people, she argued in 1911, had misinterpreted biblical teaching as promoting non-resistance. The scriptural advice to "'Love your enemies, do good unto them that hate you, and serve them that despitefully use you and persecute you'" actually was a directive to 'be active, direct and concrete.' As Gilman wrote: "'Love!' Love is not non-resistance. 'Do good!' Doing good is not non-resistance. 'Serve!' Service is not non-resistance."[48]

Throughout the war years Gilman maintained that fighting, even killing, was sometimes justified by necessity. In *Herland*, for example, written in 1915, Gilman recounted the origins of her all-female society, explaining that after warfare and a natural disaster eliminated most of the men, the few remaining ones killed all but the youngest women, whom they planned to master. The girls immediately rose up and killed their would-be masters, instead of submitting passively. Years later, in an unpublished detective story called "Unpunished," Gilman more pointedly asserted the moral righteousness of murder under certain defensive circumstances. Here she created a male character, Wade Vaughn, who was so despicably heinous behind his spotless public facade that a great many people wanted to kill him, several tried, and one actually succeeded. Vaughn is revealed to have been a nefarious blackmailer who had enslaved and tormented his wife, his sister-in-law and the two women's children. To avenge the eventual suicide of her sister and liberate the children and herself, the tyrant's sister-in-law had carefully plotted and carried out his murder. The murderer, however, was found innocent and it is evident that Gilman believed justice was achieved through the act of violence. With the notable exception of her 1911 story, "Moving the Mountain," in which Gilman sanctioned the killing of social "undesirables" by the state, she generally only regarded defensive murder as a potentially moral act. Moreover, in both *Herland* and "Unpunished" it is instructive that the killers were women, fighting off male oppressors.[49]

Gilman never actually pronounced the violence of World War I necessary or just, although she certainly came close. In the early years she argued strongly for US intervention in the conflict as a mediator, not a combatant. If she had qualms about the Allies' methods, though, she definitely sided with their cause, for as the war raged on Gilman added her voice to the increasing number of others hurling insults at Germany. While applauding some aspects of German social development, she lamented the "criminal" tendencies of the German people along with their spineless aquiescence to the ideas thrust upon them by their evil, lying leaders. Germany was a "Frankenstein among the nations," "an ultra-masculine culture, in a male world, finding natural associates among the Mohamedans, with their theory of glorified war and subject womanhood."[50] Not surprisingly, given the extent of her hostility, Gilman regarded those Germans in the US who had not applied for American citizenship with a suspicion sometimes amounting to paranoia. "Are they tourists? Visitors? Or invaders?", she asked *Forerunner* readers in 1916.[51]

Gilman's attitude towards activists in the peace 'movement' was ambivalent. Sometimes she expressed great admiration for the work they were doing, praising in particular their persistence in spite of public hostility and abuse. She never, however, rallied to support Socialist Party members and others who were jailed for their anti-war propaganda. Her sympathies were more naturally extended to reformers working for peace without blatantly agitating against the war effort. Gilman herself had accepted a charter membership in the national Woman's Peace Party at its inaugural meeting in January 1915.[52] But even this organizational network did not really rouse her enthusiasm. For instance, when Gilman's fictional character Van returned to the United States with his Herland wife and asked whether she was not pleased to see women working in the peace movement, Ellador responded casually:

> Oh, that? Talking for peace, you mean, and writing and telegraphing. Yes, that's useful too. Anything that brings women out into social relation, into a sense of social responsibility, is good. But all that they say and write and urge will not count as much as what they *do*.[53]

Ellador's almost disinterested attitude reflects Gilman's belief that ultimately war could not be eliminated by fighting or by talking and letter-writing. Gilman insisted that the question of how to stop *this* war was separate from the one of how to prevent *all* wars and ensure world peace,[54] although in practice she often amalgamated the two. When offering advice on how World War I could be stopped, she tended to focus on the role the US could play as an outside mediator between the warring nations. The American government's reluctance to intervene angered her greatly and she wrote scathing attacks on its cowardice and irresponsibility in the *Forerunner*.[55] Beyond her faith in the united ability of the outside nations to come to some agreement, some compromise, that would appease the combatants, she had few concrete suggestions to make.

Instead, she frequently slipped into what for her was the more comfortable and important question of how future wars could be prevented and peace maintained. Here Gilman was in her element, but her ideas were not necessarily original. Echoing the sentiments of Addams, Eastman and many others, she called for a "Federal Alliance of All States," a "High World-Court" that would decide international disputes, "A Strong World Force" that would back the decisions of the World Court, and "a New World-Law" to which all citizens of all nations would be bound.[56] These measures, and the world identity which underlay them, could prevent all wars from beginning. Increasingly, as individuals further developed the spirit of love, brotherhood and service, the role of such formal structures would be minimized. Ideally, nations and individuals would soon naturally live in harmony, cooperating to advance their mutual interests and the progress of the human race.

Gilman already saw promising signs of this new world spirit. Ironically, the war itself was acting as a catalyst in its growth. Hence Ellador, for whom bloodshed was unthinkable, could regard the European struggle philosophically, even positively: "What is one more [war] among so many? . . . The very awfulness of this is its best hope; that, and the growing wisdom of the people."[57] Through this war, Gilman maintained, the world was becoming "conscious": "We had thought we were but nations; now we know we are a World."[58]

Most of all, however, Gilman took heart in the signs that women were slowly gaining political power and economic independence from men. It was obvious to her that war could not be prevented and peace maintained until women were economically and socially freed from male domination and exercising their collective power in the public sphere.[59] Convinced that women's nature, their "sex instincts," made them the logical and inevitable leaders in the process leading to permanent world peace, Gilman put forth numerous proposals to prepare women for their duty. The main roadblock lay in the fact that women, having been isolated for so long in the home, were lacking in a *"sense of collectivity."* It was therefore imperative that each town form a Women's Mutual Service League committed to the goal of improving the economic, educational, social and political conditions of women. Linked together by a national federation, the Leagues could begin modestly as employment agencies and training schools for women of all classes. Women would finally begin to share their common suffering; they would "join hands and learn to help one another." As funds increased, through various initiatives by the members, the Leagues would expand to include a good club house, with a reading room, a lecture hall, evening classes and invited lectures. Soon they could boast day nurseries and kindergartens, dressmaking establishments as well as all other lines of work. "Group-houses" would be built for single women and a hot food delivery service, intended especially for married women, would ease the domestic burden.[60] Eventually, homes would be 'kitchenless' and housework would be performed by outside professionals, paid a much better salary than that presently earned by domestic servants.[61]

Through such methods women's citizenship would slowly be raised to new heights. A new womanhood would emerge and this would mean a new motherhood. "And these New Mothers will say":

We are tired of men's wars. We are tired of men's quarrels.
We are tired of men's competition. We are tired of men's
crimes and vices and the diseases they bring upon us, of this
whole world full of noise, confusion, enmity and bloodshed.[62]

Women would then limit the population and "marry only clean men, fit
to be fathers." They would not teach their children the glories of war,
but rather would instruct them in "the advantages of union, association,
interchange."[63]

When women were finally free, Gilman was certain they would
never settle for military peace alone. Women wanted economic, social,
industrial and political peace as well. Peace, if considered merely as the
absence of war, was not enough. It was only "an armistice" between
wars: "'In time of peace,' we say, 'Prepare for War!' We do. And, thus
prepared--we fight again."[64] The opposite of war, Gilman observed, is
not peace, but love, since "War means Hate, and the opposite of Hate is
Love."[65] Through the power of love, women would create a new world.
There would be no more war, no more violence, no more domination, no
more poverty. Men and women would experience together a world in a
true and total state of harmony.

Many radicals and socialists did not think that Gilman's vision of
a world in peace went far enough, especially since it dismissed class
struggle and was inconsistent about the future of capitalism in the
cooperative society she dreamed of. While she often spoke as if women
would lead the world to a totally egalitarian state, at other times it was
evident that she hoped for something less--a reformed, "benevolent
capitalism."[66] Moreover, some, like Emma Goldman, found Gilman's
exuberant faith in the liberating potential of a career for all women
naive, in light of the fact that most women's jobs were not only poorly
paid, but dreary.[67]

These criticisms notwithstanding, the world that Gilman hoped
could emerge from the ashes of the European conflict was, in fact, a
dramatically altered one. Her buoyant optimism about the future, if not
the specifics of her vision, was typical of most wartime feminists,
reformers, socialists and labour advocates. Unfortunately, the post-war
world did not bear out the promises of politicians or the prophecies of
progressives and radicals. Gilman shared in the widespread post-war
mood of disillusionment. She felt most disappointed in women,
especially the younger generation who, she thought, had replaced her
ideal of a higher morality and selfless social service with loose morals
and individual self-interest. In her autobiography she noted that the
war had heightened her sense of the differences between races. The
war, she felt, had brought out the "true colours" of nations. After
pronouncing Germany pathologically insane and grossly masculinized,
Gilman evidently turned a scrutinous eye on other nations and races.
Believing her own work had glossed over the question of racial
distinction, she insisted in her autobiography that any future theories of
social evolution would have to take race differences into serious

account.[68] Several of Gilman's friends and supporters were startled and either disappointed or annoyed by Gilman's wartime attitudes, especially her racist assaults on Germany which, they observed, contradicted her former emphasis on the unity of the human race.[69] Despite her past criticism of parochial nationalism and her appeal for a "world identity," during the war and its aftermath Gilman leaned perilously close to an attitude of bigotted patriotism.

Conclusion

Charlotte Perkins Gilman was one among many turn-of-the century women whose pacifist beliefs were premised on assumptions of biological sexual differences which relieved women of "war guilt" and regarded warfare as a natural outgrowth of "unbridled masculinity." While she respected some peace movement activists, Gilman herself was always more of a theorist than a political activist; she was always more comfortable delivering her message in conference halls, club rooms and living rooms, rather than on street corners and picket lines. It was through her theoretical writing and lecturing that she felt most politically useful. Gilman's reliance on biological explanations of male and female natures was problematic and often contradictory. And the authoritarian and racist elements which crept into her utopian writing is certainly disturbing. Nevertheless, drawing on the writings of several reform Darwinists, as well as on her personal and political understanding of patriarchy, Gilman worked out a theory of men's and women's relation to war and peace that influenced the views of feminists, pacifists and many socialists too. Despite her earlier preference for 'masculinity' over 'femininity,' she developed a sympathetic, yet still often critical, understanding of women and their oppression, and placed her hope for the future of humanity largely in women's hands. Guided by the instincts of their sex, women, Gilman believed, could arouse the world to new standards of progress, new ideals of love and mutual aid. Aiming her message primarily, though not exclusively, at women, she sought to awaken women to their social obligation to pave the way to a socialist, "humanist" world. Men, with their instincts of desire, combat and self-expression, were certainly not up to the task. Besides, they had had their chance and had failed.

Upon the outbreak of World War I, Gilman marshalled her theories about sex and gender, applying them more pointedly to the issues of war and peace. To her, the horror of the European conflict confirmed her dual fear of male sex instincts and an androcentric culture. The need for women's social mothering, she thought, was glaringly apparent. Like most feminists and reformers, Gilman would not adopt a position of 'absolute pacifism' during the war. Instead, she fired her pen at Germany and worked out a pacifist philosophy that could accommodate the necessity and moral righteousness of defensive combat. She never wanted America to feed its men into the struggle, putting her faith instead in the potential role of the US as an outside mediator in the conflict. Since America was not overtly threatened by the war, Gilman could not accept the waste of human resources resulting from Wilson's decision in 1917 to send American men overseas. But her verbal and written attacks on the German nation amounted to a kind of warfare and legitimized the Allies' cause.

Gilman did not seem to be aware of the extent to which her denunciation of the German race as insane, corrupt and masculinist betrayed her insistence on the biological sameness of the human race (except for male and female differences). Nor did she feel she was compromising her ideal of the unity of all nations under a common identity, a world nationalism. She still held to her former theories, but by the twenties she claimed to have a new understanding of the crucial differences between races, not just between the sexes. By the twenties too, Gilman had grown disillusioned with women, who seemed to have let their opportunity for and duty to social service slip through their hands. But cheered somewhat by evidence of increased female participation in the labour market, Gilman, by then in her sixties, did not let go of her faith in the international rising of women. The process would clearly take longer than she had anticipated a decade earlier. But when women finally gained their economic independence from men and unleashed their motherly energies upon the world at large, warfare would gradually become obsolete and society would function as a single, unified whole with neither nations nor individuals seeking their own advantage at the expense of the larger community. Only then, Gilman believed, could we say we lived in a world at peace.

Notes

[1]Charlotte Perkins Gilman, Herland (New York: Pantheon, 1979). Originally serialized in The Forerunner 6 (1915).

[2]See Barbara J. Steinson, "'The Mother Half of Humanity': American Women in the Peace and Preparedness Movements in World War I," in Carol R. Berkin and Clara M. Lovett, eds., Women, War and Revolution (New York: Holmes and Meier, 1980), pp. 259-81.

[3]Rebecca West, "Woman Worship," in Jane Marcus, ed., The Young Rebecca: Writings of Rebecca West 1911-1917 (London: Macmillan London Ltd., 1982), pp. 338-40; Mary Ritter Beard, Woman as Force in History, (New York: Collier, 1962), pp. 48-56, 287-95.

[4]See Berenice Carroll, "Feminism and Pacifism: Historical and Theoretical Connections," in this volume, pp. 2-28.

[5]In her biography of Gilman, Mary Hill sensitively and perceptively explores this dilemma in much greater depth than is provided here. See Mary Hill, Charlotte Perkins Gilman: The Making of a Radical Feminist, 1860-1896 (Philadelphia: Temple University Press, 1980).

[6]During girlhood and early womanhood Charlotte's most intimate bonds were with her mother and her friend Martha Luther. Her relationship with her mother was fraught with conflict, but there were times when the two were very close, especially, as Mary Hill argues, after Charlotte's father deserted the family. On these two relationships see Hill, and also Gilman's autobiography, The Living of Charlotte Perkins Gilman (New York: Arno Press, 1972; originally published New York: Appleton-Century, 1935).

[7]Gilman, The Living, p. 8.

[8]Hill, p. 61.

[9]For a fictionalized account of a woman's descent into madness based loosely on Gilman's own experience as she underwent Dr. S. Weir Mitchell's famous "rest cure" for "hysterical" women, see Charlotte Perkins Gilman, The Yellow Wallpaper, with an Introduction and Afterword by Elaine R. Hedges (Old Westbury, New York: The Feminist Press, 1973).

[10]For an account of Gilman's relationship with this woman, Adeline Knapp, see Hill, pp. 189-207.

[11]Ibid., pp. 188-9.

[12]Charlotte Perkins Gilman, Women and Economics, edited by Carl Degler (New York: Harper & Row, 1966; originally published Boston: Small, Maynard and Co., 1898), p. 51.

[13]Charlotte Perkins Gilman, The Man-Made World or, Our Androcentric Culture (New York: Charlton, 1911), pp. 20-1.

[14]"What Are 'Feminine' Qualities," Forerunner 5 (1914): 233.

[15]Gilman, The Man-Made World, pp. 28, 99, 138-40, 151.

[16]Ibid., pp. 212, 78-9. Also see p. 114. Geddes had developed a theory of sex differences based on cell metabolism. Male cells, he argued, dissipated energy; thus males were naturally aggressive. In contrast, female cells conserved energy, a function which inclined women to passivity and nurturance. On Geddes see Jill Conway, "Stereotypes of Femininity in a Theory of Sexual Evolution," in Martha Vicinus, ed., Suffer and Be Still: Women in the Victorian Age (London: Methuen, 1980). It is notable that Conway suggests Geddes' influence waned after the advent of endocrinology in 1903, which made his theories seem outmoded; yet this Geddes-like analysis was written as late as 1909-10. The Man-Made World was initially serialized by Gilman in The Forerunner 1 (1909-10) and published as a book in 1911.

[17]"What Are 'Feminine' Qualities," p. 234.

[18]Charlotte Perkins Gilman, The Home: Its Work and Influence, with an Introduction by William O'Neill (Urbana: University of Illinois Press, 1972), pp. 59-60.

[19]Ibid., pp. 57, 58-9.

[20]"What Are 'Feminine' Qualities," p. 234.

[21]Jane Roland Martin, Reclaiming a Conversation: The Ideal of the Educated Woman (New Haven: Yale University Press, 1985), p. 142.

[22]Gilman, The Man-Made World, p. 112; Gilman, Women and Economics, pp. 56-7, 38-9.

[23]Gilman, The Man-Made World, pp. 150, 235, 152.

[24]Hill, p. 268.

[25]"With Her in Our Land", Forerunner 7 (1916): 291.

[26]"Masculinism at its Worst," Forerunner 5 (1914): 257.

[27]Gilman, The Man-Made World, pp. 211, 92.

[28]"The New Mothers of a New World," Forerunner 4 (1913): 148.

[29]Gilman, The Man-Made World, pp. 215-16.

[30]Ibid., pp. 217-18.

[31]See ibid., pp. 90-6, 138-40, 213.

[32]Gilman, The Living, p. 131.

[33]Gary Scharnhorst, Charlotte Perkins Gilman (Boston: Twayne Publishers, 1985), p. 89; "Moving the Mountain," Forerunner 2 (1911): 307, 305.

[34]Gilman, The Home, p. 308.

[35]"An Unnatural Mother," Forerunner 7 (1916): 281-5.

[36]"War Waste," Forerunner 5 (1914): 286.

[37]Mary Louise Degen, The History of the Woman's Peace Party (Baltimore: John Hopkins Press, 1939), p. 16.

[38]Jill Conway, "The Woman's Peace Party and the First World War," in J. L. Granatstein and R. D. Cuff, eds., War and Society in North America (Toronto: Thomas Nelson and Sons, 1971), p. 52. Conway overstates the extent of agreement among feminists in claiming that they all believed "women were free from aggressive instincts" and were "men's moral superiors."

[39]Degen, p. 18.

[40]H. C. Peterson and G. C. Fite, Opponents of War 1917-1918 (Seattle: University of Washington Press,1957), p. 10.

[41]See Peterson and Fite.

[42]Note that even Eastman felt compelled in 1918 to state publicly that the New York Woman's Peace Party had ceased its anti-war agitation upon America's full-scale entrance into the conflict. See Crystal Eastman, "Our War Record: A Plea for Tolerance," in Blanche Wiesen Cook, ed., Crystal Eastman on Woman and Revolution (Oxford: Oxford University Press, 1978), p. 264.

[43]Wiesen Cook, "Introduction" to Crystal Eastman, p. 19; Anne Wiltsher, Most Dangerous Women: Feminist Peace Campaigners of the Great War (London: Pandora, 1985), p. 174.

[44]Alice Wexler, Emma Goldman: An Intimate Life (New York: Pantheon, 1984), p. 229. See also Peterson and Fite, chs. 5 and 15.

[45]Gilman, The Living, p. 320.

[46]"Peace in Three Pieces," Forerunner 7 (1916): 270-1.

[47]Ibid., p. 271.

[48]Gilman, The Man-Made World, p. 199.

[49]Gilman, Herland, pp. 54-5; Gilman, "Unpunished," excerpt printed in Ann J. Lane, ed., The Charlotte Perkins Gilman Reader (New York: Pantheon Books, 1980), pp. 169-77.

[50]"The War and Liars," Forerunner 7 (1916): 297; "Studies in Social Pathology," Forerunner 7 (1916): 120; "Growth and Combat," Forerunner 7 (1916): 307.

[51]"Among Our Foreign Residents," Forerunner 7 (1916): 146. See also "Is this War? Or Crime? Or What?," Forerunner 7 (1916): 27.

[52]Degen, p. 53.

[53]"With Her in Our Land," Forerunner 7 (1916): 321.

[54]"Peace in Three Pieces," p. 270.

[55]See "Why Don't We Stop It?," Forerunner 6 (1915): 244; "Why?," Forerunner 7 (1916): 5; "A Question of the Government," Forerunner 7 (1916): 4-5.

[56]"More than Peace," Forerunner 6 (1915): 37-8.

[57]"With Her in Our Land," Forerunner, 7 (1916): 318-19.

[58]"One Effect of the War," Forerunner 6 (1915): 74.

[59]See"War-Maids and War-Widows," Forerunner 6 (1915): 63-5.

[60]Ibid.

[61]For an excellent description and analysis of Gilman's proposed domestic reforms and their influence, see Dolores Hayden, The Grand Domestic Revolution: A History of Feminist Designs for American Homes, Neighborhoods, and Cities (Cambridge, Mass.: MIT Press, 1981), Part 5.

[62]"The New Mothers of a New World," Forerunner 4 (1913): 148.

[63]Ibid.

[64]"More Than Peace," p. 37.

[65]"War-Peace-Love," Forerunner 5 (1914): 333.

[66]Hayden, p. 197.

[67]To feminists like Gilman, Emma Goldman would say: "How much independence is gained [for the majority of working women] if the narrowness and lack of freedom of the home is exchanged for the narrowness and lack of freedom of the factory, sweatshop, department store or office?" Quoted in Wexler, Emma Goldman, p. 194.

[68]See Gilman, The Living, pp. 318, 258, 317, 330.

[69]Zona Gale, "Forward" to Gilman, The Living, p. xxxi. It seems that Gilman's war stand alienated a number of influential female reformers and socialists, although Gary Scharnhorst perhaps overemphasizes the impact of her wartime change of attitude in concluding from it that "Gilman had finally become an anachronism." Scharnhorst, p. 105.

PEACE-MAKING WOMEN: CANADA 1919-1939

Veronica Strong-Boag

Canadian women have rarely been the agents of official diplomacy, that ultimate preserve of elite males.[1] They have, nonetheless, made their own contribution to the Dominion's external relations. Inasmuch as Canadians have been world-minded and ultimately peace-minded, they owe much to the efforts of organized women. The 1920s and 1930s are a case in point. In those years newly enfranchised women in the United Church, the League of Nations Society, the National Council of Women of Canada (NCWC)[***] and the Women's International League for Peace and Freedom brought international affairs to the attention of large numbers of Canadians. For all their shortcomings, women in these groups were vocal champions of a more cooperative world order and an end to war. Their educational programmes, international friendships and political lobbying nourished the Canadian peace conscience during these decades and helped ensure its survival into a nuclear future.

The doctrine of maternal feminism which fueled so much of the suffrage campaigns[2] has been crucial to women's work for "world-mindedness." Many female activists believed, like Nellie McClung, that "The woman's outlook on life is to save, to care for, to help. Men make wounds and women bind them up . . ."[3] Some possessed her conviction that "if there had been women in the German Reichstag, women with authority behind them, when the Kaiser began to lay his plans for war, the results might have been very different. . ."[4] The course of the First Great War repeatedly challenged this optimism. Nellie herself came perilously close to matching the bellicose nationalism of the Imperial Order of Daughters of the Empire.[5] The suggestion of one IODE activist and future Member of Parliament that a critic of the war effort "be taken out and publicly whipped for the traitor that she is"[6] echoed not uncommon sentiments. As the autobiographical novels *Aleta Day* and the *The Staircase* by Francis

[***] My thanks to the National Council of Women of Canada for giving me access to the papers of the International Council of Women and to the SSHRCC (Research Grant #410-0087) for its financial support.

Marion Beynon and Alice Chown make vividly clear,[7] pacifist women roused a hostile response among audiences of both sexes.

Nevertheless, for all the evidence of female partisanship, the old faith in women's special proclivity for empathetic understanding, altruistic nurture and cooperation died hard. Perhaps women had learned a lesson? Some claimed to have. In 1926 Nellie McClung bitterly summed up war's accounts: "For the loan of money our nation is very, very grateful. It is only the gift of men that is forgotten."[8] One radical voiced reflections which troubled her generation:

> We knew not what we did . . .
> Our instincts we have silenced and have taught
> Our minds the truth to blear . . .
> We failed to see our Star:
> God and the world and men cried for our aid;
> We gave them guns and shells.[9]

In the years after World War I such conclusions stiffened some women's resolve to reaffirm their special mandate to work for peace.

For all the revulsion to the carnage of one war, the means of avoiding another were far from self-evident. Isolationism, pacifism and collective security were only a few of the proposals to find female advocates in the 1920s and 1930s.[10] Activist women had extensive pre-war international interests on which to draw. Many organizations, such as the YWCA, the WCTU and the NCWC, had long encouraged Canadians to think of the world beyond their borders. Friendships and commitments had followed. The inter-war years continued this development. New international associations like the International Federation of Business and Professional Women's Clubs, the International Federation of Catholic Alumnae, and the Pan-Pacific Women's Association helped keep a wide variety of women in touch with world issues. These organizational networks provided a ready-made constituency for peace programmes. This is not to suggest that women, any more than men, agreed on the means of guaranteeing or even the exact character of a warless world. A small minority of absolute pacifists, for example, broke ranks with advocates of collective security, arguing that no good could come of any solution imposed by force. Opinions were also bitterly divided about the extent of social malaise. Social democrats and socialists parted ways with the liberal mainstream when they concluded that capitalism was a major contributor to the world's problems. In a fundamentally middle-class peace movement only the very brave demanded an end both to armed conflict and to privilege. Yet boundaries between groups interested in international relations were often relatively porous. Women in the United Church, the League of Nations Society, the Councils and the Women's International League were typical in frequently being acquainted and sharing memberships as well as enthusiasm. For all their differences, internationally-minded women of many persuasions shared both a conception of their sex's particular sensitivity to the costs of armed conflict and an essential optimism about the power of education and the limitations of prejudice. By instructing children and adults in the follies of war and the ways of peace, women could prepare the way, as surely as any diplomat, for a better world.

Work within the churches was a familiar part of women's efforts to serve their community.[11] Intemperate collaboration with the war effort between 1914 and 1918 by the Methodist and Presbyterian churches was generally regretted by the United Church when it was founded in 1925. Women were especially vocal opponents of the old ways of conflict and aggression. In the religious press, Sunday schools, church meetings and children's clubs, they forged occasions to present their case for peace and internationalism. While a residual heritage of bigotry and parochialism never disappeared, many United Church women interpreted their Christian responsibilities liberally and generously. In the Women's Missionary Society (WMS) and the church in general they embodied that emphasis on education and moral suasion which characterized most women's work for peace and world cooperation. Alongside like-minded men in the largest of Canada's protestant denominations female peace-makers conducted an educational campaign which touched lives across the Dominion.

Laying the foundation for a peaceful world was a highly visible part of the labours of the Women's Missionary Society. During the inter-war years Canada's protestant missions, especially those of the United Church, underwent considerable change in response to modern biblical criticism which emphasized an historical Jesus and cultural relativism.[12] Familiar notions of Christian superiority and right to supremacy in non-Christian lands, found fewer and fewer public supporters.[13] The tone of the 1926 Atlantic City meetings of the Protestant Women's Foreign Mission Board, to which the United Church's Women's Missionary Society belonged, exemplified the new approach. Christians were asked to treat mission fields as an opportunity for toleration and humility. Practical sympathy and support for foreign populations would do more to spread Christ's message than any mechanical repetition of doctrine. In particular, old-time Christianity might well have to be re-interpreted in light of local needs, traditions and beliefs. Progressives even insisted that non-Christian peoples might have something to offer in return. At these same 1926 meetings the prominent American feminist, Carrie Chapman Catt, went so far as to wonder: "Can it be possible that out of the Orient where all the religions were born, will come an interpretation of the Christ that shall make a warless world?"[14] Some United Church women thought that Gandhi and his philosophy of passive resistance might be just that answer.[15]

Mission fields provided a practical test of the international spirit. Female missionaries were urged to groom a "generation around the world which shall learn war no more, but shall learn justice, love and mutual respect as the basis for a new world order."[16] Nurturing women were the key by which youthful hearts could be opened to Christ's pacifist message. Significant numbers of women serving overseas, especially those who remained single, appear to have identified markedly with the people they came to serve. Adoption of native children, intense friendships with local women, and support for indigenous feminism were commonplace. Some missionaries became outspoken advocates of their clients. This was true, for instance, of Martha Cartmell, who went to Japan for the Methodist Women's Missionary Society between 1882 and 1887, and whose affection for the Japanese people inspired an active interest in their welfare until her death in 1945.[17] Although it is impossible to know how much modern criticism was taken to heart, missionaries and their female supporters were sensitive to the need to foster inter-racial toleration and sympathy at home and abroad as the only sure basis for a reformed international system.

In 1938, the Foreign Mission Conference of North America met in Canada for the first time. Acutely aware of the on-going tragedy in China, the Conference reaffirmed the need for international cooperation and peace through education. Race prejudice and discrimination were repudiated as unworthy and unprofitable. The Conference identified equal partnership among races as its ultimate goal.[18] And, once again, church women were challenged to take the lead. At these meetings women participated directly, although never equally, in the reappraisal of the churches' missionary functions. In most protestant denominations they were still not eligible to become ministers and thus could rarely be counted among leading policy-makers. This bar in the United Church had ended in 1936, but effective equality remained elusive there, too.[19]

Lack of power in the highest councils of the church was not new. For many years women had found their own compensations in a separatist tradition. Church women met regularly together in Canada and supported gatherings in mission fields, such as the All India Women's Conferences in 1927 and 1935. Contributions to girls' schools at every level from primary to university in China, India and Japan also confirmed the potential for women helping women.[20] In such ways a network of feminine influence was to develop, to link a world-wide community in sisterhood. Peace and inter-racial understanding, it was hoped, would soon follow.

United Church women had their work cut out for them at home as well. Missionary society members were expected to

> inform ourselves regarding the immigration laws of our country so that we can be a help to other nationals in different nations; discard all missionary literature which tends to foster race prejudice, giving pageants and plays close scrutiny, remembering that an attitude of superiority dulls sympathy.[21]

The struggle against prejudice began in the home itself. One observer concluded unhappily that "Too many Canadian children are permitted to use the term 'Chink,' 'nigger,' 'dago,' instilling into their minds a feeling of smug superiority which characterizes many members of the white race to-day . . ."[22] Work for foreigners abroad and New Canadians in the Dominion was regularly linked up in criticism of existing practice. The connection was made very plain, for example, in the case of two Japanese-Canadian graduates of the WMS home in Victoria. First denied nurse training in hospitals in British Columbia, they met further rejection in Alberta until a United Church hospital opened its wards and classes. Rewarding their sponsors, they graduated in 1928, one with the gold medal for proficiency.[23] By spreading such 'moral tales' United Church women sponsored empathetic awareness of other peoples. Citizens sensitized to the evils of racism at home and elsewhere would be less subject to war's appeal.

The essence of the message delivered by church women in the 1920s and 1930s was captured in a poem published for young people and juniors, entitled "Growing Smaller":

Before my very eyes
This world I live in is growing smaller.
With every year that passes
I know more about the girls and boys
Of foreign countries.
They are not so different from me:
They eat, sleep, and play just as I do,
And to a large extent
They think the same thoughts.
I am learning to sympathize with them,
To understand them.[24]

While such a creed has its own arrogant ethnocentrism, it also portrays other peoples as having rights. It was indeed in their dealings with children and young people that church women were most visible in promoting "world mindedness."[25] Some eighty percent of United Church girls encountered this most fully in the Canadian Girls in Training (CGIT) founded during World War I. Leaders, frequently awakened to international issues by involvement in the YWCA, the Student Christian Movement and the WMS, encouraged members to take the cause of the League of Nations and disarmament to heart. Peace-centred themes were commonplace at meetings and typically, in November 1936, girls observed "CGIT Peace Week." In this way coming generations were groomed to take up their mothers' concern for peace. Not surprisingly peace activists such as Muriel Duckworth, later of the Voice of Women, emerged from CGIT ranks.[26] In the optimistic days following the Locarno Pact of 1925, editors of the *Missionary Monthly* hoped that thoughtful women were making the critical difference.[27] Such long-time Protestant activists as Nellie McClung hailed the leadership of women like Lady Astor, Agnes Macphail and Maude

Royden. In high spirits Nellie announced that "women in public life could help the cause of peace by their ability to compromise. They can also step down more easily than men; swallow their pride and eat humble pie. They have had to do it in this man-made world . . ."[28] In the 1930s such faith in the power of influence and conciliation faltered and then failed. World Days of Prayer, World Friendship Rallies and Peace Marches, all joined in eagerly by church women, seemed to have little impact on nations girding for war. For all the worsening picture, peace-minded women were urged not to give up. Hopes for peace and collective security depended as much as ever on their educational work.[29] Taking this advice, 103,115 United Church women lent their names to a disarmament petition of almost 500,000 signatures in 1932.[30] In May 1938 students in a WMS peace programme were urged to make it an "occasion for serious thought and study of the underlying causes of war and of dedication to those things which make for peace."[31]

Nazi terrorism had, however, to be reckoned with. The old legacy of anti-semitism dogged the United Church, but by the mid-1930s liberal-minded women joined church men in criticizing fascism.[32] In 1938 the WMS endorsed the establishment of a National Aid to Czechoslovakia Fund and a proposed Committee on Refugees and Victims of Political Persecution. A year later, pacifist sentiments had to give way before Hitler's threat to the joint heritage of Christians and Jews. Sympathy for Germany's post-war difficulties could not withstand the record of atrocities.

The impact of United Church women's labours in the cause of peace and internationalism is difficult to assess. Many church members remained untouched by pleas for greater toleration and the sharing of resources.[33] Yet some Canadians, especially young women, did indeed become more world-minded. Some of these would later lead a post-war peace crusade. In the hands of those sympathetic to a more liberal interpretation of the Bible, missions became a more tolerant enterprise. Finally, however, for all their good will, peace-minded women were in no position to impose their vision on a male-dominated political system. To be sure, the United Church's male hierarchy was largely sympathetic to the pacifist and internationalist aims of women. They could not, however, guarantee even the cooperation of their congregations. The church itself suffered from the same powerlessness which finally gave women every cause to be depressed about the future of their world.

Women, United Church members among them, also pursued their hopes for a cooperative world order in secular societies. The League of Nations Society in Canada held special appeal, embodying as it did the idealistic heritage of the 'war to end all wars.' Women could join either directly as LNS members or become associated through the corporate memberships of their own societies. The LNS's predominantly male leadership quickly came to depend on their active involvement. Founded in 1921 in an endeavour to increase public support for the League and peace, the elite-sponsored LNS found it difficult to play the prominent role its creators had envisioned.[34] The problem of simultaneously popularizing the gospel of a new cooperative internationalism while maintaining a high moral and social 'tone' for the benefit of academic, political and business leaders bedevilled the Society throughout its history.

Passions fed during the heat of war died hard. Despite an explicit commitment to peace as well as collective security, the LNS seemed from the first an uncertain home for pacifists. The opponents of World War I were, for instance, initially barred from membership in the Toronto and Montreal branches. The former quickly collapsed, a victim of post-war ultra-nationalism. Only the support of the Local Council of Women saved Montreal.[35] Similar difficulties combined with problematic leadership to plague the LNS until 1925 when a new president, Sir George Foster, a long-time advocate of female suffrage and temperance, brought with him a new consciousness of the particular value of female members. At much the same time, conduct of recruitment campaigns was assigned to women's organizations, two of which, the WCTU and the NCWC, became essential in keeping the Society before the public.[36] By 1926 forty-two of fifty-six Local Councils of Women had established League of Nations Committees. Farm women's sympathy coalesced in the pages of the Western Producer around Violet McNaughton, editor of the women's page and founder of the Women Grain Growers of Saskatchewan. The enthusiasm of women was also cultivated by female representation, after 1929, on most Canadian delegations to the League. The appointment of activists like Dame Rachel Crowdy to prominent League positions[37] was also a source of pride, as was the addition of Miss Mary Craig McGeachy, a former Ontario school-teacher and graduate of the University of Toronto, to the League Secretariat in 1928. McGeachy's regular speaking tours on behalf of the League in the 1930s, together with frequently voiced support by the first female MP, Agnes Macphail, and the first female senator, Cairine Wilson, enhanced the perception that League matters were appropriate female concerns. Taking up this challenge LNS women across the Dominion devoted themselves to making the League better appreciated. Throughout the 1920s and 1930s they conducted educational campaigns of every sort, all designed to convince citizens of the merits of cooperative internationalism. Tension mounted between pacifists and advocates of collective security, but the latter were dominant by the mid-1930s. In any case they too were reluctant to give up hope of a peaceful solution to the world's difficulty. As long as they could, they clung to the faith that education was the antidote to the forces leading to conflict.

For all their commitment to the LNS, and indeed perhaps because of it, there is some evidence that women were not entirely welcome, at least not as decision-makers. In Halifax the letters of the branch President regularly made unflattering personal references to McGeachy and complaints about the 'strong-mindedness' of the Local Council of Women's League of Nations convenor. Among her other contributions to popularizing the discussion of foreign affairs, that clubwoman established a Women's Study Group which put the staid activities of the male-dominated Society to shame.[38] Eventually even Halifax's hostile president had to give way before the fact that executive meetings saw an average of three of fourteen male and five of five female members in attendance. An independent women's unit was created, since, as the president admitted, "the men in the Branch were holding the women back."[39]

In Toronto another 'troublesome' woman, Alice Chown, a long-time anti-war activist, formed a Women's League of Nations Association affiliated with the branch. Confronted with the near-moribund state of the local organization Chown set about to liven up agendas. Her exasperation at high-brow tactics and demand for programs with broad appeal were hardly welcome as the comments of one branch president made clear: "You need pay no more attention to that wild creature, Miss Chown, who has been turned down pretty hard and has now no status with us whatsoever . . ."[40] Untamed or not, her talents were wanted in Toronto where the majority of members were female. The 1932 re-organization of the branch which saw the absorption of the Women's Society did not end differences between Chown and the largely male executive.[41] It was a testament to the hostility they provoked that neither Chown nor her Halifax counterpart ever became branch president. In 1933 Chown was also defeated in her run for the National Council of the LNS.

Such local conflict over strategy characterized a national society in difficulty. Rising levels of international violence and the League's failure to confront aggression made the LNS appear less and less relevant to those searching for solutions to world disorder. In the heightening disillusionment the Society finally accepted female leadership. In 1936 Senator Cairine Wilson, a long-time member, took on the acting presidency and, one year later, the senior position itself. By this time not only was Wilson's talent and energy abundantly clear, but elite males may no longer have thought the Society worth the effort. An optimistic liberalism still, however, nourished Wilson who claimed, "I . . . cannot remember the time when I did not regard the name of Gladstone with veneration . . ."[42] Faith in women's innate repugnance at conflict also sustained her efforts to educate public opinion and lobby government in the cause of peace.[43] She needed all the help she could get from such convictions.

LNS programmes could not keep pace with the worsening international situation. The victims of renewed aggression won the sympathy of many LNS members, including Wilson. Her presidency of the LNS-sponsored Canadian National Committee on Refugees and Victims of Political Persecution sharpened further still her repulsion at the "new barbarism" in Germany with its threat to liberally minded women and men.[44] The enforcement of collective security obligations, better late than never in the 1930s, was the only way to check such excesses. Her inability to rouse sufficient enthusiasm from Mackenzie

King or his cabinet colleagues for the tragic cases which came across her desk testified not only to the limitations of the Liberal Party, but also how far from being universal internationalist sentiments were.[45] Yet, while appeals for Jewish victims met little response, Wilson found more support for her insistence that

> . . . peace and defence . . . is the foundation of peace and security at home and . . . must be the foundation in the world at large. We as a nation must assume some responsibility for the defence against injustice and unprovoked aggression of all other nations just as we as individuals support a like assumption municipally. Our national policy must be oriented accordingly.[46]

Educating the Canadian population to the benefits of international cooperation was important work, but in the end collective security might have to be ensured by military might.

Without female support the LNS would not have survived. Yet women's prominence was far from intended by the Society's elite male founders who concentrated, at least initially, on instructing men in the rules of the new internationalism. Women were second best candidates for such information. As it turned out, however, women were much more susceptible to the appeal for world-mindedness. By the mid-1920s the organization was effectively feminized at its lower levels as women used it to further their own efforts to create a popular constituency knowledgeable about international affairs. Ironically enough, the appearance of a female president in the late 1930s only helped to confirm that the Society was far from being the authority its founders had intended. A closed, male establishment centred on the prime minister, the Department of External Affairs and the diplomatic service kept control of foreign policy firmly in their own hands.[47]

Given their at best mixed reception in male-dominated institutions, women continued to seek segregated forms of expression and power. By the 1920s the National and International Councils of Women were familiar, if often criticized, representatives of women's efforts to re-educate citizens in matters of war and peace. In recognition of its staying power the ICW was occasionally given the complimentary title, 'Grandmother of the League of Nations.' There were in fact significant similarities between the Councils and the League. Most importantly, the major impact either could have on members was moral rather than coercive.

The liberal feminist founders of the Councils planned to bring together women divided by religion, politics, class, nationality and race.[48] So as not to place too great a strain on patience and tolerance, the Constitution of the NCWC, like that of the ICW, affirmed that the Council "is organized in the interests of no one propaganda, and has no power over the organizations which constitute it beyond that of suggestion and sympathy."[49] Controversial political and religious questions were avoided lest they disturb a tenuous consensus. The long International presidency of Lady Aberdeen, who was also founding president of the NCWC in 1893, helped confirm this orientation.[50] Much molded by her exposure to highly partisan Canadian politics and her fervent life-long Gladstonian liberalism, Ishbel Gordon believed that prospects for reform were best when it remained cautious and non-confrontational. In order to preserve contact among women of dramatically opposed views, she led resistance in Canada and in the International to discussion of such subjects as birth control and the exact implications of collective security. Her strategy, much like that of her admirer, the Canadian liberal, William Lyon Mackenzie King, was to trust that agreement would ultimately surface. Until that time, debate, with its potential for permanent alienation, should be postponed.

Canadians sometimes disappointed their founder. Her determination to welcome German and Austrian women back into the ICW after the war was strongly resisted. Anti-German feelings ran high at NCWC meetings in 1918 when a leading westerner warned that there existed "strong suspicion of something within the Council connected with Internationalism which makes for pacifism."[51] Tempers were still hot later when an old Canadian ally warned the ICW President to bar former enemies from the forthcoming Congress.[52] Aberdeen's response was forceful:

> Do you really wish the I.C.W. to be utterly paralysed and useless at this time of the world's great need, that this great federation of organized women's societies should confess itself unable to call its members together to confer how best they can take up again their work of healing and good will.[53]

In a later exchange she blamed IODE influence, concluding, "We will never get any further until we have learned to drop these extreme nationalistic ideas."[54] The election of Sophia Sanford of Hamilton, an active supporter of the ICW, to Canada's presidency in 1920 brought an end to the official breach, but strain remained.

Despite this inauspicious beginning, the persistence of faith in women's special proclivity for peaceful solutions, ICW ties, and patriotic desires to affirm Canada's status in the world of nations encouraged Council to view international relations as an important area of attention in the 1920s and 1930s. The appointment of NCWC members as official Canadian delegates to world conferences--such as Dr. Ritchie England of Montreal to the Pan-American Conference of Women in 1922--was prized as bringing not only the Dominion but its new voters more to the forefront of world affairs. By the mid-1920s, NCWC members had taken up the cause of the League of Nations. The result was the formation of League Standing Committees and corporate membership in the LNS. The exact meaning of this allegiance was not debated at annual meetings, presumably lest it pit one member against another. In general, however, the NCWC spoke for collective security rather than outright pacifism.

The first LN national convenor, simultaneously member of the International's Peace and Arbitration Committee and a future national president, Henrietta Wilson, worked hard to keep local convenors and the annual meetings abreast of latest League developments. The need to educate Canadians in world-mindedness emerged as an early and persistent refrain. Lectures, study groups, pen pals, essay contests and oratorical contests were organized by local councils across the Dominion. Like Canadian delegates to Geneva, Wilson and her successors could not resist presenting the Dominion "as an example with her vast unprotected borders and her mere skeleton of defence force."[55] In neither case was the relevance for Europeans of the North American model debated.

The Council retained close ties with the LNS throughout the 1930s, but enthusiasm depended on the individual convenor. In 1933, for example, only sixteen of forty-four local councils submitted annual reports.[56] Most activities focused either on lobbying Ottawa or, more often still, on educating the electorate. In one typical initiative the federal government was urged to support the 1932 Disarmament Conference. One measure of NCWC prominence was the appointment of President Winnifred Kydd as a Canadian delegate. Her subsequent tour of the Dominion stimulated interest in disarmament, including demands for government control of the manufacture and trade in war material.[57] Work was not always so rewarding. Convenors of the League Committee had to remind listeners that "The menace to world peace is very great. No one can afford to be indifferent."[58] Yet world issues rarely provoked the concern NCWCers hoped for. One convenor complained that "while the year has been productive of much study throughout the Councils, much more could be done if only the women of Canada knew the power that lies in their hands to mould public opinion in favour of a Peace Policy for Canada."[59] As optimism waned in the late thirties a national League of Nations convenor became difficult to secure. Yet as the 1938 report admitted, the League, for all its failings, had no substitute.[60]

Deteriorating world conditions shifted attention to urgent causes such as the Canadian National Committee on Refugees and Victims of Political Persecution. Here, however, were new dilemmas for those fearful of controversy. The observation of one prominent NCWCer reveals the Canadian Council's sensitivities regarding immigration and Jews:

> The main point that has been stressed in all discussion and publicity is that, the National Committee on Refugees and Victims of Political Persecution is only asking for a selected group to be admitted . . . and are stressing the point that, less than half of those who have to seek a new home as a result of policies of Germany, the absorption of Austria and the dismemberment of Czechoslovakia are Jews.[61]

As was only too often the case, proposals for greater world responsibility had to take old prejudices into account. For all the liberal views of many members, the Council always found it extremely difficult to advance beyond the opinions of the conservative.

Ties with the ICW also reminded Canadians of international obligations and sympathies. Just as with many internationally-affiliated bodies, intense friendships stemming over years had grown up. Lady Aberdeen was the centre of the Council network, but ties went far beyond her, reinforced as they were at every Quinquennial. Yet there were problems. In the first place, contact was frequently uncertain. The costs and complexities of involvement in the International often kept Canadians marginal actors. They were, however, conscious of the International's manoeuvres to take command of the women's peace movement. The predicament of the ICW, like that of the NCWC, centred on a means of avoiding the shoals of controversy while at the same time retaining authority. In some ways this was an acute case of the problem facing all women's educational efforts. At what speed should a reform-minded organization advance, in order neither to lose momentum on the questions of the day nor alienate prospective sympathizers not yet persuaded by wiser associations and counsels? Such a *modus operandi* prepared the way for less consensus-oriented and more homogenously radical or conservative organizations to seize the initiative. Rivals like the International Woman Suffrage Alliance, later the International Alliance of Women for Suffrage and Equal Citizenship (IAW), and the Women's International League for Peace and Freedom (WILPF) had the advantage of smaller constituencies. On at least two occasions Aberdeen tried unsuccessfully to absorb the more progressive IAW, despite some Canadians' arguments that amalgamation "will kill the N.C.W."[62] WILPF differed still more sharply from the slow-moving and cautious Councils. Carrie Chapman Catt summed this up in her assessment of two rival peace conferences in 1924:

> The Peace and Freedom League represents the extreme left-wing of the Peace movement and the kind of people who are interested in it are not those who would go to your meetings. They believe in cutting into the heart of present difficulties and finding a remedy . . . In many countries their chief members are those who are so radical, that they do not have a great deal of influence with the masses. On the other hand, your Congress, leaving out discussion of the Great War and the present day problems and devoting itself only to the general question, will only make an appeal to the very moderate and conservative.[63]

Matters got still more difficult when the ICW had to make allowance for fascist national councils.[64] Carrie Carmichael of Canada had, for instance, to report after a recruiting trip to South America that

181

the Argentine Council was "wholly irregular," excluding as it did all suffrage and reform groups.[65] Juggling diverse opinions made decisive action on the peace question all the more unlikely, as the ICW's failure to condemn outrightly the Japanese invasion of Manchuria indicated.[66] Mounting evidence of German atrocities including attacks on Jews, feminists among them, made Aberdeen's balancing act impossible. The disappearance of the German and Austrian Councils proved that the rational discourse the Council movement depended on had become a victim of forces which had no respect for such liberal niceties.

The Canadian Council shared its parent's dilemma. Peace and internationalism became intensely controversial once discussion advanced beyond platitudes. In Canada the effort to appear always moderate and respectable was handicap enough; in the world at large it was still more debilitating. Councils were almost invariably liable to the charge of conservatism and complicity in reform setbacks. The fact that the right wing in Canada, as in fascist nations, made precisely contradictory charges made the search for a liberal consensus, in peace-making as in other situations, a distinctly problematic business.

Dissatisfaction with existing women's organizations, including the Councils, helped create the Women's International League for Peace and Freedom in Paris in 1915. Founded by the prominent American social reformer and pacifist, Jane Addams, WILPF represented the left wing of the organized women's peace movement during World War I and the inter-war decades. A few Canadians, such as Dr. Julia Grace Wales of the University of Wisconsin, author of a plan for mediation without armistice in 1915,[67] were early proponents but it was not until the beginning of the 1920s that there were sufficient numbers, and even these were small, to establish Canadian branches. Typifying both the high quality of WILPF's small Canadian band and its social democratic character were women like Laura Jamieson, juvenile court judge in Burnaby, B. C., Agnes Macphail, Progressive M.P., Lucy Woodsworth, wife of J. S. Woodsworth and peace activist in her own right, and Violet McNaughton. Such women sometimes worked with churches, the LNS and Local Councils of Women but in the main they found those more conservative bodies far too timid.

Not surprisingly WILPF Canada was never as sanguine as more moderate organizations about the League of Nations. Many WILPFers considered the League compromised by association with a defective peace treaty. These critical observers also suspected that the proceedings in Geneva often camouflaged the defence of vested economic interests. Substantial issues set WILPF apart--notably its preoccupation with the economic causes of conflict, its left-wing sympathies and its special attraction for all-out pacifists. In the years leading up to 1939 WILPF grew more insistent that lasting peace was not possible without some redistribution of resources. For many Canadians this advice was unacceptable.

Yet for all their disagreements with conventional women's groups, WILPFers like Jamieson and Woodsworth evoked a faith in women's special qualities which Cairine Wilson and Nellie McClung would have found familiar. Differences emerged, not so much about the nature of women, as about the nature of the world itself. Just as importantly the League members shared that capacity for female friendship which formed the backbone of women's efforts elsewhere. Affection linked activists like Jamieson and McNaughton. Nor were friendships restricted to Canada. McNaughton's correspondence bound her and other Canadians to League activists in the US and Europe. Such relationships provided the essential introduction to the feminist world outside the Dominion. McNaughton's advice to Irene Parlby, Member of the Legislative Assembly of Alberta and Canadian delegate to the League of Nations in 1930, to visit WILPF's Maison International, an "informal gathering place for women delegates to the League where they meet other outstanding women who happen to be in Geneva at the time,"[68] exemplified how loyalties were fostered and information exchanged.

After the war the League became a favourite target for super-patriots. In March 1920, for example, Toronto's jingoistic *Telegram* helped force the cancellation of a visit by Jane Addams and later on attacked a tour by Austrian and German members.[69] Support for WILPF's mixture of feminism and pacifism really materialized after the 1924 International Congress in Washington when Canadians invited European members to include the Dominion in their North American tour.[70] The Canadian women's peace movement had found its most ardent advocate.

WILPF's left leanings never endeared it to large numbers, and leaders like Jamieson, the first National Secretary, remained sensitive to the need for diplomacy. As president of the Parent-Teacher Federation of British Columbia she explained to McNaughton that:

> The programs are innocuous in some ways, but we couldn't start out very strongly--have had criticism already. At least they will serve to form a 'peace background' for children's minds.[71]

Two years later, in 1927, she remained circumspect but forceful while conducting a *de facto* WILPF tour under the auspices of the Canadian Clubs. In the same campaign for credibility she and other Vancouver sympathizers cooperated with the local League of Nations Society to stage peace conferences during Armistice week and with the WCTU to embargo war materials to Japan. Such cooperative efforts typified WILPF's educational programme. It mattered little whether the pacifist message was carried by the LNS, the Pan-Pacific Women's Association, the Women's Missionary Societies or the Vancouver International Folk Festival, so long as it was heard.[72]

This choice of strategy reflected an assessment of WILPF's prospects as a radical group. Not until the 1930s was it even possible to establish an official Canadian Section to coordinate small branches in

Toronto, Winnipeg and Vancouver and the official groups among farm women's organizations and the WCTU on the prairies.[73] This structure, with the addition of several affiliates in the west, including in 1937 branches in Jasper and Edson, Alberta, remained much the same until the outbreak of war. WILPF's numbers are impossible to estimate. Actual members were always too few, as the difficulty in finding a replacement for Jamieson as National Secretary in 1930 suggests, but the editor of *Pax International*, the WILPF magazine, claimed that Canada ranked third in the number of paid subscriptions in 1930.[74]

Yet, in the hands of its dedicated membership, WILPF had an impact out of all proportion to its size. Perhaps more than any other peace-minded group, it kept Canadians thinking. Citizens were both shocked and informed when WILPF sponsored a survey of militarism in history textbooks and took up a tireless campaign against cadet training. Consciences were also unsettled by news of peace rallies and lectures, the initiation of a massive disarmament petition in 1932 and the embargo of ships carrying war materials to Japan in 1939.[75] Prominent international WILPFers, such as Emily Greene Balch, American pacifist and later Nobel Peace Prize winner, and Maude Royden, a charismatic Congregational preacher and anti-war activist from Great Britain, also turned up in halls and churches to keep WILPF's message before the public. Many programs were undertaken in cooperation with other groups, but the WILPF 'touch' was unmistakable. More than the United Church, the LNS, or the NCWC, WILPF endeavoured to leave audiences with some awareness of the connection between conflict and oppressive political and social structures. Good will was not sufficient to cure abuses; some fundamental restructuring of national and international priorities had to take place.

Canadians did not appear as major actors in the parent body. After 1924 they took part regularly, if in small numbers, at world Congresses, but distance made it difficult for them to follow or to influence the League elsewhere.[76] During the 1920s and 1930s the International was more and more sharply divided between, broadly speaking, French and German members convinced of the need to use force to redress social and economic injustice, and British, American and Scandinavian members more optimistic about solutions in education, conciliation and compromise.[77] The worsening international situation, which brought the persecution and arrest of League members in Germany and Austria, exacerbated tensions. During the 1934 Zurich Congress a fierce battle raged over the relative priority to be assigned the goals of social transformation and peace. More left-wing members from Continental Europe, favouring a greater commitment to major structural changes in society, won the day.[78] The British attempt to weaken the executive's power of independent action and to decentralize authority in the hands of individual national sections also failed. More unanimous was the outrage against anti-semitism. In September 1935 WILPF called "to those who still have the courage and freedom to do so to speak out and to join us in expressing public execration of all programs, open and secret, and of the hideous challenge to civilization which Hitler has brought upon Europe."[79] Hitler's forced union with Austria shocked even the "most ardent sympathizers with Germany's just grievances."[80] The dismemberment of Czechoslovakia in 1938 effectively ended calls for patience. WILPF's frantic efforts at further peace research, conferences and proposals began to appear increasingly irrelevant in the hard light of Europe's dawning conflict. Thoughts turned inexorably to urgent work for refugees.

As war neared in the spring of 1939 the U.S. section demanded stronger neutrality legislation and the Canadian section urged Ottawa to prohibit the export of all war materials. Canadian WILPF was, however, sharply divided as to the proper course of action. Some, like Mildred Farnhi of B. C., remained unalterably opposed to war in all its guises. Others, like Agnes Macphail who voted for Canada's declaration of war, had finally to conclude that "contemplating a world without opposition to Hitler seemed more terrible than even war."[81]

Like women in the United Church, the League of Nations Society and the Councils, women in WILPF concentrated on education in international affairs and an admission of past errors as the surest route to a warless world. As a more uniformly radical group they were especially aware of the economic causes of conflict. This insight drew many to the Cooperative Commonwealth Federation in the 1930s. Such adherence highlighted the difference between WILPF members and more conservative peace workers. Yet the conviction that women possessed a surer grasp of peace's value and their optimistic trust in education linked WILPFers to a feminist and gradualist tradition which could be found in the other bodies as well. Finally, of course, all were powerless to redirect fundamentally a state or an international community directed by men.

The search for peace and international understanding during the inter-war years was difficult for any Canadian. The choice of many women was to pursue familiar educational and lobbying strategies. This was the first impulse of women in the United Church, the League of Nations Society, the National Council and the Women's International League. And although many citizens had their awareness of world issues raised, female activists in the Dominion, as elsewhere, found their methods an inadequate response to the dilemma of the times. They depended on levels of receptivity, tolerance and common sense which were all too rare. Nor were women the major actors. The Canadian government and the Department of External Affairs, like the world of nations, was overwhelmingly in male hands and this was never effectively challenged.

And yet to place the actions of women in these four groups in a different perspective, the inter-war years were not a time when many women or men of good will were to feel their labour brought desired results. Regrets abounded on every side. The Conservative Martha Black reflected bitterly in 1940:

As in Britain we were all sheep herded by the Pacifists . . . It seems to me that I could write a book, entitled Mine the Fault. For four years I sat in the House of Commons knowing as well as moving pictures could tell us, all that travellers were telling us, all that men in the regular Force were telling us yet only once did I have either the brains or the GUTS . . . to raise my voice . . . In those times if one so much as ever raised a whisper about soldiers and armament we were simply put down as War Mongers. So cowards that we were we remained mum or timidly suggested inadequate help. I could kick myself around the block now. . .[82]

Black's frequent critic, the WILPFer Agnes Macphail, was equally tormented over the events of the 1930s and her own role in them. She voted for war because of her hatred of Hitler but she confessed to a longtime pacifist,

I still do not know what was the right and wrong of it. I hate war and death to liberty which it brings--but then liberty was dead anyway.[83]

Such reflections testify not only to the difficulty of decisions during these years, but also to the range of the opinion on the proper course of action among women. Their hopes for a better world foundered, as did those of other Canadians, on the reality of Nazi terrorism and their own limited power to influence the course of events. The cause of peace would have to be taken up again by the survivors of the Second Great War. Women would be essential in that campaign as well.

Notes

[1]See J. L. Granatstein, The Ottawa Men. The Civil Service Mandarins, 1935-1957 (Toronto: Oxford University Press, 1982), p. 4.

[2]For a useful discussion of this philosophy in the Canadian context see W. R. Morrison, "'Their Proper Sphere': Feminism, the Family, and Child-Centred Social Reform in Ontario, 1875-1900," Ontario History 68, 1/2 (March/June 1976).

[3]Nellie L. McClung, In Times Like These (Toronto: University of Toronto Press, 1972), p. 23.

[4]Ibid., p. 89.

[5]See Gloria Geller, "The Wartimes Elections Act of 1917 and the Canadian Women's Movement," Atlantis 2, 1 (Autumn 1976): 88-106.

[6]Toronto Public Library, Baldwin Room, (henceforth TPL, BR) (Peggy) Ann Merrill Papers, Martha Black to "Dearest Pegg", September 13, 1920.

[7]For more details on Beynon and her views, see Ramsay Cook, "Francis Marion Beynon and the Crisis of Christian Reformism," in Carl Berger and Ramsay Cook, eds., The West and the Nation (Toronto: McClelland and Stewart, 1976). Unfortunately no sustained treatment of Alice Chown yet exists. Some information is available in the excellent thesis, Thomas Socknat, "Witness Against War: Pacifism in Canada, 1900-1945" (Ph.D. thesis, McMaster University, 1981), especially p. 106, and M. C. Tutton, "An Outrageous Idealist," Canadian Comment, October, 1935, p. 8, and Tutton, "From Geneva to Canada," Canadian Comment, November, 1935, pp. 8-9, 19.

[8]Nellie L. McClung, "Men and Money," All We Like Sheep and Other Stories (Toronto: Thomas Allen, 1926), p. 61.

[9]Margaret Fairley, "A Woman's Confession," Canadian Forum, August, 1921, p. 333.

[10]For a review of Canadian attitudes in one decade, albeit one which ignores the views of women, see Robert Bothwell and Norman Hillmer, The In-Between Time, Canadian External Policy in the 1930s (Toronto: Copp Clark, 1975).

[11]See, for example, Wendy Mitchenson, "Canadian Women and the Church Missionary Societies in the 19th Century," Atlantis 2, 2, Part 2 (Spring 1977): 57-75, and Christopher Headon, "Women and Organized Religion in Mid and Late 19th Century Canada," Journal of the Canadian Church Historical Society 20, 1/2 (March-June 1978): 3-15.

[12]For a discussion of the debate see Stephen Endicott, James G. Endicott: Rebel Out of China (Toronto: University of Toronto Press,

1980), chs. 3-5; see also Richard Allen, The Social Passion (Toronto: University of Toronto Press, 1970), ch. 19.

[13]For a discussion of these changes, see William R. Hutchinson, "Modernism and Missions: The Liberal Search for an Exportable Christianity, 1875-1935," in J. K. Fairbank, ed., The Missionary Enterprise in China and America (Cambridge: Harvard University Press, 1974).

[14]Catt as cited in Mrs. John MacGillivray, "The Missionary Boards of North America in Conference," The Missionary Monthly, March, 1926, p. 363.

[15]See Mildred Fahrni, "My Visits with Gandhi," International Fellowship of Reconciliation Report, April, 1983.

[16]Mrs. Nicholson as cited in MacGillivray, "The Missionary Boards of North America," p. 364.

[17]See Archives of the United Church of Canada, the Strachan-Cartmell Collection.

[18]See "The Foreign Missions Conference," Missionary Monthly, March, 1938, pp. 111-13.

[19]For an appraisal of some of the issues surrounding the ordination question in Canada, see Mary Hallett, "Nellie McClung and the Fight for the Ordination of Women in the United Church of Canada," Atlantis 4, 2 (Spring 1979): 2-16.

[20]See, for example, "The All-India Women's Conference," Missionary Monthly, July/August, 1927.

[21]Mrs. Nicholson as cited in MacGillivray, "The Missionary Boards of North America," p. 365.

[22]Barbara Gibson Wyld, "Strangers Yet Brethren," New Outlook, March 28, 1928, p. 11.

[23]See W. H. Pike, "Two United Church Japanese-Canadian Nurses," Onward, August 23, 1930.

[24]Palm Branch, October, 1928, p. 7.

[25]See Margaret Prang,"'The Girl God Would Have Me Be': The Canadian Girls in Training, 1915-39," The Canadian Historical Review LXVI, 2 (June 1985): 171-2, 175-6, for her discussion of the internationalist sympathies of the CGIT.

[26]See Prang, ibid., p. 166. On the Voice of Women see Kay MacPherson and Meg Sears, "The Voice of Women: A History," in G. Matheson, ed., Women in the Canadian Mosaic (Toronto: Peter Martin, 1976).

[27]See, for instance, "Women and World Peace," Missionary Monthly, September, 1929, front cover.

[28]Nellie L. McClung, Leaves from Lantern Lane (Toronto: Thomas Allen, 1936), p. 135.

[29]See, for example, "Fear Not," Missionary Monthly, December, 1931, p. 530.

[30]"United Church Women Lead," Missionary Monthly, March, 1932, pp. 100-1.

[31]Winnifred Thomas, "The Theme for May," Missionary Monthly, April, 1938, p. 169.

[32]For a discussion of the range of opinion, see Alan Davies and Marilyn Felcher Nefsky "The United Church and the Jewish Plight During the Nazi Era 1933-1945," Canadian Jewish Historical Society Journal 8, 2 (Fall 1984): 55-70. By the mid-1930s considerable sympathy for Jews was evident. See, for example, (Mrs. Meyer) Mattie Rotenberg, "Christian and Jew--Their Common Heritage," Missionary Monthly, June, 1939, pp. 247-9; "Ten Commandments of Good Will," ibid., January, 1939, p. 16.

[33]See the critical discussion in Marilyn Harrison, "The Social Influence of the United Church of Canada in British Columbia 1930-1948" (M.A. thesis, University of British Columbia, 1975).

[34]See Donald Page, "Canadians and the League of Nations Before the Manchurian Crisis" (Ph.D. thesis, University of Toronto, 1972).

[35]Ibid., pp. 183-7.

[36]Ibid., pp. 275-6.

[37]A prominent English feminist and reformer who became head of the League's Social Section.

[38]Public Archives of Canada (henceforth PAC), League of Nations Society in Canada Papers, v. 3, folder "Halifax Branch 1936," letters by C. N. Mercer to R. B. Inch.

[39]D. J. Herperger, "The League of Nations Society in Canada during the 1930s" (M.A. thesis, University of Regina, 1978), p. 100.

[40]W. Grant to G. Meredith, February 1930, as cited in Herperger, ibid., p. 59.

[41]See PAC, R. Inch Papers, v. 5, folder 125 "Chown, Alice."

[42]Canada, Senate, Debates, February 25, 1930.

[43]See ibid.

[44]PAC, Canadian National Committee on Refugees, v. 7, folder 15, typescript memo, Cairine Wilson, "Statement on World Situation Issued to the Press . . .," October 2, 1938.

[45]For a discussion of this refusal to act see Irving Abella and Harold Troper, None Is Too Many: Canada and the Jews of Europe 1933-1948 (Toronto: Lester and Orpen Dennys, 1982).

[46]PAC, Cairine Wilson Papers, v. 8, Scrapbook, unidentified clipping, undated but probably 1938, "Viewing Munich from League of Nations Angle."

[47]See H. Blair Neatby, William Lyon Mackenzie King 1924-1932 (Toronto: University of Toronto Press, 1976); see also C. Ritchie, The Siren Years, A Canadian Diplomat Abroad 1937-1945 (Toronto: Macmillan, 1974).

[48]See V. Strong-Boag, The Parliament of Women (Ottawa: National Museum, 1976), especially chapter 5.

[49]"Constitution," Women Workers of Canada, 1894, p. 22.

[50]See Strong-Boag, op. cit., pp. 131-47.

[51]PAC, International Council of Women Papers (henceforth ICWP), v. 33, folder 494, "Extract from Minutes of the Annual Meeting of the International Council of Women of Canada, June 1918," typed.

[52]PAC, ICWP, v. 33, folder 493, Emily Cummings to Lady Aberdeen, December 1, 1919.

[53]PAC, ICWP, Aberdeen to Cummings, December 19, 1919, copy.

[54]PAC, ICWP, Aberdeen to Cummings, March 12, 1920.

[55]Henrietta Wilson, "League of Nations," Yearbook of the NCWC, 1926, p. 57.

[56]Hilda Laird, "League of Nations," Yearbook of the NCWC, 1933, p. 86.

[57]Ibid.

[58]Jean Lickley, "League of Nations," Yearbook of the NCWC, 1935, p. 100.

[59]Ibid., p. 102.

[60]Minnie E. Thomson, "League of Nations," Yearbook of the NCWC, 1938, p. 113.

[61]Laura T. Hardy, "League of Nations," Yearbook of the NCWC, 1939, p. 109.

[62]PAC, ICWP, v. 8, folder 8, Carrie Carmichael to Aberdeen, May 30 [1923].

[63]PAC, ICWP, v. 27, folder 399, Catt to Aberdeen, January 12, 1924.

[64]Italy was an especially pernicious example, dominated as it was by the Fascist Countess di Robilant.

[65]PAC, ICWP, v. 1, folder 11, Carmichael to Aberdeen, April 10, 1923.

[66]See letters debating the action to be taken regarding Manchuria, PAC, ICWP, v.26, folder 391. Aberdeen held the line but there was bitter resistance within the ICW itself to her failure to act.

[67]G. Bussey and Margaret Tims, Women's International League for Peace and Freedom 1915-1965 (London: George Allen and Unwin Ltd., 1965), pp. 18 and 20.

[68]Saskatchewan Archives Board Saskatoon (henceforth SABS), Violet McNaughton Papers (henceforth VMP), v. 18, file 54, McNaughton to Parlby, August 15, 1930.

[69]Page, "Canadians and the League," pp. 183-4.

[70]Socknat, "Witness Against War," pp. 206-10.

[71]SABS, VMP, v. 15, file 34, Jamieson to McNaughton, April 24, 1925.

[72]The Folk Festival operating in Vancouver in the 1930s was a typical example of WILPF interest in popular education.

[73]It is difficult to estimate the exact number of groups which were operating at any one time. The McNaughton Papers seem to provide the best available guide.

[74]SABS, VMP, v. 38, folder 95 (1) "Laura Jamieson to Friends," June 25, 1930.

[75]For a useful review of these activities see Deborah Powell, "Women's Peace Organizations in Canada 1920-1970" (Research Essay, Political Science 498, Carleton University, April 1983).

[76]See McNaughton's frustration with inadequate information, SABS, VMP, v. 38, folder 95 (1), McNaughton to Mme. Camille Drevet, July 6, 1932, and folder 95 (3) McNaughton to Drevet, May 16, 1933.

[77]See Bussey and Tims, Women's International League for Peace and Freedom, chs. 11 and 12.

[78]Ibid., pp. 120-2.

[79]As cited in ibid., pp. 128-30.

[80]Ibid., p. 159.

[81]PAC, Edith Holtom Papers, v. 1, Macphail to Mrs. Holtom, May 2, 1940.

[82]TPL, BR, Merrill Papers, Black to "My Dear Peggy Anne," December 20, 1940.

[83]PAC, Holtom Papers, Macphail to Holtom, May 2, 1940.

VERA BRITTAIN AND THE PEACE PLEDGE UNION: WOMEN AND PEACE

Yvonne Aleksandra Bennett

> If women are indifferent--
> If they remain politically non-conscious--
> If--in brief--they choose not to choose--
> Then they are indirectly but none the less
> certainly assisting those forces which are
> pushing civilization towards chaos.

Vera Brittain, "How War Affects Women," 1937.[1]

A direct product of the "never again" mood so pervasive in Great Britain during the 1920s and 1930s, the Peace Pledge Union was founded by an Anglican priest, Canon 'Dick' Sheppard, in October 1934. The Union fast became Britain's premier pacifist organization, claiming over 100,000 members by the summer of 1939. Vera Brittain was one of its most influential leaders and arguably the most important woman pacifist to emerge in twentieth-century Britain.[2]

Mindful of the theme of this anthology, I would like to examine Brittain's writings on the responsibilities of women to peace; secondly, to consider an early attempt on the part of women to organize for peace, namely, the Peace Pledge Union's wartime Women's Peace Campaign; and lastly, to sketch Vera Brittain's own work for peace during the Second World War both as an individual and as a member of the Peace Pledge Union.

Vera Brittain and the Peace Pledge Union

Vera Mary Brittain was born in Staffordshire, England in 1893 and died, at the age of 77 years, in March 1970. By profession a writer, she is probably best known for her autobiographical work, *Testament of Youth*, first published in 1933.[3] The book describes Brittain's provincial, late-Victorian upbringing; her struggle, as a woman, to acquire a higher education for herself; her nursing career in the Great

War and her subsequent readjustment to peacetime; her work for the League of Nations Union; her disenchantment with liberalism and her consequent embrace of socialism. But above all the book is a statement against war and, as such, ranks as a classic.

Brittain had decided upon a literary career at a young age,[4] and, to further her goal of becoming a writer, decided to attend university, a proposal which her parents greeted with dismay; an early marriage and motherhood were the expected developments for a woman of the provincial upper middle classes. It was thus against significant odds that Brittain won a place at Somerville, and she keenly anticipated going up to Oxford in the autumn of 1914 to read English, in the company of her brother Edward and three of his friends, one of whom, Roland Leighton, was shortly to become her fiancé. But the outbreak of the European War shattered her hard-won dreams.[5] Her brother and his companions immediately volunteered for service and were commissioned. Unable to endure life on the sidelines at Oxford, and aware of the privations suffered by the four, Brittain became a Voluntary Aid Detachment nurse.[6] Life certainly did not spare her sensibilities: in three years Roland, Edward and their two close friends were killed. These successive deaths and the daily, unremitting suffering she saw in the field hospitals on the Western Front caused her to begin to question the popular, unexamined enthusiasm and patriotism aroused by the war.[7] Indeed, the seeds of her gradual conversion to pacifism were sown in the summer of 1917 whilst Brittain was nursing at a military hospital in Etaples.

One day, when I finished the gruesome and complicated dressing of a desperately wounded prisoner, a disturbing thought struck me. Wasn't it somehow odd that I, in Etaples, should be trying to save the life of a man whom my brother up at Ypres had perhaps done his best to kill? And didn't that argue the existence of some fundamental absurdity in the whole tragic situation?[8]

Such thoughts of tragic irony did not emotionally catapult Brittain into pacifism. It was only with great reluctance that she admitted the bankruptcy of the trust she placed in the League of Nations for a new world order. Her pacifism, from its inception, was rationally and pragmatically inspired, although in later years an overriding Christian dimension came into play.[9] In short, Brittain's move to pacifism was not sudden. Her personal journey to Damascus involved the gradual, and at times unconscious, adoption of a set of beliefs and values which only later crystallized into a total renunciation of war.

By the end of the 1930s Brittain could not ignore the fact that the leadership of the League of Nations Union (LNU), an organization formed to advance the goals of the League of Nations, was becoming uninspiring and myopic, whilst the organization as a whole was systematically ousting the left-wing element to which Brittain belonged.[10] Furthermore, Brittain was also of the opinion that in England the League of Nations platform was being used to advocate rearmament, not so much in the name of collective security, but as a pretext for strengthening Britain militarily.[11] Indeed, by the summer of 1936, Vera Brittain was forced to admit that the LNU was no longer a body which she, in conscience, could support. Accordingly, in January 1937, she responded positively to an invitation from Canon Sheppard to become a sponsor of the Peace Pledge Union.[12] Twenty years later Brittain gave an account of the rift which the escalation of European tensions in 1935 and 1936 had caused to open between the advocates of collective security--reinforced by military sanctions--and their former pacifist allies:

> For fifteen years after the First World War [the] . . . wide moral division between the supporters of collective security and the exponents of revolutionary pacifism had always existed but had not been emphasized. But with the threat of a second World War, the gulf became clear. Individuals who believed that war was wrong in all circumstances could no longer join with those who were prepared to fight in the last resort.[13]

Vera Brittain's personal belief in pacifism and the institution of the Peace Pledge Union had their roots in this shared realization.

Vera Brittain on Women and Peace

Yet there were also other variables at play. For Vera Brittain, her feminism was an integral part of her pacifism, and *vice versa*. In the 1920s and early 1930s her literary and journalistic output, her public addresses and lectures, all revolved around feminist themes and women's issues. But following her conversion to pacifism, there was a marked change in her concentration and much of her energy was devoted to discussing questions of war and peace. Yet Vera Brittain never lost sight of her early commitment to feminism. In 1941 she wrote:

> The women's movement . . . began when civilization reached the point at which a sufficiently large enlightened minority perceived that the operation of reason was superior to force as a factor in human affairs.
> That is why the struggle against war, which is the final and most vicious expression of force, is fundamentally inseparable from feminism, socialism, slave emancipation and the liberation of subject races.[14]

Indeed, the cumulative intensity of her commitments to feminism, to socialism and to pacifism, produced innumerable articles and lectures combining these themes.

In February 1934 Brittain published one of her first articles on the subject of women and war, entitled "Can the Women of the World Stop War?"[15] Although the metaphor is singularly inappropriate to the subject, Brittain came out of her corner swinging. She seldom wrote with subtlety and her journalistic efforts (which were, in my opinion, far superior to all her literary efforts, barring *Testament of Youth*) show off Brittain's punchy style to good advantage. A short, sharp delivery where motive and purpose did not require complexity suited her approach to writing best of all. In this article, published in the *Modern Woman*, Brittain referred to the ". . . terrible, inert mass of lethargic womanhood."[16] In an apparent effort to shake women out of their collective apathy Brittain made a number of stinging criticisms which proved to be recurring themes in her articles on women and war. Writing against the backdrop of the failure of the Geneva disarmament conference which opened in 1932, the accession to power of Adolf Hitler in 1933 and a crisis in the Far East, Brittain stated that a woman whose interests revolved only around the world of domestic details and one who

> . . . refuses to accept what Sir Norman Angell has called 'the moral obligation to be intelligent', is guilty of gross irresponsible selfishness toward her children and society.[17]

Brittain believed women could bring an end to war if they overcame their domestic myopia. To achieve this, women involved in the peace movement needed, in Brittain's opinion, to take a leaf out of the book written by the militant suffragettes and be prepared to adopt militant tactics involving civil disobedience.[18] In another article of Brittain's on "Women and Disarmament," which was published in the same month, Brittain suggested a General Strike on the part of women:

> What more effective General Strike could ever be proclaimed than a strike of women who refused to mend another garment or cook another meal until the sums intended for additional bombing-planes or new 9,000 ton cruisers were dedicated instead to their health and their housing?[19]

But to effect such a strike Brittain was well aware that the collective political and international consciousness of women would have to be raised and that women would have to begin to take an interest in events "beyond their own little doorstep."[20] Brittain also advocated that women join organizations, "from the right-wing League of Nations Union to the Anti-War Movement on the extreme left."[21] For Brittain the necessity of political awareness and the ability to translate consciousness into effective action was a paramount concern.

Vera Brittain had no illusions about the enormity of the task she was advocating. One of the largest obstacles she perceived as lying in the path of women was the "infinite capacity of most women for resignation . . ." which she understood not only to be a severe handicap for women themselves, but also "a menace to the civilization which their united efforts could save."[22] She understood women's uncomplaining endurance in the face of unnecessary adversity to stem from a lack of education and confidence.

> Any system of education which inculcated in women a truer valuation of their needs and functions would. . .mean a real service to the cause of disarmament.[23]

For Brittain education was the critical factor. Her own experiences had given her a keen appreciation of the value and importance of educational opportunity. Ignorance ensured inequality and deprived women of the confidence and ability to express themselves and to exercise their rightful influence at the domestic and international levels.[24]

In the late 1930s Vera Brittain believed that the thraldom of the majority of women to domesticity, and what she understood as the inherent tendency of the domestic routine to anaesthetize, numbed the intellectual development and capacity of women.[25] Righting this wrong was not simply a question of extending educational opportunities for women, although Brittain understandably was a fierce advocate of university education for women. Rather, Brittain was anxious that the provision, for example, of communal domestic services would enable women to have the choice and the possibility of involving themselves in activities outside the home.[26] Through widening the bounds of awareness Brittain hoped that the political consciousness of women would be awakened, not least because it was a necessary prerequisite for political action:

> Progress for women has been rapid where it depended on political action, slow where it depended on changes in heart and habits.[27]

The task as Brittain understood it, however, would be a complicated one, since in the 1930s women were still new to the exercise of political responsibility, and the early political education of women was lamentably lacking.[28] Brittain, for example, faulted the women's magazines for encouraging apolitical attitudes in women through a failure to address political problems in their columns, implicitly suggesting that political issues did not interest or affect women. Caustically, Brittain noted that even men's sporting papers oftentimes included items of political interest.[29] Education and increased awareness were a means of overcoming such obstacles, not least because "no sudden advance is possible over ground which has not been prepared."[30]

Yet education was not the only issue raising serious difficulties in the way of the successful involvement of women in the peace movement. The peace movement itself, in Brittain's opinion, badly needed an image change. War was glorious, exciting and rousing, whilst peace, on the other hand, simply did not "appeal to the imagination, and has, therefore, no glamour."[31] The answer, as Brittain saw it, was to instill "a spirit of adventure in the peace movement."[32] She suggested the launching of a giant peace crusade which would employ the advice of "several advertising experts who have studied the psychology of human response to every kind of appeal, and who would know how to invent slogans to arrest popular attention."[33] Dramatic methods and daring initiatives would revitalize and rejuvenate the movement.

Money? Well, it would be needed, of course, but money is apt to flow in whenever a movement is dramatically presented as a life-or-death issue. Organisers? They should be forthcoming quickly enough, as they have been for Fascism, if peace were associated with action and initiative instead of being identified with perpetual pamphlets and the droning of tired voices in somnolent lecture halls.[34]

Given the experience of the last few years, Brittain's ideas cannot be easily dismissed as occupying a position somewhere out in left field. The women of Greenham Common most certainly would have had her wholehearted support.[35] The large peace demonstrations held in so many of the world's major cities in recent years, the protests of the women of Northern Ireland and those of the mothers of the missing in South America are an eloquent witness to the possibility of realizing goals Brittain voiced for women and for the peace movement half a century ago.[36]

The Peace Pledge Union's Women's Peace Campaign

The organization through which women were able to organize and to work for peace in the late 1930s was the Peace Pledge Union (PPU), which celebrated the fiftieth anniversary of its founding in October 1984. In October 1934 Canon Dick Sheppard made his private, national appeal through advertisements in the British press, asking the men of Britain to pledge themselves to "renounce war and never again, directly or indirectly [to] . . .support or sanction another."[37] His appeal brought an immediate response, but wishing first to assess and to consolidate his support, Canon Sheppard did not form any coherent or official body until July 1935.[38] The Sheppard Peace Movement, as it was initially named, became the Peace Pledge Union in May 1936.[39] It should be noted that Sheppard's appeal to renounce war was not widened to include women until 1936.[40] But by September 1937 roughly 64,364 men and 18,670 women had signed pledge cards and by the summer of 1939 these figures had grown to roughly 86,000 men and 43,000 women. Women in the Union consistently comprised a third of its overall membership.[41]

The Peace Pledge Union was a very active organization. Some of the most popular forms of publicizing peace used by the Union were poster-parades, mass demonstrations and open-air meetings--although the English weather was not always on the side of the organizers of the latter![42] Groups and individuals were rarely at a loss for striking ways to dramatize their case. One PPU member was arrested

> . . . for panicking the crowd which had gathered in Downing Street on the eve of war in September 1939 by lobbing tennis balls--which were mistaken for hand-grenades--into its midst as a means of demonstrating the horror that war would bring.[43]

As well, a PPU Group in Peckham planned a poster-parade on bicycles and received the following advice from the Legal Department of the National Council for Civil Liberties: "The cyclists . . . should be careful not to obstruct other traffic. Needless to say the posters should not in any way affect the proper control of their bicycles."[44]

The attitudes of the general public towards pacifists in the opening months of the war were very mixed, ranging from overt hostility through studied indifference to latent sympathy and open admiration. Mass Observation, the pioneering social survey organization, conducted a survey in Fulham, a mostly working-class district of London, in April 1940. Respondents were asked what they thought about pacifists and some of the answers gathered included:

> Bloody awful. If we were all pacifists the Fuehrer would be here tomorrow.[45]
> I think they're a lot of twirps.[46]
> Needs a lot of pluck don't it?[47]
> I reckon they're bloody heroes.[48]

It was against this not altogether encouraging backdrop that the Peace Pledge Union's Women's Peace Campaign emerged.

The Campaign was not launched by the PPU's National or Executive councils but began with a Liverpool woman's solitary march from Liverpool to London in September 1939. Mary Taylor carried a banner which bore the words, "For the Sake of Children Everywhere, I appeal to Men to Stop This War." Her effort was reported in the back pages of *Peace News*, the PPU newspaper edited by John Middleton Murry.[49] On 13 October 1939 Taylor planned to lead a women's peace march thorough Liverpool,[50] and by the end of that month her idea began to find a response.[51] On Friday, 3 November 1939, *Peace News* reported that on the preceding Tuesday a procession of women, which stretched out of sight, had marched for peace through Holborn. On Wednesday a second parade had left from the Methodist centre in Kingsway which the police tried to stop. The marchers had demanded to know "what new regulation they were infringing . . . " and since an answer could not be supplied, they were provided, instead, with "a huge and very benevolent sergeant in a blue steel helmet."[52] It was at this point that some PPU officials began to respond to the women's protest.

In mid-November John Barclay, the PPU's National Development Officer, proposed a peace march by all the women of Great Britain.[53] The response was apparently very encouraging[54] and by the end of November the Peace Pledge Union established a Women's Committee under the direction of Mary Gamble, and the Women's Peace Campaign came into being.[55] To launch the campaign a rally was called for the Central Hall, Westminster. In *Peace News* Gamble declared:

> This campaign is designed not only to give expression to women's revolt against war, but to their demand that the Government should, at the earliest possible moment, use the method of negotiation to secure a lasting peace.[56]

The organizers had planned that women would walk in silence from the Embankment to the Central Hall for the meeting. But the police had other ideas. Sir Philip Game, the chief of the London police, banned the march as politically motivated.

> The ban was imposed in accordance with an order issued under the Defence Regulations by the Home Secretary, Sir John Anderson, on November 28, prohibiting 'processions of a political character' in the London area for three months dating from December 2.[57]

Undaunted, the Women's Peace Campaign committee made plans for a national campaign in February 1940, declaring Saturday, 17 February 1940 Women's Peace Day. Arrangements were made for processions in Newcastle, Birmingham, Nottingham, Liverpool, Sheffield and Manchester.[58] Yet the results of the day, even in light of the unusually bitter weather, were decidedly disappointing. In Central London 140 women marched; in Cardiff 53; in Nottingham 30 and in Manchester 116.[59] Nevertheless, the Women's Peace Campaign persisted and in mid-March announced the launching of a nationwide petition:

> We women address this appeal to the governments of the nations to stop the war and meet together to discuss peace.[60]

But by the end of April it was apparent that the petition and the Campaign were both floundering.

The "bore" war had become a real war. The totality of the demands made by escalating conflict bit into the fabric of English life and the strictures and exactions upon society and the wholehearted response of the vast majority of the population meant that pacifists were exceedingly hard pressed in maintaining their witness. Of the petition Sybil Morrison, the secretary of the Women's Peace Campaign, admitted that:

> The invasion of Scandinavia has, of course, made it much more difficult now to approach people about signing an appeal for negotiations because opinion is hardening against the pacifist.[61]

One woman probably captured the emotional response of many:

> In the last war I personally used to think it rather brave of conscientious objectors to stick to their principles but that was because my boy was safe in his cradle. Now that he is fighting I feel very angry with them. . . .The sight of a notice in the window with the words "Peace Pledge Union" now makes me furious.[62]

On June 21, one day before the French surrender, Morrison, in an article entitled "Women's Peace Campaign Must Go On," implicitly acknowledged that support and enthusiasm for the campaign were rapidly waning.[63] Indeed, news of the campaign virtually disappeared from the pages of *Peace News* until December 1940.

This eclipse of the nationwide, public campaign of the Women's Committee can undoubtedly be largely explained by the increasingly perilous situation of the Allied and British war efforts against Nazi Germany in the second half of 1940. The obstacles in the way of campaigning for a negotiated peace under such circumstances were colossal. But there were also other considerations. Although the campaign sought to mobilize women, its central theme was a call for a negotiated peace. This, however, duplicated the Peace Pledge Union's official Stop-the-War campaign launched within days of the outbreak of hostilities. The Stop-the-War campaign, from its inception, was beset by difficulties and differences within the Union as to its appropriateness and effectiveness. These divisions within the PPU concerning the campaign only escalated in gravity as the war proceeded.[64] The Women's Peace Campaign unfortunately suffered an identical fate and, because it was a second-string effort, its fortunes faded even more rapidly.

In December 1940 the low-profile successor to the Women's Peace Campaign made its appearance in the form of a weekly "Women's Section" column in *Peace News*.[65] But the column, which continued the appeal for a negotiated peace, had a decidedly humanitarian as opposed to socialist or feminist orientation and was phased out after only seven months. This was probably because, by the summer of 1941, differences over the pacifist campaign for a negotiated peace had produced a "distressing division . . . that involves a conflict of opinion which is weakening to our witness and may easily be damaging to our unity."[66]

The state of the debate within the PPU was summarized in a pamphlet written by Alex Wood, the PPU's chairman, and published in late 1941. Wood concluded:

> The end of the fighting is the first condition of a successful attack on the evil . . . [of war]. Peace by negotiation is therefore always our policy although not always our tactic. We can never retreat from it although at any given moment it might be unwise to campaign on it.[67]

The Women's Peace Campaign collapsed in the summer of 1941.[68] The Peace Pledge Union's main campaign for a negotiated peace persisted, however, until the autumn of 1944, when it, too, had to be abandoned. This was probably mainly on account of a critical dilemma crystallizing in the minds of a number of pacifists.

> If the Nazis have really been guilty of the unspeakable crimes circumstancially imputed to them, then--let us make no mistake--pacifism is faced with a situation with which it cannot cope. The conventional pacifist conception of a reasonable or generous peace is irrelevant to this reality.[69]

It was a dilemma not faced directly by pacifists before the end of the war.[70]

Vera Brittain--At War for Peace, 1939-1945

Vera Brittain was conspicuous by her absence from the Women's Peace Campaign. In an article which appeared in *Peace News* in the issue following that which carried the last Women's Section column, Brittain explained her position:

> The Women's Section was originally started in the autumn of 1939 to organize a limited series of meetings under the name of 'The Women's Peace Campaign.' Some of us who have worked for years on behalf of equal rights and opportunities between men and women felt misgivings about both this campaign and its perpetuation as a 'Women's Section', for we regarded its conception as reactionary and its methods out of date.
>
> The time is past when women, by organizing themselves into separate groups have to demonstrate their ability to work politically at all. The modern phase of the women's struggle is the much more difficult one of equal . . . co-operation.[71]

It was in this spirit and with this understanding that Brittain threw herself into wartime peace work. Brittain was a woman of fierce determination and will power, moral courage and conviction of purpose, indefatigable energy and industry, and a remarkable consistency of belief. Without these driving qualities Brittain could not have accomplished a fraction of the tasks she set herself. My intention here is only to sketch Brittain's activities in order to provide a composite picture of their variety and scope.

Brittain earned her living by the pen and it was to the pen she turned to make her first contribution to wartime pacifism. War had immediately created an increase in Brittain's correspondence from fellow pacifists concerning issues relating to war and to peace. In order to cope with the volume of questions she received, Brittain conceived the idea of a fortnightly newsletter maintained by individual subscription. The idea proved successful enough to sustain the project and Brittain published the newsletter, without interruption, throughout the war.[72] Indeed a Cabinet memorandum issued in May 1940 singled out Brittain's *Letter to Peace Lovers* as one of the most successful publications of its sort.[73] In addition to the newsletter Brittain also published five books during the war, two of which addressed themselves directly to the subjects of pacifist and military issues. *Humiliation with Honour*, written in the form of explanatory letters from a woman pacifist to her adolescent son, sought to provide a readily intelligible explanation of the pacifist position to a general audience.[74] But the most controversial of her wartime books was *Seed of Chaos, What Mass Bombing Really Means*.[75] A powerful indictment of saturation bombing, the book has withstood well the test of time.[76] The publication received little attention in England and was chiefly to be noted for the savage criticism it provoked from George Orwell.[77] But extracts from an earlier version of the book were also published in the United States. Twenty-eight leading American Protestant clergymen appended their signatures to a postscript supporting Brittain's critique of mass bombing, producing a "'furore' . . . [which] had even inspired three and a half columns of adverse criticisms in the *New York Times*."[78] In addition to these major works Brittain wrote a number of small pamphlets dealing with pacifism, food relief for occupied Europe and mass bombing.[79] Brittain also contributed innumerable articles to national and provincial newspapers, as well as to *Peace News*, on these and related subjects. Furthermore, she used to very good effect the "Letters" columns of these papers to make her case, or to explain and defend the pacifist position, seeking always to remind the public audience of the values she understood the world to be abandoning at its peril.

Brittain also travelled extensively through wartime England lecturing to small PPU groups as well as to larger public gatherings.[80] The considerable influence which her high profile as a successful writer and popular speaker enabled her to exert upon large audiences was conceded by the government. Indeed the government viewed Brittain-- from its perspective--as a political trouble-maker.[81] She was referred to by two different government officials as "a determined pacifist" and as an "aggressive pacifist"[82] whilst another gave the following assessment:

She is of the kind that thrives on opposition and counterblast
will merely call forth counterblast and give her more publicity
than before.[83]

Brittain was clearly not a woman easily ignored, even by the
government's reckoning!

Within the Peace Pledge Union Brittain poured her tremendous
energies into her responsibilities as a member of the Union's Executive
and National Councils. Her views and opinions carried considerable
weight within the PPU, especially in terms of moving the Union away
from the sectarian tendencies inherent in the pacifism of people like
Middleton Murry. She advocated the increased, active involvement of
pacifists in political, humanitarian and relief activities, irrespective of
whether or not one's co-workers were fellow pacifists.[84] Brittain gave
very concrete expression to the position in society and wartime work she
advocated for pacifists by becoming a founding member of the Bombing
Restriction Committee and the tireless chairperson of the PPUs Food
Relief Campaign.[85] Her wartime witness, like that of other women
pacifists, was one of constant struggle. But for Vera Brittain the belief
that her life as a pacifist contributed positively to the long-term goals of
peace and a war-free world absorbed the disappointments and
frustrations of apparent failure in the short term. The logic was that of
the Cross. Christ had died believing that whatever the immediate
results

of a course determined by conviction and ending in failure,
His Father would reveal in time's long perspective that the
action performed in accordance with the Divine Will would
produce the results desired for His world.[86]

It was in this faith, whether understood in religious or moral terms,
that Vera Brittain and other women pacifists endeavoured to witness to
their pacifist commitment during the Second World War.

Comments

Alison Prentice

I'd like to ask a question that arises out of Deborah Gorham's
presentation which alerted us to the importance of people's personal
family relations, and their personal relations generally, for their
political outlook. Maybe you could tell us a little bit more about Vera
Brittain's feelings about her children, how they changed or developed. I
would particularly like to hear about that book that was evidently
addressed to an adolescent son. I know that she sent her children to the
United States during the Second World War. I read *The Testament of
Experience* in which she expresses very strong feelings about the

situation of her children. I'd be interested in your perspective on the problem that she faced, that is, sending her own children away in order to do this war work and her ambivalent feelings about that.

Yvonne Bennett

Yes, this was certainly something which caused her a great deal of suffering. I think her son John was born in 1927 and her daughter Shirley Williams, who, of course, is well known as a founding member of the Social Democrats in Britain, was born in 1930. So when they went to the United States early in the war, they were very young and this, I think, was something which weighed very much on Brittain's mind during the war and indeed subsequently. There are some beautiful letters in the Brittain collection that she wrote to her children, some of which one almost feels one shouldn't be reading, and some equally beautiful letters back from them. The children returned before the war's conclusion and Vera was very, very glad of that because she felt that her children were just at the age that if they stayed away longer than the two or three years that they were away that there would be an irreparable rift in the mother-child relationship.

Ruth Roach Pierson

A point that I think the paper raised in passing that might have got lost in our discussion over the last two days is the dilemma that the Peace Pledge Union was put into when it learned of the creditable evidence of the mass murdering of Jews and others designated undesirables by the Nazi regime. In these papers there have been on the one hand people who are absolute pacifists and on the other hand people who are what one might call politically or historically specific pacifists. What sort of discussion emerged within the Peace Pledge Union when they were faced with the revelations of the unspeakable Nazi horrors?

Yvonne Bennett

Yes, this is a very critical point. It certainly became critical for pacifists after the war when the evidence was simply there for all to see and was indisputable. The little piece there that I read from John Middleton Murry was in fact a part of an editorial on the whole question of the final solution and pacifism's response to that. Initially, though, in pacifist circles, and this was certainly true I think until the Americans entered Bergen-Belsen, the pacifist response simply was incredulity--total disbelief that human beings could do this to one another. In the Brittain collection there are two very interesting letters written by Corder Catchpool who was a very prominent Quaker, active in the Peace Pledge Union. And Corder Catchpool's interpretation of the photographs and of the evidence was simply that the allies were trying to disguise the effects of allied bombing on Germany and that, in actual fact, was what people were seeing. He simply couldn't believe or accept the revelations. In terms of Vera Brittain's own response, I think that the answer to the question is as follows: here we're looking at pacifists, particularly absolute pacifists, in Britain during the Second World War. Almost all of those who clung to their witness and who lived their witness, were, in fact, the religious pacifists, the Christian pacifists. And that meant that even in spite of these unspeakable horrors that they were seeing, they believed that somehow so long as they lived according to their conscience and to their beliefs, things would ultimately work themselves out and that time was in God's hands and not in theirs.

Veronica Strong-Boag

I'm interested in some of your observations about how the pacifists dealt with the information that was coming out of Germany because I think your distinction between the religious pacifists, and, let's say, the secular pacifists is very important. Certainly the ones that remained firm pacifists throughout the war were the religious ones in Canada and they were very few in number. But I think what is also quite clear amongst the internationalist pacifists in Canada was that by 1933 and certainly by 1935 feminists were also victims of Nazi persecution (and indeed feminists ended up in large numbers of Nazi concentration camps). Many Canadian pacifists had connections with just those feminists and they were getting information both from the Women's International League and through the Council that feminists were dying in these camps. Efforts to aid political refugees were beginning in Canada, certainly, by 1937. The pacifists were very attentive to those refugees who were bringing more information. That did certainly change secular pacifists' minds about what their response to the war would be. They had a lot of information.

Yvonne Bennett

Yes, they did. In fact, on that score the Quaker "intelligence service" was pretty good, too. It was really almost as good as the government's. Corder Catchpool, for instance, was receiving letters which were smuggled from Germany. Vera Brittain, of course, was part of the literary circle; she was a member of PEN, (Poets, Essayists and Novelists). Storm Jameson, the first woman president of PEN, renounced pacifism in 1939 because her work helping Jewish writers had demonstrated to her the gravity of the situation.

Deborah Gorham

I would like to comment in general on the whole dilemma of World War II and the absolutist pacifist. The war was not fought by the Allies to defend world Jewry; the Jews of Europe died anyway. That is one thing to remember. I think Vera Brittain realized that. She was involved to a certain extent in helping to get Jewish refugees out and that is one of the things that one could have done, and one of the things that people did do. And one of the things also, of course, that governments and individuals did not do enough of, those who were gung-ho supporters of the war, so I think that point has to be made.

Jo Vellacott

I just want to comment on alternate ways of working for peace by absolute pacifists. A lot of that can be summed up in the phrase "removing the causes of war." Kathleen Lonsdale, for instance, wrote on that subject and it has to do with education. The pacifists were nearly all involved in campaigns against militarism in schools and in favour of positive peace education and changing the climate of education and the content of education, as well as personal witness.

Notes

[1]Vera Brittain Collection (hereafter cited as VBC), McMaster University, Hamilton, Ontario. F289, Vera Brittain, "How War Affects Women," Lecture given at Rockford Women's Club, Rockford, Illinois, 30 November 1937.

[2]For a full history of the wartime Peace Pledge Union see Yvonne Bennett, "Testament of a Minority in Wartime: The Peace Pledge Union and Vera Brittain, 1939-1945" (Ph.D. thesis, McMaster University, 1984).

[3]Vera M. Brittain, Testament of Youth: An Autobiographical Story of the Years 1900-1925 (London: Victor Gollancz, 1933). The book, to this day, ranks as the best seller ever published by the Gollancz publishing house. In 1978 Virago, the London-based feminist publishers, reissued Testament of Youth. See John J. O'Connor, "'Testament of Youth'--An Early Feminist Story," New York Times, 30 November 1980, and Janet Watts, "Women at War," Manchester Guardian Weekly, 30 April 1978. See also Alan Bishop, ed., with Terry Smart, Vera Brittain. Chronicle of Youth: War Diary 1913-1917 (London: Victor Gollancz, 1981).

[4]Brittain produced her first novel at the age of seven and a further four before the age of eleven. Her determination to achieve her literary ambitions was fortunately unbounded since she had to overcome both parental and societal constraints. But Brittain did find support at her boarding school--St. Monica's in Kingswood, Surrey--where the progressive headmistress, Miss Heath-Jones, nurtured and encouraged Brittain's nascent feminism. See also VBC/G490, Vera Brittain, "Were Women Meant to Have Brains?," Quiver, February, 1935.

[5]

> In cities and in hamlets we were born,
> And little towns behind the van of time;
> A closing era mocked our guileless dawn
> With jingles of a military rhyme.
> But in that song we heard no warning chime,
> Nor visualized in hours benign and sweet
> The threatening woe that our adventurous feet
> Would starkly meet.

Vera Brittain, "The War Generation: Ave," in Poems of the War and After (London: Victor Gollancz, 1934).

[6]Both Roland Leighton and Edward Brittain wrote detailed,

graphic and poignant letters to Vera Brittain. These may be found in VBC, McMaster University.

[7]This mood is perfectly captured in the poetry of Rupert Brooke. The reality of the horrors and suffering of trench warfare is to be found in the poetry of Siegfried Sasson, Isaac Rosenberg and the matchless work of Wilfred Owen.

[8]VBC/H341, Vera Brittain, "From War to Pacifism," published in Forward, 9 September 1939 under the title, "What can we do in War Time? Work for a Sane Peace."

[9]See VBC/I74, Vera Brittain, "The Kind of God I Believe In" [c. 1945].

[10]The aim of the League of Nations Union was to advance the work of the League of Nations. See E. Bramstead, "Apostles of Collective Security: The L.N.U. and its Functions," Australian Journal of Politics and History 13 (1967): 347-64, and George W. Egerton, "Collective Security as Political Myth: Liberal Internationalism and the League of Nations in Politics and History," International History Review 5 (1983): 475-627.

[11]VBC/Correspondence: Vera Brittain to Miss Jarrett, 5 March 1937. Also VBC/H274, Vera Brittain, "Germany and the League of Nations," n.d.

[12]VBC/Correspondence: Dick Sheppard to Vera Brittain, 27 January 1937 and Vera Brittain to Dick Sheppard, 28 January 1937. See also Vera Brittain to George Catlin, 21 June 1936; Brittain to Sheppard, 3 July 1936; Brittain to Philip Mumford, 28 October 1936; Brittain to Miss Stancer, 27 January 1937.

[13]Vera Brittain, Testament of Experience: An Autobiographical Story of the Years 1925-1950 (London: Victor Gollancz, 1957), p. 168. See also VBC/G794, Vera Brittain,"The Things of Peace--3," Reconciliation, March, 1961, p. 46, and VBC/G523, Vera Brittain, "No Compromise with War," World Review of Reviews, May, 1937.

[14]Vera Brittain, "Women and Pacifism," Peace News, 15 August 1941, p. 3.

[15]VBC/G444, Vera Brittain, "Can the Women of the World Stop War?," Modern Woman, February, 1934, pp. 7 and 62.

[16]Brittain, "Can the Women. . .," p. 7. See also VBC/G445, Vera Brittain, "Women and Disarmament," Highway, February, 1934, p. 2 and VBC/F21, Vera Brittain, "How War Affects Education," Lecture [n.p.], 23 January 1934.

[17]Brittain, "Can the Women. . .," p. 62.

[18]Ibid.

[19]Brittain, "Women and Disarmament," p. 3.

[20]Brittain, "Can the Women. . . ," p. 62.

[21]Vera Brittain, "Can the Women. . . ," p. 62. That Brittain spoke to all women, as women, and not out of some vested political interest is given credence by the fact that she encouraged women to join the peace organization best suited to their own political persuasions.

[22]Brittain, "Women and Disarmament," p. 3. Three years later

Brittain was still concerned with the resignation of women--"This apathy constitutes as great a threat as fascism." Brittain, "How War Affects Women."

[23]Brittain, "Women and Disarmament," p. 3.

[24]VBC/G530, Vera Brittain, "Women Still Wait for Equality," Daily Herald, 26 March 1938.

[25]Brittain, "How War Affects Women." See also VBC/G509, "Women and the Next War," British Legion Journal, April, 1936.

[26]Brittain, "How War Affects Women."

[27]Eleanor Rathbone, quoted in Brittain, "How War Affects Women."

[28]Brittain, "How War Affects Women."

[29]Ibid. It should be noted, however, that Brittain was well able to translate her case for the necessity for women's involvement in the peace movement into a strictly domestic language geared to touch the "lethargic mass." See VBC/G513, Vera Brittain, "A Shadow Which Mothers Dread. Tell Your Children the Truth About War!," Yorkshire Evening News, 11 November 1936 and VBC/G528, Vera Brittain, "To Mothers Especially," PPU Leaflet, 1937.

[30]VBC/G757, Vera Brittain, "Dissent by Demonstration," Nation, 21 March 1959, p. 252.

[31]VBC/G482, Vera Brittain, "Why Not a Real Peace Crusade?," published in a pamphlet, "The Lighter Side of Peacemaking," Quarterly News, 1934, p. 37. This was a point made very strongly by Vera Brittain in Testament of Youth.

[32]Brittain, "Why Not a Real Peace Crusade?," p. 39.

[33]Ibid.

[34]Ibid.

[35]In the 1960s London's Trafalgar Square witnessed a number of CND demonstrations. One such demonstration, led by Bertrand Russell, had been banned by the police, but the protesters ignored the ban. The police cordonned off the Square to prevent others from joining those already sitting in. Vera Brittain, in her seventies, was among those protesters who found their way blocked by the police and promptly sat down in the middle of the road, later to be gently carried away by police constables. Interview with Harry Mister (London), 22 December 1980.

[36]In 1961, in a letter to The Times, Brittain wrote:

Sir, - Lord Coleraine's disparaging comments on the Committee of 100 in your issue this morning recall the criticisms of the suffragette movement that I read in my schooldays. Mrs. Pankhurst, the reviled leader of the "screaming sisterhood," ended up with a statue in Westminster and Lord Russell will doubtless do the same. [He did, in Red Lion Square!]

The sacrificial fervour of great idealistic crusades begins to capture public imagination and achieve its ends when it takes an active and "dangerous" form. Not only the suffragette movement, but Mahatma Gandhi's civil disobedience campaign in India, bears witness to this uncomfortable historical fact.

VBC/G809, Vera Brittain, "Anti-Nuclear Campaign," The Times, 19 September 1961.

[37]Sybil Morrison, I Renounce War: The Story of the Peace Pledge Union (London: Sheppard Press, 1962), p. 100, and Martin Ceadel, Pacifism in Britain, 1939-1945: The Defining of a Faith (Oxford: Clarendon Press, 1980), p. 178.

[38]Martin Ceadel, Pacifism in Britain, p. 178; Sybil Morrison, I Renounce War, p. 10.

[39]Martin Ceadel, Pacifism in Britain, p. 222; Anonymous, "Christian pacifism: Canon Sheppard's pacifism," Tablet, 25 April 1936, p. 516.

[40]H. R. L. Sheppard, "Women and Peace," New Statesman and Nation, 4 July 1936, p. 11.

[41]VBC/F289, Vera Brittain, "How War Affects Women." The response was somewhat of a disappointment for Sheppard, who had frankly anticipated a far greater one.

[42]See report on the Bermondsey Group Meeting, Peace News, 2 February 1940. Also "Letters," Peace News, 12 January, 1940.

[43]Ceadel, Pacifism in Britain, pp. 228-9.

[44]National Council for Civil Liberties (NCCL) Archives, University of Hull. PPU/NCCL, 16/3, 1939-1940, Legal Departments, NCCL to L. H. Hislom, PPU, Peckham, n.d. For an important discussion of the history of civil liberties in England and the Government's Emergency Powers, see A. S. Kileman, "Emergency Powers and Liberal Democracy in Britain," Journal of Commonwealth and Comparative Politics 16 (1978): 190-211. Also Neil Stammers, Civil Liberties in Britain in the Second World War (London: Croom Helm, 1984); Angus Calder, The People's War: Britain 1939-1945 (London: Panther, 1971), pp. 35-6 and 123-4; Robert S. W. Pollard, Conscience and Liberty (London: George Allen and Unwin, n.d. [c. 1940-41]), especially pp. 43-4 and 83-94.

[45]Mass Observation Archive (hereafter MO), University of Sussex. MO Box 311B, File B, Pacifism Interview, female respondent, aged 40, middle class.

[46]MO, Pacifism Interview, male respondent, aged 35, skilled.

[47]MO, Pacifism Interview, male respondent, aged 25, skilled.

[48]MO, Pacifism Interview, female respondent, aged 40, unskilled.

[49]Anonymous, "Liverpool to London Lone Peace Pilgrimage Gives a Lead to Women," Peace News, 6 October 1939, p. 7.

[50]Anonymous, "Women's Peace March Tomorrow," Peace News, 13 October 1939, p. 5.

[51]In the October 27th issue of *Peace News* it was reported that more than forty women had marched through London's West End.

[52]Anonymous, "They Marched for Peace," Peace News, 3 November 1939, p. 5.

[53]John Barclay, "War--A Challenge to Women," Peace News, 17 November 1939, p. 6. The activities of women pacifists brought an Armistice Day telegram from a Lillian Westall of Ottawa, Ontario. "Sincerest wishes to all the London women marchers and all meetings today." Anonymous, "Cheer from Canada," Peace News 24 November 1939, p. 3.

[54]John Barclay, "Women Accept the Challenge," Peace News, 24 November 1939, p. 6.

[55]John Barclay, "Mobilizing the Women," Peace News, 1 December 1939, p. 6.

[56]Anonymous, "Women May Send Peace Call to Queen," Peace News, 1 December 1939.

[57]Peace News, 8 December 1939, p. 1. Vera Brittain, Sybil Thorndike, Ruth Fry and Mary Gamble were among the speakers in the Central Hall. Brittain's address may have been VBC/F51, "Pacifism 1939." Explaining the ban, Sir John Anderson said:

The march which the Women's Peace Campaign proposed to organize was clearly a procession of a political character designed to further a political object.

Anonymous, "Ban on March Explained," Peace News, 12 January 1940, p. 4.

[58]Anonymous, "Plans for Women's Peace Day," Peace News, 9 February 1940, p. 8. See also Sybil Morrison, "Women's Peace Campaign. Nation-Wide Drive Next Month," Peace News, 19 January 1940, p. 1. Other centres planning activities were Cardiff, Croydon, Dartford, Eastleigh, Glasgow, Guildford, Hull, Leeds, Nottingham, Romford, Sheffield, Watford, Wembley.

[59]Sybil Morrison, "Where Women Marched," Peace News, 1 March 1940, p. 7.

[60]Sybil Morrison, "Women's Peace Campaign Petition Launched," Peace News, 15 March 1940. The campaign hoped for one million signatures, obtained by going "to every tea party, sewing party, Church service or Guild and. . .[asking] to be allowed to explain the appeal and invite signatures." Dorothy Evans, "Why Must Our Boys Die? Women's Appeal to Governments," Peace News, 5 April 1940, p. 1.

[61]Sybil Morrison, "Signing Them on For Peace," Peace News, 26 April 1940, p. 1.

[62]Mass Observation, Directive Replies (Women), October 1942. The respondent is G. Hartland.

[63]Sybil Morrison, "Women's Peace Campaign Must Go On," Peace News, 21 June 1940, p. 4.

[64]For a full discussion of the Stop-the-War campaign--which was successively known as the "Armistice Now" and "Negotiated Peace Campaign"--see Bennett, "Testament of a Minority in Wartime," Chapter Six.

211

[65]The first column was written by a veteran Quaker pacifist, Ruth Fry, and was entitled, "War on the Home." Fry wrote: "As never before ... this war is directed against women, and they have a right and a duty to make known their opinion about it." Peace News, 27 December 1940, p. 3.

[66]Charles Raven, "Negotiation or Revolution?," Christian Pacifist, April, 1941, pp. 128-9. See also PPU London Area Minutes, 10 August 1941; G. Lloyd Phelps, "Against Negotiation Now," Christian Pacifist, April and July, 1941 and Charles Raven, "Negotiation or Revolution?," Christian Pacifist, September and November, 1941.

[67]Alex Wood, Peace by Negotiation (London: Peace Pledge Union, n.d., [probably between September 1941 and February 1942]). See also Peace Pledge Union, Minutes of National Council Meeting, 15-16 March 1941.

[68]Another problem may have been possible editorial opposition to the campaign on the part of Peace News editor John Middleton Murry. Both Sybil Morrison and Vera Brittain frequently found themselves at odds with Murry and the coverage and space given to the Campaign in Peace News would seem to suggest that Murry was not supportive. See Frank Lea, John Middleton Murry (London: Methuen, 1959), pp. 310-11. Sybil Morrison commented in an interview that there was great admiration for Middleton Murry as a literary critic but the joke among the Peace News staff was to call him "God" (behind his back!) and to genuflect outside his office. Morrison also corroborated Brittain's written opinion that Murry had a "D.H. Lawrence inspired attitude toward women," agreeing that "he had a frightful attitude." Interview with Miss Sybil Morrison (London), 6 July 1979 and VBC/Correspondence, Vera Brittain to Andrew Dakers, 9 November 1942.

[69]John Middleton Murry, "Lublin," Peace News, 22 September 1944, p. 2.

[70]Surprising though it may seem, the principal reason for the lack of a pacifist response was utter incredulity; that human beings could commit such heinous crimes was beyond the comprehension of most pacifists. See VBC/Bombing Restriction Committee File, 1945-1946, Corder Catchpool to Vera Brittain, 19 April 1945 and Catchpool to Brittain, 25 April 1945. Also Bernard Wasserstein, Britain and the Jews of Europe 1939-1945 (Oxford: Oxford University Press, 1979).

[71]Vera Brittain, "Women and Pacifism," Peace News, 15 August 1941, p. 3.

[72]Brittain, Testament of Experience, pp. 219-21.

[73]PRO CAB 75/7 HPC (40), 103, Memorandum on Anti-War Publications, 4 May 1940. See also CAB 73/3 CDC (40), 8, "Home Front Propaganda," Memo by the Minister of Information, 3/3/40.

[74]Vera Brittain, Humiliation with Honour (London: Andrew Dakers, 1942). See VBC/A11.

[75]Vera Brittain, Seed of Chaos. What Mass Bombing Really Means (n.p. [London?]: New Vision Publishing Co., 1944).

[76]For a fuller discussion of the bombing question see Yvonne Bennett, "The Pacifist and Quasi-Pacifist Critique of the Strategic Bombing Policy of the Allies During the Second World War," paper presented at the Duquesne History Forum, Pittsburgh, October 1979. Also Bennett, "Testament of a Minority," Chapter Six.

[77]For an excellent discussion of the exchanges between Brittain and Orwell, and for an assessment of the research, argumentation and conclusions contained in Seed of Chaos, see Alan Bishop, "Vera Brittain, George Orwell, Mass Bombing and the English Language," paper presented to McMaster English Association, McMaster University, February 1984. See also George Orwell, The Collected Essays, Journalism and Letters of George Orwell, Vol. 3, As I Please 1943-1945, pp. 179-81 and 213-15. Also Orwell in the Observer, 8 April 1945 and Tribune, 23 June 1944. Also VBC/G594 and VBC/G612.

[78]Brittain, Testament of Experience, p. 331. Also Brittain, "Massacre by Bombing," Fellowship X, March, 1944, pp. 332-6.

[79]See for example: Vera Brittain, One of These Little Ones (London: Andrew Dakers, 1943); Stop Bombing Civilians (London: n. p., 1943); Vera Brittain Writes on How Shall the Christian Church Prepare for the New Order? (London: Anglican Pacifist Fellowship, n.d., [c. early 1942]).

[80]One product of her travels was Brittain's England's Hour: An Autobiography 1939-1941 (London: Macmillan, 1941). See VBC/A10.

[81]PRO FO 371/24245, FO Minute from Charles Peake to Mr. Scott, 2 January 1940. Marked Confidential. File: Visit of Miss Brittain to the United States of America.

[82]PRO FO 371/24245, Peake to Scott and PRO FO 371/24245, FO telegram to Lord Lothian, 10 January 1940.

[83]PRO FO 371/24245, FO Minute dated 13 January 1940, signature indecipherable.

[84]Many absolutists or, to use my own terminology, 'high pacifists,' seriously questioned involvement in relief work--especially with non-pacifist co-workers--on the grounds that it compromised pacifism's complete and utter rejection of war and all its works. Vera Brittain maintained that the high pacifist position, in its most orthodox sense, became untenable for the vast majority of pacifists and liable to be construed as hand-washing by the majority of non-pacifists. For a full discussion of this issue, see Bennett, "Testament of a Minority," Preface and Chapter Five.

[85]For a discussion of both campaigns, see Bennett, "Testament of a Minority," Chapter Five.

[86]Brittain, Testament of Experience, p. 172; VBC/Correspondence, Brittain to J. S. Barr, 27 May 1941; Stuart Morris, The Creed of a Christian Pacifist (Manchester: Co-operative Union, 1937).

PART III

CONTEMPORARY PRACTICES

TEACHING FOR PEACE IN THE SECONDARY SCHOOL

Margaret Wells

As is probably true for most teachers, I have always regarded a classroom of students engaged in a vigorous debate as a sign that my teaching has been successful--I have stimulated their interest and they are grappling with the issue. Teaching about nuclear issues has forced me to reconsider this notion. I have begun to question what the focus of these heated discussions is for my students. Do they feel the need to defend their own point of view by attacking the opinions of others or do they want to establish some mutual areas of understanding? I have to admit that the former is more likely the motivation and that the way in which I framed the discussion of the issue might be encouraging the students' confrontational attitudes. Somehow the nuclear issue demanded a different approach.

In this paper, I intend to outline the development of my own approach to peace education in the context of the growing support for peace studies by the Toronto Board of Education for which I work.

My own interest in teaching about peace began approximately ten years ago when I was working in a school which held a weekly speaker's hour at which various community people were asked to address the students on a wide range of topics. Around Remembrance Day we would use this hour to hear people such as Setsuko Thurlow (a social worker with our board, a Hiroshima survivor and a peace activist; also a contributor to this volume) or to view a film such as *The War Game* produced for BBC television. We hoped to counter the glorification of war which was sometimes associated with November 11th and to remind our students of what war means in a nuclear age. These events often led to stimulating discussion in the school, but the problem was that they were isolated occurrences remaining largely unconnected with what was happening in the regular curriculum.

I had an opportunity to improve this situation a few years later when I began teaching the compulsory history course at the intermediate (i.e., grade nine and ten) level. The Ontario Ministry of Education published a support document entitled *The Canadian Military: Evolution of a Peacekeeper* to provide an example of how to handle an issue of concern to Canada and to the world which was required to be included in the course. Although this document emphasized Canada's role in United Nations peacekeeping operations and did not even consider our role in the nuclear arms race, it at least legitimized introducing issues of war and peace into the curriculum.

I taught a unit on the threat of nuclear war, using the ministry document but including material which examined Canada's role in selling nuclear technology and our participation in the arms race. Generally my students responded very positively to the unit.

In 1980, I began teaching a course called World Issues which is a study of development. As I became more familiar with the work being done in development education, I realized that it was important not to concentrate solely on third world countries but to examine the unequal pattern of development and the social costs of high technology within "advanced" countries. As I began to emphasize the interdependence of the world community, the social and economic costs of militarism throughout the world became an important theme in the course. In addition this course encouraged me to broaden my own and my students' outlook on the world so that every issue was not seen as part of the east-west confrontation. Nations which were working towards a third path to development challenged us to examine our "either . . . or" thinking on many important issues, including those related to peace and war.

During the fall of 1981 a trustee of the Toronto Board, Fiona Nelson, concerned that there was no programme planned to observe Disarmament Week in the schools, called together a group of teachers and some prominent people in the community, such as Clark MacDonald, former moderator of the United Church, and George Ignatieff, former Canadian ambassador to the United Nations. By focusing on issues in the world which tend to be at the root of much conflict, the group hoped to develop suggestions for activities and resources to be used in the schools. Some material was field tested in a series of student workshops in the spring of 1982; as a result of this work a conference for three hundred secondary students was planned for the fall of 1982. Students were involved in pre-conference workshops and were encouraged to develop ideas for activities within their schools.

Ms. Nelson's group felt that a different pedagogical approach was necessary to teach the critical contemporary issues which they wanted to see included in school programmes. As a result, they persuaded the board to sponsor a two-day workshop for teachers in the fall of 1982, in order to explore such a pedagogy.

In the spring of 1983, knowing that there was support from all the senior curriculum officials, the group decided that it was appropriate to become an official committee of the board. Previously Ms. Nelson had reported on the group's activities to the School Programs Committee. Ms. Nelson demonstrated her political astuteness in waiting to constitute her group as an official board committee until she had established its credibility and support for its work. It is at least questionable whether or not the board would have created a committee to promote the study of disarmament in the schools without this careful preparation.

216

The Thinking and Deciding in a Nuclear Age Committee stated that its goal was:

> to further the study of critical contemporary issues in world affairs--issues that are complex and controversial, intellectually and emotionally challenging, and rarely treated in textbooks.[1]

They hoped to accomplish this goal by assisting teachers and students with curriculum materials and resources, encouraging in-service educational opportunities for teachers and generating co-curricular activities to complement the regular classroom programme. The committee adopted a five-year plan for the consideration of the following issues: nuclear disarmament, the impact of technology on the world of work, equal rights, north/south disparities, and pollution and resource depletion.

Since its inception as an official board committee, Thinking and Deciding in a Nuclear Age has sponsored another conference for secondary school students, a five-day in-service program for secondary school teachers, a rewriting of the booklet outlining activities for the observation of Remembrance Day, the preparation of an annotated resource list on nuclear weapons issues for teachers and the creation of student resource kits on war and peace. During the the summer of 1984 the committee hired a team of writers to prepare a policy paper on the teaching of controversial issues which was designed to empower teachers to raise issues, such as the threat of nuclear war, and to establish some guidelines for how this should be done.

As a result of the first teacher training workshop in the fall of 1982, approximately twelve teachers met to form an organization of educators to address the threat of nuclear war. Some of us wanted an organization which would focus on the development of a nuclear issues curriculum and peace studies in general; others wanted an organization which would be primarily a pressure group encouraging teachers' federations and boards of education to take a stand in favour of peace education. After several months of discussion, it was decided that Educators for Nuclear Disarmament[2] would serve both purposes. In the spring of 1983, END began publishing a newsletter directed at teachers. Since then it has held several public meetings with prominent guest speakers and sponsored two conferences on peace education, the second on November 10, 1984. In addition, END has supported and contributed to the work of the Thinking and Deciding in a Nuclear Age Committee and has been instrumental in the creation of a Nuclear Disarmament Education Committee in our local branch of the Ontario Secondary School Teachers' Federation.

Part of the inspiration for the creation of END came from Roberta Snow, a Boston educator who was hired by the board to lead the in-service programmes for teachers in the fall of 1982 and 1983. Ms. Snow was one of the founding members of Educators for Social Responsibility in the United States. She is also one of the authors of a curriculum entitled *Decision Making in a Nuclear Age* which states in its introduction:

> More than nuclear facts, interpretations and opinions, this course makes use of the classroom as a vehicle to develop the social insight, interest and skills students need to create and participate in a democracy . . . students are encouraged . . . to recognize that history is not inevitable; every decision they make, or leave to others, involves a choice.[3]

At the teacher workshops, the participants held widely divergent views on the nuclear issue and much of the time was spent arguing out these opinions as well as discussing how to present issues related to nuclear weapons to our students. Throughout these discussions Ms. Snow was an excellent model of how a teacher can raise controversial issues in a way which encourages dialogue instead of confrontation.

Although *Decision Making in a Nuclear Age* is an excellent curriculum, some of us who have attended the teacher workshops feel the need for a Canadian curriculum. As one participant explained:

> It's not just that Canadians need to learn about the Gouzenko case and not just the Hiss case. It's also that being in a different country it is most important for us to know the particular way this problem of war and nuclear arms has emerged for us. Different aspects of the problem stand out for us. Different strategies are often necessary.[4]

The development of such a course must be a priority for Canadian educators. In the meantime we must continue to raise the issue in our classrooms with the available resources. What I hope to do in the rest of this paper is to outline some general principles which should guide any course dealing with nuclear weapons issues and discuss how I have tried to apply them in my own practice.

A curriculum dealing with issues of war and peace must involve students in inquiry and in making value judgements, a process which is often described as critical thinking and, by John Dewey, as reflective thinking. Methodology which will encourage such critical or reflective thinking cannot be reduced to a set of mechanical procedures because the personalities of the teacher and the students create the dynamic in any classroom. A pedagogy for peace education must be tested in practice and revised continuously; it must also be adapted by each teacher to her own particular situation.

The first important principle which should guide such a curriculum is that knowledge be seen as a human creation and, therefore, tentative. Knowledge is a social product, that is, it grows out of human interaction. It is created and not consumed. In this view, knowledge is not seen as a static and neat package which is passed on to the learner but as a dynamic process in which the learner must be involved. As the well-known document on language policy in British schools, the Bullock report, states:

> It is a confusion of everyday thought that we tend to regard knowledge as something that exists independently of someone who knows. 'What is known' must in fact be brought to life afresh within every 'knower' by his or her own efforts.[5]

Because knowledge is a human creation, it shares with humans the quality of fallibility. Of course some things are more knowable than others, but, particularly in dealing with issues around nuclear war, one is forced to recognize the tentative nature of human knowledge. No one knows positively what would happen in the event of a nuclear war and we do not have certain knowledge of how to prevent such a catastrophe. There are no definitive answers to the many questions raised by the existence of nuclear weapons. As the physicist Jacob Bronowski states:

> There is no absolute knowledge. And those who claim it, whether they are scientists or dogmatists, open the door to tragedy. All information is imperfect. We have to treat it with humility.[6]

The implication for the teacher in accepting this approach to knowledge is a movement away from an emphasis on the "right" answer. Sometimes academically successful students who are well versed in the rules for winning in school have particular problems with this emphasis on tentative answers that are always open to revision.

I begin the nuclear weapons unit of my World Issues course with a Ray Bradbury short story, "The Flying Machine," about an ancient emperor who orders the execution of the inventor of a flying machine out of fear that the machine will be used in the future to attack the kingdom. The story raises several questions: should scientific knowledge be controlled? How should decisions about applications of scientific knowledge be made in a democracy? When do we have enough information to make such decisions? What is worth preserving? What means are acceptable for preserving what we value? In discussing these questions, I encourage the students not to feel the need to give definitive answers but to see the classroom as a safe forum for working through their ideas on these issues. By insisting that they suspend judgement, especially in the early stages of discussion, I am discouraging them from advocating simple solutions to what are often complex issues.

It is important to note that this view of knowledge as tentative should lead neither to a cynical notion that there is no way for a person to test the validity of his/her theories nor to a bland relativism which accepts all opinions as being of equal value. As Henry Perkinson, an American educational theorist, states in his book *The Possibilities of Error*:

The critical approach will make students uncertain about their knowledge. Uncertainty means openness, flexibility; it holds out the possibility for intellectual growth. Part of the intellectual function of the teacher is to raise her students' tolerance level of uncertainty.[7]

Mention of the "intellectual function of the teacher" brings us to an important consideration in any peace education program--should the teacher assume a neutral position or is it acceptable for her to advocate a particular position on how peace can best be achieved?

The Thinking and Deciding Committee stated as one of its objectives: "to encourage teachers to consider and express their positions on contemporary issues as part of their professional responsibility."[8] However, they added the note:

While it is important that teachers support students' responses to critical issues, they must be careful not to enlist them in their own personal causes. Teachers and students must be free to explore together many points of view and to formulate co-operatively questions, answers and methods of investigation.[9]

Certainly students are adamant that they do not want to be taught *what* to think about important societal issues but *how* to think about them.

So where does this leave the teacher? Must she refrain from expressing her opinion on issues of nuclear war and peace? The Canadian educator William Hare states in his book *Open-Mindedness and Education*:

the rejection of propaganda does not force us to adopt neutrality; and the open-minded support of a particular view by the teacher is perfectly consistent with having the pupils treat all views according to consistent *critical* principles.[10]

Certainly advocacy of a particular position is seen as acceptable and even necessary to meet one's professional responsibilities and one's moral responsibilities as a citizen when dealing with such issues as sexual and racial equality.

In deciding what role to adopt in the discussion of nuclear weapons and peace, the teacher must be aware of what messages are being given to students. By adopting a neutral position, the teacher may give the impression that she does not have an opinion and that it is not important for people to form carefully considered positions on these issues. By expressing her opinion and indicating that she is prepared to subject it to the same critical scrutiny applied to the students' views, the teacher can demonstrate the ability to take a stand without being dogmatic.

As is clear from the Thinking and Deciding Committee's statement on the role of the teacher, peace education requires that teacher and student be seen as co-learners. This does not mean that the teacher will abandon her responsibilities to create a conducive learning climate and to introduce materials appropriate to the students. What the teacher must abandon is what Paulo Freire calls the "narrative" quality of much education. The student must be seen as an active learner, not a passive recipient. The students' thinking on these issues should be the starting point and the continual reference point in the curriculum. For example, once when my class was involved in a study of a history of the arms race, one bright and generally well-read student expressed shock when she learned that the United States and the Soviet Union had been allies during World War II. Her admission that she thought that the two powers had "always" been enemies provided us with an opportunity to discuss the process by which a nation moves from the status of ally to enemy or vice versa.

A significant part of this curriculum should involve the students in reflection on their own thinking. The use of journals can help students to understand their own thinking better and to see how their thinking changes as they go through the course. The journal allows the students to personalize the class discussions, to integrate the information, concepts and attitudes developed into their own frameworks. Through this process students come to own their knowledge and their values.

In any such curriculum, discussion must be a central teaching strategy. Discussion is not to be understood as a cathartic experience that might be no more than a pooling of ignorance and prejudice. Rather, discussion is seen as a forum for students to expand their information on an issue, to develop skills in analyzing and synthesizing this information, to test the feasibility of proposed solutions to issues and to develop the courage to take a stand on the issues, a stand open to revision.

Discussion about issues of war and peace should be in the form of dialogue rather than debate. Dialogue suggests respect for the views of others even if they are different from one's own views. It also requires that participants will be open to the possibility of broadening their perspectives on an issue through listening to different viewpoints.

As a result, it is important that students examine many perspectives on these issues. This should not be reduced to the simplistic and confrontational notion of looking at both sides of the issue. Instead, this approach recognizes that there is a wide spectrum of opinion on how best to create a peaceful world and that there is a possibility of a fruitful dialogue amongst people holding these various opinions. A student understands a position better if he/she understands possible objections to it and still considers it a sound position, the more so because it has been critically examined. As Andrew Blair says in the special issue of *Ethics in Education* devoted to peace education:

> Whatever approach to peace you may have, whether you tend toward the need for military strength or a military reduction, you cannot reasonably be confident that your view is right until you have heard, and understood, what the opposing views are. This is something which young people need to learn. Until they learn to engage in dialogue, they will not be able to see the elements of truth in all sides of an issue or synthesize them into the complex position necessary for a fruitful approach to peace.[11]

In teaching about these issues another important consideration is that intellect and emotion not be separated. Our opinions are the result of emotional and intellectual processes. If, as the United Nations' statement suggests, wars begin in the hearts and minds of people, it is crucial that a curriculum dealing with these issues addresses our students' hearts as well as their minds. We do not want to produce skilled technocrats but wise citizens of a peaceful world community.

Many writers about peace have commented on the distorted reasoning which allows military strategists to plan for the destruction of vast numbers of human beings. We must help students to move away from such compartmentalization of feeling and thought. We must help them to see that logic need not require the blunting of emotion and moral sensitivity. One useful strategy to accomplish this goal is to have students critically examine the language used in the nuclear weapons debate and the implications of such language.

Students must be encouraged to use this curriculum as a support to wise action. Awareness of the fallibility of human judgement and the tentative nature of knowledge does not absolve us from acting. In fact, this is the human condition--we must act in spite of uncertainty and ambiguity.

Our students want to apply what they learn to their lives. I quote from one student's journal, an entry in which she was evaluating the course:

> Many courses teach you a lot, but this one teaches you how to think, how to understand, evaluate and put into place thoughts or information. Not just to store them away, and not do anything with the information given to you.

A curriculum dealing with issues of war and peace must not overwhelm such students, leaving them with a sense of powerlessness or cynicism about the effectiveness of action.

Through the process of critical thinking practised in discussion, students can develop value judgements and the courage to act on their values. Such action will be based on students' views of a better world. It is important that a peace curriculum does not concentrate on preventing war; instead it must focus positively on building a peaceful society. Both students' fears and their hopes for the future must be addressed in the curriculum. Students should be asked to imagine what a peaceful society would be like as a first step in the creation of such a society. The world desperately needs the resources of these young people who have hope for a better world because they realize the future will be the result of human choice, young people who are compassionate human beings with a vision of a just and peaceful world and an openness to working with others to create it.

Comments

Deborah Gorham

How do you deal with the fear that children and adolescents might have? Even those who go on peace marches are terrified--it's just such a difficult thing, when you're scared of death anyway, to separate out your own personal death from total annihilation.

Margaret Wells

It's a very individual thing; students deal with it in different ways. Journals are a very useful tool for dealing with that because some students feel that they can say things in a journal that they don't want to say in class. Other students deal with it by talking a lot. I don't think that there's one definite way that you deal with those fears. It just has to be included in the discussion. You can't tell them not to be afraid.

Notes

[1]From minutes of the Thinking and Deciding in a Nuclear Age Committee (now called Critical Issues in the Curriculum Advisory Committee), June 13, 1983, pp. 1-2.

[2]There was discussion about whether the name Educators for Nuclear Disarmament would limit membership in the group to those people who had worked through their thoughts and feelings on the topic and were prepared to take a stand in favour of disarmament. Some members felt that a name such as Educators for Social Responsibility might open the organization to teachers who were still in the process of forming their opinions. That name was adopted in spring 1986.

[3]Chris Austill, ed, Decision Making in a Nuclear Age (Weston, MA: Halcyon House, Inc., 1983), p. 2.

[4]Bob Davis, "War and Peace: What did you learn in school today?," Mudpie, February 1984, p. 19. Mr. Davis was the representative from an organization called Parents for Peace at the 1983 fall in-service.

[5]Alan Bullock, A Language for Life (London: Her Majesty's Stationery Office, 1975), p. 6.

[6]Jacob Bronowski, The Ascent of Man (Boston: Little, Brown and Company, 1973), p. 353.

[7]Henry J. Perkinson, The Possibilities of Error: An Approach to Education (New York: David McKay Company, Inc., 1975), p. 36.

[8]Minutes of the Thinking and Deciding in a Nuclear Age Committee, June 13, 1983, p. 2.

[9]A staff report on Issues and Directions for the Thinking and Deciding in a Nuclear Age Committee, p. 2.

[10]William Hare, Open-mindedness and Education (Montreal & Kingston: McGill-Queen's University Press, 1979), p. 70.

[11]Andrew G. Blair, "The Way to Peace," Ethics in Education 3, 10 (June, 1984): 2.

THE ATOMIC BOMBING OF HIROSHIMA AND NAGASAKI: THE ROLE OF WOMEN IN THE JAPANESE PEACE MOVEMENT

Setsuko Thurlow

During centuries of feudalism and civil war, the women of Japan had been considered inferior to men according to the Confucian philosophy. Lacking in legal, economic or political rights in the patriarchal family system, they had little choice but to obey their parents as children, obey their husbands when married, and obey their sons when widowed. When Japan abandoned feudalism in the second half of the nineteenth century, the growing militarism joined the remnants of feudalism as the exploitive milieu for women. Now, in addition to being economically productive, women were expected to dedicate their reproductive function to the state, to bear many children and to send their sons off to die for the Emperor. After flirting briefly with democracy in the Taisho Period (1912-1926), the militarists steadily increased in influence and power, though not without resistance. The form of resistance taken by such women as Raicho Hiratsuka was consciousness raising regarding the low status of women through their writing, rather than direct political action. Because of this background of inequality and oppression and the role models providing a tradition of resistance, Japanese women enthusiastically welcomed their new rights under the post-war democratic Constitution, using them to struggle against any revival of militarism or, more broadly, the political, economic or social conditions which had kept them in subservience for so long.

This paper is intended to deal briefly with the psycho-social impact of the atomic bombings of Hiroshima and Nagasaki upon the populations involved and upon the nation in general and to examine the role of women in the post-war Japanese peace movement which has been so profoundly affected by the wartime nuclear bombings and the subsequent nuclear arms race.

The details of the atomic bombings of Hiroshima and Nagasaki are related in many other works and so will not be dwelt on here. Suffice it to say that, at 8:15 a.m. on August 6, a uranium atomic bomb exploded over Hiroshima, emitting blast, heat and radiation. Devastation extended to a radius of about two kilometres and the number of dead by the end of 1945 is estimated at 140,000 out of a population under 400,000, 90% of whom were civilians. Three days later, on August 9, a plutonium bomb exploded over Nagasaki levelling the district of Urakami and bringing death to some 70,000 people by the end of 1945.[1] These weapons were instruments of mass, indiscriminate slaughter whose effects continue to the present day.

The suddenness and totality of the destruction were simply too much for survivors to comprehend for some time. Many felt as though the end of the world had come. In addition to deaths from burns and other injuries, more and more people began to die from the effects of radiation which struck seemingly at random in a mysterious, eerie way, and this intensified the fears of the survivors. For most, the struggle to live was all they could cope with in the face of the loss of loved ones, the continual anxiety about their own health, the destruction of their social, political and economic structures, and social discrimination as carriers of the taint of radiation. Many who moved to other cities hid their identity as A-bomb survivors. Dr. Robert Jay Lifton, the American psychiatrist who has done the most thorough psychological study to date on the survivors, coined the term "psychic numbing" for this condition of conscious and unconscious avoidance and denial of the trauma.[2]

While the atomic bombings were indeed catastrophic, the survivors initially could still cling to their traditional value system and to the faith that Japan would still prevail in the war no matter how onerous the burden became for the Japanese people. But then on August 15 came the Emperor's broadcast announcing Japan's surrender. This was a devastating experience psychologically because it destroyed the foundation of the society's value system and took away the anchor of stability for people undergoing terrible suffering and deprivation.

Japan's surrender and the beginning of the country's occupation by the United States of America brought the most drastic and sudden social changes in Japanese history: a redistribution of the land, the democratization of education, the legalization of labour unions and the break-up of the great business corporations or *zaibatsu*. There was also the new and democratic Constitution which, among other changes such as renouncing war, officially abolished the old patriarchal family system and gave women full political and civil rights on an equal basis with men. It should be noted that on August 25, just ten days after the surrender, Raicho Hiratsuka had organized a group to lobby the Japanese government for women's suffrage.[3] On October 10, the day before the order of General MacArthur, the Supreme Allied Commander, to do so, the new Japanese cabinet decided to grant the vote to women. A core of well-educated and politically aware women was ready to take advantage of the new rights. In the first post-war general election, held on April 10, 1946, thirty-nine women were elected members of the Diet.

Not all the policies of the Occupation were as beneficial as these, particularly the policies relating to the atomic bombings. From

September 1945 the Occupation imposed the Press Code which meant a rigid censorship on any materials critical of the United States or connected with the atomic bombings. The American authorities confiscated photographs, films, poems, novels, scientific studies, medical records and specimens, indeed materials relating in any form to the cataclysmic events of August 6 and 9. It actually became illegal for Japanese doctors to conduct medical studies on the effects of the A-bomb on human bodies. Just at the time when the survivors most needed the support of their countrymen and women as well as of the outside world for further material and psychological survival, writers and journalists were largely prevented from publishing information about the plight of these desperate people. The Press Code meant that they had to suffer alone, in silence and with a sense of abandonment.[4]

In addition, the United States established its own Atomic Bomb Casualty Commission to study the effects of the bomb upon human bodies. While tens of thousands were suffering from inadequate medical care, the ABCC studied them but did not offer treatment and even withheld their findings from Japanese doctors. The survivors' anger at being treated like guinea pigs had to be repressed, for the world was to be kept from learning the truth about nuclear war.

Not all survivors, however, meekly accepted this suppression of evidence and experience, and the resistance that developed during the Occupation helped to prepare the way for what was to become the powerful Japanese anti-nuclear peace movement of the post-Occupation period. This resistance began largely with a few women writers and poets, survivors such as Sadako Kurihara, Shinoe Shoda and Yoko Ohta from Hiroshima, and Sumako Fukuda from Nagasaki. Shinoe Shoda published 150 copies of a book of poems secretly and illegally through a friend working in the Hiroshima Prison. She personally distributed them to other survivors giving them hope and encouragement by articulating their pain and assisting their grieving. The following are two examples of her writing, considered unacceptable by the Occupation authorities and passed secretly from hand to hand under threat of prosecution.

> A buckle
> Inscribed with a name
> And just a mass of charcoal.
> The mother, embracing them,
> Weeps over what was her son.

> * * * *

> Isn't there any operation
> To cut off my memories
> And let me break with the past?
> Give me some treatment
> Or I shall go mad.[5]

In March 1946 Sadako Kurihara, in partnership with her husband, attempted to publish a collection of writings and poems on the atomic bomb experience. Certain sections which were considered too graphic had to be deleted, as were any indications of censorship. Several times Mr. Kurihara was summoned to the local headquarters of the US Counter-Intelligence Corps and threatened with court-martial and exile to Okinawa. He answered quietly that it was his understanding that America was a democratic nation that espoused freedom of expression, but that this persecution to which he was being subjected was making him lose faith in America.[6] In the end the work was published in a softened version, omitting overt criticism of America, but still making its contribution to the building of a resistance movement. One of the selections published was the following poem, based on a true story, by Sadako Kurihara.

> It was night in the basement
> Of a shattered building.
> Those wounded by the atomic bomb
> Filled up the dark basement,
> Without the light of a single candle.
> Amid the smell of blood,
> The stench of dead bodies,
> A sweaty stuffiness and sound of moaning.
> Out of them a strange voice was heard:
> "A baby is being born!"
> In the hell of a basement like this
> A young woman is in labour at this moment.
> What should the people do
> In this darkness, without a match?
> The people huddled there
> Were anxious about her,
> Forgetting their own pain. Then--
> A voice sounded: "I am a midwife!
> I will assist at the birth!"
> It was a severely wounded person
> Who spoke, who had been moaning
> A moment ago. Thus, in the dark,
> In the bottom of the hell, a new life
> Came into the world. The midwife
> Died before dawn, covered with blood.
> Let new life be born! Let new life be born!
> Even if one must pay with one's own life.[7]

In 1949 as the Cold War grew more intense with the Berlin Blockade, the creation of NATO and the Soviet explosion of their first atomic bomb, the political restrictions of the Occupation became more severe. For example, the authorities prohibited the discussion of the atomic bombings at public meetings. But on October 2, 1949, at a meeting in the auditorium of Hiroshima Jogakuin (the writer's *alma mater*), a Grade 5 boy stood up unexpectedly, related the loss of his older brother in the atomic bombing and expressed his desire for a world free of atomic bombs. A woman jumped up and, regardless of the possibility of prosecution by the Occupation, proposed an emergency resolution appealing to the world to abolish all atomic weapons. This resolution struck a responsive chord in the hearts of the long-repressed citizens and was enthusiastically and unanimously passed. This was the first such appeal made at a public meeting in all Japan and may be considered to be the real birth of the Japanese anti-nuclear peace movement.[8]

The beginning of the Korean War in 1950 brought the start of Japanese rearmament with the creation of the National Police Reserve. Peace activities were seen as leftist and anti-American by the authorities and even the memorial ceremonies in Hiroshima on August 6 were restricted. Nevertheless, 6 1/2 million signatures were collected in Japan for the 1950 Stockholm appeal for an end to the nuclear arms race.[9]

After the signing of the Peace Treaty in 1952, which ended the Occupation and restored sovereignty to Japan, it became possible at last to examine and analyze the atomic bomb experience. It was learned, for example, that the Pentagon had recommended to President Truman that the target cities be left undamaged by conventional bombing, the better to assess the effects of the new bomb.[10] Another discovery was that the Interim Committee had recommended to the President that the bombs be used on Japan as soon as possible, without warning, and on military or industrial targets surrounded by residential areas."[11] Japanese journalists and historians increasingly came to the conclusion that, in addition to the desire to experiment with the two revolutionary new weapons of different types on living, intact cities, the primary American motives for the bombings were political rather than military. Truman's justification of the American action, that it had eliminated the necessity for a costly Allied invasion of Japan, lost much of its validity when it was learned that the invasion was not scheduled until November 1, 1945, and that the United States government knew that the Japanese had already initiated peace proposals.[12] The Japanese perceived an obvious political motive for the bombing in the deteriorating relationship between the United States and the Soviet Union in 1945 and the desire of the former to force a quick Japanese surrender before the Soviets could enter the war against Japan and claim the territorial rewards promised at the Yalta Conference. Rather than having been sacrificed on the altar of war for the sake of peace, the survivors saw themselves as victims in the opening moves of the Cold War between the United States and the Soviet Union. This realization was intensified by the deepening Cold War of the 1950s and by further developments in the nuclear arms race between the superpowers.

The ability to see the experience of the atomic bombings in historical perspective and global context, to realize the truth of nuclearism and recognize the secrecy and deceit, the enforced silence, the misinformation, the efforts to prevent the world from knowing the truth, assisted those survivors who were capable of conceptualizing all this to come out of their psychic numbing and victim consciousness. By articulating these ideas in writing, in art, in music, and on film, they rejected their role as victims and pawns, asserted their resistance to militarism, and expressed their commitment to peace and their appreciation of life. By thus transcending their own personal trauma and tragedy and by taking on the prophetic mission of warning the world of the dangers of nuclearism, their psychological recovery was strengthened and they experienced a release of energy and empowerment to remove the original cause of their trauma and to become role models for thousands who would follow in their footsteps.

The following poem by Sadako Kurihara gives powerful expression to the impulse to shoulder the prophetic mission of warning the world of the horrors of nuclear weaponry.

I who survived wish more than anything else to be a
human being.
Especially as a mother, fearing a day
When the blue sky above the apple-cheeked children
With their promising futures
May suddenly be torn apart,
All their bright futures incinerated:
I would pour my tears over the living rather than the
dead,
And protest all war more than anything else.
Even if I should be persecuted
For refusing to let my child be killed in any war,
Because the hell of that fateful day
Was so strongly burned on my retina,
I will never hide myself, never!
It was August 6th in 1945,
Soon after the sun began to shine
And people were humbly starting the day.
Suddenly--
The city was blown away,
People were hideously blistered and swollen,
And the seven rivers were filled with bloated corpses.
Even if there would be a story
Of a person who, having glimpsed hell,
And warning others of its horror,
Was immediately called back to hell
By the lord of the inferno,
Even then, I who survived Hiroshima
Will witness wherever I go,
And sing with all my heart,
"No more wars on earth!"[13]

It was, however, the American test of an H-bomb at Bikini Atoll on March 1, 1954, which resulted in the death of a member of the crew of a Japanese fishing vessel and the hospitalization of the rest of the crew, that mobilized the opinion of the entire nation about the threat of the continuing nuclear arms race. As this news hit Japan, along with the fact that the catch of the vessel had to be buried as dangerously radioactive and fish caught by other vessels in the Pacific were also radioactive, the people's anxiety turned to anger. Again, it was a small group of women who took the initiative. A study group composed of housewives in the Suginami Ward of Tokyo made up a petition to all nuclear-armed states demanding the total abolition of the production, stockpiling, use or testing of nuclear weapons. Carrying the petitions in their shopping baskets on their daily trips to the markets, the women stopped passers-by for their signatures. Almost overnight this became a nation-wide movement collecting 20,000,000 signatures[14] and stimulating the passage of resolutions for the abolition of nuclear weapons by practically all municipal and prefectural governments, as well as by both Houses of the Diet, professional associations, religious organizations, trade unions, women's groups and student and youth groups. This phenomenon of far-reaching and unforeseen consequences, the first mass movement in Japanese history to be initiated from the grassroots level rather than from the higher levels of the hierarchy, was started by a small group of ordinary women. The natural outcome of this nationwide mobilization of the public was the holding of the first annual World Conference Against A- and H-Bombs in Hiroshima in August, 1955.

This movement also enabled the general public to identify with and empathize with the plight of the survivors who, for their part, experienced for the first time a strong sense of public support. This was a significant step in the survivors' process of psychological regeneration and enabled them to take an important leadership role in the peace movement. It also became possible to organize the National Confederation of Survivors' Groups in 1956, and as a result of its political pressure, the A-Bomb Victims' Medical Aid Law was enacted in 1957, marking the first recognition by the national government of a special responsibility to the survivors.[15]

Not surprisingly, however, the nation-wide peace movement that had emerged spontaneously among people of strong psychological motivation and moral commitment was lacking in structure, financial resources, and experienced leadership. It soon was, in fact, in imminent danger of losing its momentum. At this point, however, the Socialist Party, trade unions and the Communist Party stepped in to provide the necessary funds and leadership for the fledgling peace movement. This development was a mixed blessing. While it enabled the peace movement to survive and achieve some important objectives, such as pressuring the government of Japan to adopt the three non-nuclear principles of no production, no possession and no introduction of nuclear weapons, and the passage of the A-Bomb Victims' Medical Aid Law, it instilled potentially divisive ideological factors and alienated many Japanese from the movement. The Japanese peace movement now, with the centralization of power, lost its uniqueness as a grassroots movement and in 1961 and 1962 split into two distinct organizations, *Gensuikyo* and *Gensuikin*, the former loyal to the Japanese Communist Party and the latter following the Socialist Party and the *Sohyo* Federation of trade unions. This division brought further disillusionment and alienation on the part of many survivors and other Japanese.

There have been serious but only partly successful efforts at reconciliation and co-operation between the two rival organizations, with women's groups and other citizens' organizations attempting, usually without success, to mediate between the two. Efforts at co-operation have been most successful in the planning of the annual World Conference Against A- and H-Bombs, in the 1977 International Symposium on the Damage and After Effects of the Atomic Bombing of Hiroshima and Nagasaki, and in preparation for the two UN Special Sessions on Disarmament in 1978 and 1982.

The annual World Conference Against A- and H-Bombs has become the focal, unifying point of the entire diverse Japanese peace movement, which includes a wide range of women's groups, old and new, large and small. Some examples are the YWCA, the Women Voters' League, and a federation of women's groups called the *Fudanren*, an affiliate of the Women's International Democratic Federation.

The common concern of these women's organizations is to keep Japan from ever being involved in another war and to prevent nuclear war in general because it threatens the very survival of humankind. They have had it with war to the very marrow of their bones. No more will they tolerate the cruelty and inhumanity of militarism and war; no more will they receive the ashes of sons and husbands in little boxes. Their consciousness has, however, broadened from the sense of being victims of the system to a realization that they were also accomplices of the militarism and aggression which made victims of so many of our fellow Asians. With a sense of repentance, Japanese women have tried to develop support for and solidarity with the people, and particularly the women, of Vietnam, the Philippines, Korea, the Pacific islands and elsewhere. They see that Japanese military imperialism has been replaced by economic imperialism and even "sexual imperialism," with prostitution tours arranged to Korea, the Philippines and Thailand.

The basic philosophy behind the women's movement in Japan is the realization that each human being has the right to be treated with dignity and respect and to have a life that is fulfilling and productive. They have seen that war is the denial of all this and that without justice there is no peace. For them, the issues of peace, development, democracy, equality and respect for women are all interrelated. Having achieved their rights, women are going to struggle to keep them. As with earlier Japanese women activists, they have continued with efforts at consciousness raising, but to this has been added political action in the form of petitions, demonstrations and lobbying. They maintain constant vigil on government policies, ready to take action, as recently when the history textbooks were revised to excuse and downgrade the significance of Japanese aggression in Asia. They see the Japan-US Security Treaty as the source of much evil, infringing on Japanese independence by tying their country to the American military system and by involving Japan in the militarization of the Pacific.

The future presents the challenge of transmitting these values to the next generation in the face of the complacency of affluence, the ignorance of the suffering and heartbreak of war and the revival of militarism encouraged by a conservative government. There is a sense of urgency about this challenge as the older generation of women with first-hand experience of war and exploitation dies off. Under the nuclear shadow no one knows when time will stop.

Sadako Kurihara's poem about the child born in the darkened basement may be interpreted this way. The darkness and stench represent war and militarism; the midwife represents the innocent who died without seeing the dawn; the mother represents women, and the baby stands for the future of our species. Humanity must survive! Civilization must continue!

> "Let new life be born! Let new life be born!
> Even if one must pay with one's own life!"

Comments

Unidentified Woman

You mentioned that one of the first experiences of the survivors was the social discrimination associated with the radiation, and I find it interesting that once the grassroots anti-nuclear weapons movement started there was such massive support for it. I'd like to know what you think about how people across the country moved from the position of social discrimination against the survivors to one of wholeheartedly supporting that movement. Was there a change in attitude that it might be helpful for you to explain? I'd just like to say that I feel it's important to understand this because of all the prejudices that keep people inactive and keep them from engaging in important social movements like this.

Setsuko Thurlow

Yes, many people came out of hiding and joined the peace movement. But I must say that people who are actively involved in the peace movement are still a small minority of all the survivors. When we say survivors that means not only the people who were actually in the cities at that time but the people who went into the city in search of their loved ones and who were exposed to the radiation. Today there are about 350,000 people who carry the survivor's certificate which ensures free medical treatment if a problem develops. Your question concerns the process of coming out of that psychic numbing and taking a public stand. I think when we lose our loved ones we go through a certain period of grieving during which we need the support of the people around us who understand what we are going through. And after a certain period with all the support and encouragement and love and warmth you can come out of the grieving period. So try to put yourselves in the survivors' situation, when practically the whole city was blown up and many, I know this was true of many of my classmates, had lost every member of their family. At that time, when they needed the emotional support, the political and social milieu was a very restrictive one. You were not supposed to talk about it. One very practical way of dealing with trauma is to articulate our pain and to share it with our loved ones. But we were not allowed to do that. We weren't supposed to talk about it publicly. It would have been nice if the survivors could have come together for group sessions just to cry on each other's shoulders and offer mutual support, but this was discouraged in that political milieu. So you can imagine the pain and agony they went through. The people in Tokyo didn't know much about the suffering of the survivors in Hiroshima and Nagasaki because the newspapers were not free to publish the details. In spite of this, they knew that the atomic bomb was a horrible thing and, as I have said in my paper, under the impact of the Bikini incident they started a nationwide movement and for the first time the Hiroshima and Nagasaki survivors felt widespread public support.

Notes

[1] Committee for the Compilation of Materials on Damage Caused by the Atomic Bombs, Hiroshima and Nagasaki (New York: Basic Books, 1981), pp. 363 ff.

[2] Robert Jay Lifton, Death in Life (New York: Basic Books, 1967).

[3] Research Division on Women's Issues, Fusenkaikan, Fujin Sansei Kankei Shiryoshu (Tokyo: Fusenkaikan, 1975), p. 5.

[4] Hiroshima and Nagasaki, pp. 14, 497, 508.

[5] Japan Council Against A- and H-Bombs, White Paper, n.d., p. 15.

[6] Seiji Imabori, Gensuibaku Jidai, vol. 1 (Tokyo: Sanichi Shinsho, 1959), p. 26.

[7] Sadako Kurihara, Chugoku Bunka (Hiroshima: Chugoku Bunka Fukkoku Kanko no Kai, 1946), p. 21.

[8] Imabori, op. cit., pp. 34-5.

[9] Han Genbaku no Tatakai (Hiroshima: Gensuibaku Kinshi Hiroshima Ken Kyogikai, 1975), p. 12.

[10] Robert Jungk, Brighter Than a Thousand Suns (Harmondsworth: Penguin Books, 1956), p. 164.

[11] Ibid., p. 168.

[12] Fletcher Knebel and Charles W. Bailey, No High Ground (New York: Bantam Books, 1960), p. 20; Winston S. Churchill, Triumph and Tragedy (Boston: Houghton Mifflin Co., 1955), p. 628.

[13] Sadako Kurihara, Hiroshima To Iu Toki (Tokyo: Sanichi Shobo, 1976), p. 22.

[14] Imabori, op. cit., p. 134.

[15] Hiroshima and Nagasaki, pp. 542 ff., 625.

INDEX